SOCIAL CHANGE IN
FAMILY AND KIN

The *Social Change in Western Europe* series developed from the need to provide a summary of current thinking from leading academic thinkers on major social and economic issues concerning the evolving policies of Western Europe in the post-Maastricht era. To create an effective European Union governments and politicians throughout the region must work to provide satisfactory social, economic and political conditions for the populations of Europe, and each volume affords an opportunity to look at specific issues and their impact on individual countries.

The series is directed by an academic committee composed of Arnaldo Bagnasco (Turin University), Henri Mendras (CNRS, Paris) and Vincent Wright (Nuffield College, Oxford), assisted by Patrick Le Galès (CNRS, Rennes), Anand Menon (University of Oxford) with the support of Michel Roger and Oliver Cazenave (Futuroscope in Poitiers). This group forms the *Observatoire du Changement Social en Europe Occidentale* which was launched in Poitiers (France) in 1990 with the generous funding of the Fondation de Poitiers headed by René Monory.

SOCIAL CHANGE IN WESTERN EUROPE

IN THE SAME SERIES

SOCIAL CHANGE IN WESTERN EUROPE

FAMILY AND KINSHIP IN EUROPE

edited by
MARIANNE GULLESTAD
and
MARTINE SEGALEN

PINTER

London and Washington

PINTER
A Cassell Imprint
Wellington House, 125 Strand, London WC2R 0BB
PO Box 605, Herndon, Virginia 20172

First published in 1997
© Observatoire du Changement Social en Europe Occidentale 1997

British Library Cataloguing in Publication Data
A catalogue record for this book is available from the British Library.
ISBN 1 85567 476 9 (hb)
    1 85567 477 7 (pb)

Library of Congress Cataloging-in-Publication Data
Famille en Europe. English
    Family and kinship in Europe / edited by Marianne Gullestad and Martine Segalen.
        p.   cm.—(Social change in Western Europe)
    Translation of La famille en Europe.
    Includes bibliographical references and index.
    ISBN 1-85567-476-9.—ISBN 1-85567-477-7 (pbk.)
    1. Family—Europe.   2. Parenthood. I. Gullestad, Marianne. II. Segalen, Martine. III. Title. IV. Series.
HQ612.F3414   1997
306.85'094—dc21   96-49948
                                                                                  CIP

Typeset by York House Typographic
Printed and bound in Great Britain by Biddles Ltd, Guildford and King's Lynn

CONTENTS

NOTES ON CONTRIBUTORS

Claudine Attias-Donfut is a sociologist who is the research director at the Caisse nationale d'assurance vieillesse (NAV) and is also affiliated to the EHESS (Ecole des Hautes Etudes Sciences Sociales). Among her publications are: *Sociologie des générations, l'empreinte du temps*, 1988, PUF; *Générations et âge de vie*, 1991, *Que sais-je*; and *Les solidarités entre générations. Vieillesse, familles, Etat* (ed.), 1995, Nathan.

Marzio Barbagli is a lecturer in sociology at the University of Bologna. He has worked principally on the history of the family and of education in Europe, also on social mobility and criminality. He has published *Educating for Unemployment. Politics, Labor Market and School System, Italy, 1859–1973*, Columbia University Press, 1982; *Sotto lo stesso tetto. Mutamenti della famiglia in Italia dal XV al XX secolo*, 1984, Il Mulino; and *Provando e riprovando. Matrimonio, famiglia e divorzio in Italia a negli altri paesi occidentali*, 1990, Il Mulino.

Joan Bestard Camps is a lecturer in social anthropology at the University of Barcelona. His research has centred on Formentera in the Balearic Islands. He has published *What's in a Relative? Household and Family in Formentera*, 1991, Berg.

Jesus Contreras Hernández is a professor in social anthropology at the University of Barcelona. His research has to do with the Peruvian Andes and with Catalonia. He has published *Subsistencia, ritual y poder en los Andes*, 1985, Barcelona; and (with Joan Bestard Camps) *Barbaros, paganos, salvajes y primitivos*, 1988, Barcelona, and *Doce historias de familia: una historia familiar*, 1997, Barcelona.

João de Pina-Cabral is a professor in social anthropology and Rector of the Universidade Atlântica (Oeiras, Portugal). He has published *Sons of Adam, Daughters of Eve: The Peasant Worldview of the Alto Minho*, 1986, Clarendon Press; *Os Contextos da Antropologia*, 1991, Difel, Lisbon; and *Aromas de Urze e de Lama*, 1993, *Fragmentos*, Lisbon; and he has coedited (with J. K. Campbell) *Europe Observed*, 1992, Macmillan.

Ali de Regt teaches in the Department of Sociology, University of Amsterdam. In 1993 she published a study of financial relations within the family under the title *Geld en gezin*.

Janet Finch is Vice-Chancellor of the University of Keele. She has published *Family Obligations and Social Change*, 1989, Polity Press, and (with J. Mason) *Negotiating Family Responsibilities*, 1993, Routledge.

David Gaunt researches at the Department of Ethnology at the University of Stockholm and is a research director in the Social Sciences Division. He has written a number of books and articles on the development of the family. At present he is studying the problems of assimilation faced by immigrant families in Sweden.

Marianne Gullestad is a social anthropologist and research professor at the Norwegian Centre for Child Research at Trondheim. Her many publications in English include *Kitchen-Table Society*, 1984, Scandinavian University Press; *The Art of Social Relations: Essays on Culture, Social Action and Everyday Life in Modern Norway*, 1992, Scandinavian University Press; *Everyday Life Philosophers: Modernity, Morality and Autobiography in Norway*, 1996, Scandinavian University Press; and the edited volume, *Imagined Childhoods: Self and Society in Autobiographical Accents*, 1996, Scandinavian University Press.

Hervé Le Bras is a director of research at the Institut National des Etudes Demographiques (INED) and director of studies at EHESS (Ecole des Hautes Etudes Sciences Sociales). His publications include *Les trois France*, 1987, Odile Jacob/Le Seuil; *Marianne et les lapins: l'obsession démographique*, 1991, Olivier Orban; *La Planète au village*, 1993, Editions de l'Aube; and *Les limites de la planète, mythe de la nature et population*, 1994, Flammarion.

Didier Le Gall is co-director of the Department of Sociology and director of the Laboratoire d'Analyse Socio-Anthropologique du Risque at the University of Caen, and associate researcher at the Centre de sociologie de la famille at the University of Paris–V (CERSOF). He has published several studies with Claude Martin including *Les familles monoparentales*, 1987, ESF, and a chapter in *Les recompositions familiales aujourd'hui*, 1993, Nathan. He has also published *Approximación Sociológica al Estudio de la Familia*, 1994, Ediluz, Venezuela; and edited *Approches sociologiques de l'Intime*, 1997, Mana, Revue de Sociologie et d'Anthropologie.

Claude Martin is in charge of research for the CNRS at the Centre de recherches administratives et politiques and lectures at the Institut d'études politiques in Rennes. He is also responsible for the Laboratoire d'analyse des politiques sociales et sanitaires (LAPSS) at the Ecole nationale de la santé publique in Rennes. His research is on the family and social politics. He has published *Home-based Carer, the Elderly, the Family and the Welfare State: an International Comparison*, 1993, University of Ottawa Press (with F. Lesemann); *Familles et politiques sociales*, 1996, L'Harmattan (with D. le Gall); and *L'après-divorce. Lien familial et vulnérabilité*, 1997, Presses universitaires de Rennes.

Franz Schultheis teaches sociology at the University of Geneva. His research is mainly directed towards social history and intercultural comparison of welfare state, sociololgy of the family and social stratification. His publications include *Sozialgeschichte der französischen Familiepolitik*, 1988, Campus; *Affaires de famille, affaires d'Etat*, 1991, Ed. de l'Est (co-edited with F. de Singly); and *Familien & Politik*, 1987, Universitätsverlag Konstanz.

Martine Segalen is a professor in social anthropology at the University of Paris X-Nanterre and a former CNRS research director. Her field in social anthropology is centred on urban sociability and the family. Her publications include *Sociologie de la famille*, 1996, Colin; *Nanterriens: les familles dans la ville*, 1990, PUM, Toulouse; *Les enfants d'Achille et de Nike. Une ethnologie de la course à pied ordinaire*, 1994, Métailié; *Jeux de famille* (ed.), 1991, Presses du CNRS.

INTRODUCTION

Martine Segalen

Family patterns in Europe are becoming increasingly indistinguishable. Over recent years population studies focusing on statistics for marriage, fertility and divorce have tended towards this prediction. There will come a time when we shall lose our national and regional distinctions and uniformity will reign with European families responding in the same way to a common policy. Yet such a prospect is certainly not recognized as inescapable. A combination of population factors clearly shows the coexistence of several models within one and the same national entity. Nor is there general acceptance for the view that the family consists only and necessarily of husband and wife (in both their traditional and reconstituted forms) together with their children, as population experts more often than not choose to assume. The collateral and particularly the intergenerational dimension to family relationships, that is becoming increasingly evident as people live longer, is once more a reality. Three, even four generations are present as kin together, interacting materially, emotively, socially and symbolically. The kinship networks that have been made so much of by anthropologists in regard to rural or non-European societies have become a reality in our own society. Those in retirement can be seen as constituting two age groups: one flourishing and still active, the other becoming more or less dependent; and these new factors call for a reappraisal of the family against the background of welfare provision.

Recent studies carried out into the institution of the family in France have drawn attention to the significance of these aspects of continuity. Is this a specifically French characteristic? Are other European countries dissimilar in this respect? Does the intergenerational dimension take on different characteristics in northern and in southern Europe? The present volume is concerned to respond to questions such as these.

When dealing with the family in all its contemporary complexity, any allusion to kinship needs to be justified. Those of us who, since the 1970s, have made use of this term or concept in studying rural and/or urban societies, have had the feeling of being thieves (or smugglers perhaps) appropriating a resource from a realm which we did not belong to – that of social anthropology.

Kinship elsewhere and here

Talking of kinship elsewhere and here is one and the same, for when we talk about others we are also talking about ourselves. The first anthropologists to discover kinship across the diversity of nomenclature systems attempted socio-historical classifications from the most archaic to the most highly developed. Hence the Western family in the experience of Morgan, Maine or, a few years later, Durkheim is placed implicitly at the apex of an evolutionary scientific construct. With the British structuro-functionalist school, kinship studies occupy a central place in anthropological accounts which conceive society as an organic whole and bring out the close connection, indeed degree of overlapping, between kinship and religious, political and economic functions; in so doing, these studies shifted Western societies in the spectrum of world societies and, in contrast to the 'others', made kinship within societies of which the anthropologists were members appear as the poor relation of the social function. Overturning the proposition of earlier analysts, this second generation of anthropologists used Western civilization as a mirror for social constructs whose richness and complexity are to be found elsewhere.

Since the 1970s, several types of critique have added a further component to the complex treatment of kinship. David Schneider (1968, 1984) has criticized the ethnocentrism implicit in descriptions offered, maintaining that to the extent that Western kinship is biologically rooted, we bring our own biologically focused model to the study of other societies. But ties of blood have not elsewhere the primacy we attribute to them in Europe and North America; moreover, the words we use are not neutral and when we translate one or another kinship term used in a distant society by brother, uncle or cousin, for instance, we load these words with historical, symbolic and social content that relates to us and may be inappropriate in the situation as it applies to them (Geffray, 1990). The dialogue between us and the others seems to resume itself into a dialogue between the biological and the social. Yet do we really accept the thesis of the exclusively 'biological' viewpoint to Western kinship and the exclusively 'social' to kinship elsewhere? In this light the proposition put forward by Maurice Godelier is certainly ambiguous, when he writes: 'Kinship constitutes a sphere in every society, but it does not follow from this that kinship everywhere has the same status or displays the same structure as it does or has done in the contemporary western world' (1993, p.1192); as if the problem was settled on our side and there was general agreement on what we in the West mean by kinship.

Hence the problem of 'decentring in relation to the west' (ibid.) remains essential. But when anthropologists talk of kinship, they imply very different things: some schools see the essence of kinship in affiliation and descent across the manifold social functions it gives rise to beyond the domestic sphere; others place emphasis on the principles governing marriage; others stress the relationship between social change and change in kinship systems; more recently, in the mid-1970s, the questioning of biological assumptions has developed. Against this background of discord, kinship studies in European societies have taken on new vigour, in a new encounter with history, as shown by Jack Goody (1985). Research, principally involving rural societies, has made an attempt to link questions concerning the mode of reproduction of domestic groups with the diversity of modes governing the handing down of property (Augustins, 1990).

'Kinship' is not then a term about which there is agreement in our own case any more than it is in that of others. Is there one definition of kinship in modern Western society, modern being taken in the sense of urban, industrial and tertiary sector society, in which the social and territorial bonds require to be examined in a way that is radically different from those we encounter in traditional rural societies? Studies make constant mention of the enquiry conducted in the 1950s in a working-class district of London, Bethnal Green, which functioned as a 'village within the city' (Young and Willmott, 1957), but such urban communities built up on ties of family have disappeared in the same way that the rural communities of the past have. Kinship in a modern and contemporary setting is organized on the basis of social bonds that are radically different, whose context is wage-earning and the welfare state.

The rediscovery of forms of kinship in our society

Acknowledgement that there existed bonds of kinship in modern society was not a foregone conclusion. The compartmentalization between anthropology and sociology until well into the 1980s (unlike the early days of the discipline) produced a split between family and kinship studies whose damaging effects have been condemned by Jack Goody:

> In encyclopedias each of these subjects is treated separately, one by anthro-pologists, the other by sociologists, and thus the picture is one-sided. This state of affairs originated with studies undertaken during the nineteenth century which were based on the theory that the notion of 'family' did not exist in primitive societies; though now discredited, this view still exercises an influence on the manner in which different specialists approach the subject. Anthropologists give much attention to preferential marriage choice but little to marrying age; those who study population give detailed study to marrying age but tend to treat preferential choice - if they treat it at all - as statistical material rather than as a norm. Sociologists isolate the conjugal couple from the kinship network. (1994, p.7)

Furthermore, with the growth of institutional religion, the develop-ment of capitalism and the centralized state, the West invented the division of social labour, relegating the family to the confines of biolog-ical sexuality, producing and socializing children and ensuring the material and emotional well-being of its members. The radical expul-sion of the economic function from the family has had an adverse effect on the study of kinship in modern societies. And where anthropologists studying other societies tried to recompose all these spheres, sociolo-gists segregated their observation of contemporary society still more, fragmenting social behaviour into so many particular fields with little passage between them - work, housing, education, leisure and so on (Mendras, 1995). Added to this, the development of state welfare appeared to deprive the family of its traditional role in providing care and the expansion of wage-earning struck at the notion and role of inheritance.

The rediscovery of kinship in modern societies is the result of several factors combined. First, feminist sociology in the 1970s led to the reintegration of the economic factor into kinship: with regard to non-European societies, anthropologists denounced the rift established by Meyer Fortes, isolating the the domestic element from the social (Yana-gisako and Collier, 1987). The mass entry of women into the labour market was part instrumental in promoting cross-disciplinary studies into the interrelationship of family, work, fertility, leisure and environment. The reappearance of the economic factor thus brought kinship back into focus, providing as it did the setting for economic activity. And there are other reasons. A longer life span, the decline of the welfare state, the new celebration of family values all conduce to the new visibility given to ties of kinship in our society (Segalen, 1991, 1996). But if one allows that these ties exist, one must ask to what purpose.

To none, in theory. Modern societies are wage-earning societies, in which social ties are largely deterritorialized. At their basis lies the cult of autonomy, performance and the ethic of self-actualization, all of which conspires against the perpetuation of family. Leaving aside socialization within the family for which today there is no guarantee apart from a father and mother's affection and, less directly, fondness on the part of older generations, society has taken over the family's role: wage earning is a function of an individual's potential; the state through its systems of insurance provides support in the manifold circumstances of living. The fact of having kin is of little theoretical significance in today's society. However, just as active sports have developed to counter the sedentary way of life that society inflicts upon us, so ties of kinship take on the appearance of a form of resistance on the part of the individual who seeks dialogue other than with the state and its administration. When families choose to live fairly close to one another, celebrate occasions together, provide support for their younger members in their job-searching or for their older ones when forced to cope on their own with the administrative complexities they are faced with, they assert a countervailing force, their own power in fact.

Moreover, contemporary social innovations, for which no historical precedent exists, pose the question of intergenerational links in a new way. One has only to consider the social and cultural consequences of a longer life span on kinship, or observe new forms of behaviour: kinship is no longer created by marriage; new forms of union call into question the mechanism for turning non-relatives into relatives by marriage, thus becoming blood relations of the following generation. Recent debate on the subject of reconstituted families (Meulders-Klein and Théry, 1993) has focused in particular upon claiming a social place for the new relative. So, if this place is not recognized between parent and child, all the more reason for it not to be established as generation succeeds generation. Can the 'moral force of ties of blood' be converted into the moral strength of ties of pseudo-kinship? Can one be considered as a parent (in the context of the reconstituted family) for a few years, then abdicate the place? And if so, what happens to the generational ties which accompany the parental situation? Does a pseudo-parent break the genealogical chain?

Along with the development of such questions that follow necessarily from changes in marriage, the biological obsession of our society raises the question of family self-perpetuation in terms that are equally new. New techniques of contraception, in the 1970s, then of procreation, in the 1980s, have shattered the biological assumptions given universal credence until then – dissociation between sexuality and procreation, multiple progenitive parents possibly, or possible disruption in the order of births and in the order of generations. Even if assisted procreation in the end accounts only for a small number of births, it has a markedly disruptive effect on all the notions surrounding parenthood, giving precedence as it does to the biological factor as well as trying to apply all the developing resources of biological engineering to providing a couple who make the request with a child of their own. This is an area where anthropologists and psychologists meet. Maurice Godelier, apropos the great debate on the extent to which indigenous peoples are aware of the mechanisms of procreation, has written: 'sexuality functions as a form of ventriloquism whereby society speaks of itself' (1993, p.1191) and Geneviève Delaisi de Parseval for her part observes that 'assisted procreation constitutes a type of resonance-box for a "story" in the midst of existential crisis – that of procreation itself' (Delaisi and Verdier, 1994, p.42). This is tantamount to saying that biotechnological innovations threaten the way we construct what we represent to ourselves. In the course of virulent criticism of the socio-medical environment of assisted procreation, Delaisi mentions that 'assisted procreation lays stress on a very general feature of society by posing the central question of successive generations, a question which makes it clear that the key term here is almost certainly child-bearing as *obligation*, far truer than the epiphemonen of "desiring a child" or "planning a child". We feel it our duty to have a child in order to discharge a transgenerational debt. And we owe a grandchild to our parents.' (p.43)

The rightness of this remark cannot fail to strike home, if we decline to shatter the edifice of universal principles upon which our system of parenthood rests. The several responses that Europe could make to these questions in political terms would be likely to lead to radical diversification in the nature of parenthood. Induced pregnancy in elderly mothers is legal practice in one country, in another not; in one, a child born as a result of artificial insemination has a right to know who his father is, not so in another; and what of embryos that have been frozen and are implanted a matter of years – or generations – after they are formed, bearing in mind the disturbing effect of implanting embryos, conceived by a woman and her husband, in the woman's mother's womb?

The disruption and turmoil thus experienced in modern society inclines us to examine the nature of the intergenerational bond which ensures that the family is perpetuated.

Dimensions of kinship in contemporary France

It is not unlikely that the international celebration of 1993 as the year of solidarity and 1994 as the year of the family prompted a new, and indeed spectacular, interest in sociological studies of family relationships. Le Play's work received much attention (1994), the part of kinship in contemporary societies was examined by Bawin-Legros (1994) as was the role of memory within the family (Coenen-Huther, 1994) and generational relationships (Coenen-Huther, 1994; Attias-Donfut, 1995). In Switzerland a national survey was undertaken into networks of solidarity within the family (Coenen-Huther, Kellerhals and Von Allmen, 1994) and in France another looked into family interaction across three generations; it was supervised by the CNAV and will be referred to in this volume. Pioneer work done by Roussel (1976) and Pitrou (1977) was followed up by a theoretical study of intrafamily relationships (Jean-Hugues Déchaux, 1994).

The present volume sets out to reflect and develop this debate in an international context. The task of enquiry is twofold: in the first instance, to discover to what extent and in what ways the perpetuation of family shows itself in different European countries; secondly, to record its distinguishing characteristics in the light of two significant factors that now affect the family – fragile unions and, to use Claudine Attias-Donfut's term, 'generational co-longevity'. A response to these questions merits a closer look, in the French context, at the three most common dimensions of modern kinship – sociability, support and transfer.

Day-by-day relations, on a regular basis or on festive occasions, are many and various. Their frequency provides a subject for analysis in terms both of proximity and accessibility of one home to another and the degree to which relations between generations are easy or subject to conflict. Whatever forms sociability takes, contemporary experience reflects a growth in intensity given that individuals and families have more time and more money at their disposal and that health is less of a problem in the process of ageing. The women in the family tend to be the agents of sociability and the pivots are the grandchildren with the capacity they have of turning stepmothers into grandmothers.

The forms of assistance implied by the support function are of a different order. In a downward direction, one thinks of all that the elder generation may transfer to the younger generation. In the France of today, pensioners are well-provided for and two-thirds of them own their own home. Maintaining young people till they are able to find a job and providing gifts on appropriate occasions or when they set up home on their own constitute a steady flow which will be reversed when parents become old and physically dependent. Here again, women tend to be vectors of the relationship.

The third sphere of contemporary kinship – representing a traditional function, yet in a new form – has to do with inheritance and the handing down of property. The inheritance from older generations is on the increase and the generational effect of its transfer is significant. Most probably it involves the main home, perhaps a second home too; frequently, in the instance of France at least, a house has symbolic importance as a fixed point for the entire family. In Britain, 75 per cent of families are homeowners, in Italy 68 per cent, more than 50 per cent in France, 47 per cent in the Netherlands and so on. Moreover, as a form of capital it provides a background to the transformations the family undergoes. In the case of divorce and remarriage, considerations of the line of descendants may outweigh those of joint estate. But there is a further consideration: mindful of the dividends currently distributed by the welfare state, is one to 'live off one's property' so as to provide for the afflictions of old age – an attitude that tends to prevail in Anglo-Saxon countries – or else do one's best to keep such capital intact so as to pass it down – an attitude favoured in France and Mediterranean countries?

The forms, thus summarized, in which contemporary kinship is exercised produce tension between biological and social factors, between what is private and what is public and between the individual and the family group. Across these three spheres families are perpetuated. What we are here dealing with is kinship in its pure state whereby an individual is not in the main assigned a social place, while its members struggle to give life to a notion of kinship which takes the form of a group of cognate lines motivated by the desire to remain as it is, while undergoing transformation, at the same time existing in the consciousness of its members. Both objectives are distinct. The concept of self-perpetuation is wider than that of reproduction which has more to do with social status; the point at issue is not so much that of moving up or down on the social scale as remaining oneself in the conditions of modernity that apply.

As Pierre Bourdieu says, 'the family unit exists for and by accumulation and transmission. The "subject" of most strategies of reproduction is the family acting as a sort of collective subject, not as a simple aggregate of individuals' (1994, p.11). Even so, unlike rural societies in which the individuals constituted a family resource (an unpaid workforce ensuring the perpetuation of the line and of the inheritance), modern kinship has become a resource for individuals (a resource financially and in terms of identity). For the young in France who typify the new middle strata, the perpetuation of the family implies unfailing family support, more particularly to enable them to continue into higher education or in times of difficulty (divorce, sickness or unemployment); it implies a family memory rooted in a precise location and frequent family get-togethers; in short, the basis for an individual identity with a perspective of both the past and the future. The perpetuation of family is a construct, constantly reasserted in terms of duration – the span of a life, the span of generations – which is why the term 'exchanges', so often used in research, seems inappropriate since it takes little account of the temporal factor. The items – goods, services, assistance, advice – circulating among relations represent neither an equivalent amount nor an equivalent substance. Parents during a period in their lives give to their children, who, will in all probability help them later on in their old age while they provide for their own children as well. The reciprocity which the notion of exchange implies is neither immediate nor identical; rather, as Lévi-Strauss remarks in regard to the exchange of wives, it is generalized. It would be more appropriate to refer to cycles insofar as this concept takes the notion of deferred return into account.

The give-and-take that characterizes contemporary kinship is in keeping with new prescriptive codes where the precondition of obedience has given way to a complex set of negotiations. Family and individual combine and if, as stated by Fortes 'kinship unites . . . creates rights and moral obligations which cannot be abdicated' (1969, p.242), the obligations so created are far from being predetermined rules, but represent a flexible framework that is fashioned by social, cultural and economic forces. Respective undertakings are negotiated situation by situation and, if necessary, reassessed.

Finally, insofar as sexuality and procreation are dissociated, and social and biological ties superimposed, surveys conducted in France lead us to recognize kinship as a group of persons with ties of blood and of union (marital or not) in whom are identified not a common body of ancestors, myths or property, but complementary rights and duties that spring from the very nature of their relationships, built essentially upon the presence of children born of them and/or nurtured by them.

Such is a summary analysis of kinship and the perpetuation of family in French society at the close of the twentieth century. Can one predict the durability of this model, while taking into account – as one must – the socio-historical context particular to every generation? With the maintenance of kinship relations being conditioned in part by factors such as the level of income of those in retirement or the respective impact of generations, it is almost a foregone conclusion, as Attias-Donfut emphasizes, that these ties will be further strengthened in the years to come, since they are bolstered for a further generation at least by an age group that is well provided for and strongly committed to younger and older ones alike.

European diversities

If these various questions have received plenty of attention in France, Belgium and Switzerland, how has the situation developed in other European countries in regard to family networks, kinship and descendants, and the will to perpetuate the family? This is the main thrust of the present volume. It has to be said at once that international studies on so complex a social question are not easy to conduct. One further aim here is to present an array of contributions outlining various cultural aspects of kinship, which at the same time discourage any illusion of these being comparative studies.

To start with, we do not necessarily attach the same meaning to the terms we use: 'familie', 'family', 'famille' have not the same semantic content. In the perspective of constructing Europe and setting up common policies, questions of comparability take on crucial importance. Where family comparability is concerned, studies are mainly based on figures that reveal behaviour patterns by means of socio-demographic indicators or define the size and structure of families and the forms of organization they adopt – what Franz Schultheis describes as the 'preponderance of the statistical argument'. Hervé Le Bras deconstructs the standard index used to measure fertility so as to bring to light the relatively different trends in operation in Europe; and he puts forward the hypothesis that family systems which are overexacting have the effect of stifling fertility, which may go to explain its spectacular fall in Mediterranean countries. From another angle, Marzio Barbagli adds strength to the hypothesis in showing that nowhere else in Europe are family relations as close as they are in Italy, where fertility has in fact fallen spectacularly.

Further to this, a simple examination of the ways in which indices are constructed reveals significant differences between nation states as to the concepts round which family policy is framed. German law, for instance, is based on the notion that kinship comes into existence with marriage, whereas in France and Britain, the family's centre of gravity is the child rather than the couple (Hantrais and Letablier, 1994, p.5); at the same time, both Germany and Britain adhere to the notion that family is a private concern, whereas in France it constitutes an 'affair of state' (de Singly and Schultheis, 1991). Then the perpetuation of the family, a subject that particularly concerns us, is in France given special prominence in its political and symbolic aspects, whereas in Britain it is treated in a utilitarian way with the cross-generational solidarity between family, government and market services being seen as balancing out. Again, in the approach to cultural factors, comparability is made the more hazardous, reflecting, as it will, the diversity of academic traditions, itself a reflection of social and historical traditions that are distinct to each country.

The study of family relationships in France has been largely dominated by Lévi-Strauss's approach to marriage systems and it required a consolidated breakthrough on the part of sociologists studying current trends, bringing their concepts of networks and interdependence and their reflexions on the links between family and welfare systems, in order for ethnographic studies and micro-sociology to advance. Research conducted in Britain has been still more sensitive to criticism of the ethnocentrality of Anglo-Saxon studies on the part of Edmund Leach (1980), with the result that studies of home-based kinship are provided – not to say encumbered – with a dose of self-reflexiveness: saying who one is, where one is speaking from and what social group one represents is now a regulation assignment that precedes analysis, indeed sometimes takes the place of analysis.

Marilyn Strathern's *After Nature* (1992), which has to do with kinship in Britain at the present time, is no more than indirectly concerned with the problem of determining the field of kinship or of examining the substance of ties between those related by blood or marriage; its concern is rather to analyse how notions of 'relatedness', nature and biological constitution act on ideas of what determines kinship. The prime aim is to make explicit what was implicit. Breaking with the social tradition of British anthropology, Strathern's endeavour is to dwell on the cultural aspects of kinship. Though she may point to 'the individuality of persons as the first fact of English kinship' (p.14) and 'diversity as a second fact of modern kinship' (p.22), making for a British specificity, her book treats the substance of the subject no more than marginally. It has fallen to a sociologist, Janet Finch, to open the discussion on the generational impact in contemporary British society (Finch, 1989), a discussion which she continues here by examining competition between blood and marriage ties in the matter of inheritance.

If the significance of kinship is self-evident in Scandanavia or in the Mediterranean countries, this is far from being the case in Germany, where the absence of kinship studies can be related specifically to historical experience; in Germany, too, refusal to consider intergenerational ties has come to influence practice itself, as is well shown by Schultheis.

However diverse academic traditions may be, it has to be granted that international comparisons can be more or less problematic in considering one or other of the three areas identified above – sociability, support or inheritance. At times one may – indeed, has to – question the impact of national attitude on the nature of kinship relations, developing a comparison for instance between the law as it relates to inheritance, the operation of welfare provision, or the historical contexts for the governing ideology of the family. At other times, the nation state does not appear as a pertinent unit of comparison, in particular when cultural considerations are stressed; here regional patterns may be more significant in accounting for behaviour and attitudes inherited from past social structures. This is shown in the analysis of cohabitation between generations in certain parts of France (Claudine Attias-Donfut) or the role of 'peerdom' in Catalonia (Joan Bestard and Jesus Contrerás) or again in the varying potency of family interaction in different regions of Italy (Marzio Barbagli).

In spite of such reservations, the volume constitutes a first step towards a cross-cultural understanding of European countries, in regard to facets of family experience that are not susceptible to an orthodox statistical approach. It may claim originality insofar as it is concerned to look at aspects of kinship that do not generally receive consideration, that is, interchange and interdependence, and to point to influences that may help or hinder the perpetuation of the family and to the conditions that render it visible or invisible. On the basis of cases examined, a few provisional conclusions may perhaps be drawn.

The perpetuation of the family (or, more generally, experience of family) in Europe cannot be fully understood outside its socio-historical context. Portrayal and practice as it becomes enshrined in legislation is in essence and emphasis long-lasting. Thus Germany is still grappling with the father relationship, shrouded, as it was, in a mythology of authoritarianism before the trauma of the Nazi period, and now demystified following a far-reaching ideological metamorphosis; in Britain, individualism, in respect not only of couples but of individuals, is given an antecedence as early as the thirteenth century.

Secondly, modern conditions of living make do with kinship networks which at times resemble clanship, often based on individual homes or a common neighbourhood (as in Italy, Portugal and Spain; and in Sweden, too).

New family patterns (in particular, involving reconstituted families) incline one to view kinship as being governed by tension between biological and social factors. And one of the questions treated in this volume has to do with the decisions family members make in regard to the perpetuation of the family when a marriage is unstable. On the one hand, even when the relationship is a lasting one (and increasingly in such a relationship), there seems to be implicit mistrust of the children in the practice of making settlements in favour of the surviving spouse; on the other hand, instances of remarriage reveal a degree of uncertainty in handing down estate and evident hesitation between the need to provide support for the surviving partner and what is due to the children.

Finally, the change in the ideological context is paramount, as Marianne Gullestad rightly emphasizes. The line must go on, with the role of inheritance assured and with aspirations and identity finding expression; at the same time those newer values that enhance self-fulfilment must be recognized and promoted.

Factors connected with the perpetuation of the family are likely to require strengthening in the years ahead through the process of settlement and inheritance as well as through symbolic and material acts of transfer between generations. In Bourdieu's term, the contemporary family is clearly a 'continuous creation' (1994, p.10). Kinship at the close of the twentieth century is not a vestige of society but well and truly evidence of its modernity.

1

FERTILITY: THE CONDITION OF SELF-PERPETUATION. DIFFERING TRENDS IN EUROPE

Hervé Le Bras

Fertility has been subject to precise measurement in Europe for more than a century now. Yet its fluctuations and levels in individual countries remain largely unexplained. This has much to do with the fact that a particular indicator is used – the 'total fertility rate' or 'cross sectional index' – whereas there are many other approaches for observation and analysis available to specialists.

The problem with the total fertility rate is that of being equally sensitive to circumstantial and structural change, equally sensitive to changes in motherhood schedules and in lifetime fertility. By correcting this indicator so as to account in particular for changes in marriage (essentially the age at which women marry) and contraception (implying the spacing out of births or 'delayed contraception'), one aspect of the enigma surrounding changes and differences in level disappears while another can be better understood. Instead of proposing a description where entirely dissimilar past patterns, across the experience of war and economic crisis, are reconciled in the post-war period through a baby boom shared in common, followed by a general unexplained drop in birth rate after 1965, which for all western European countries implies falling below the generation reproduction threshold, a different picture emerges without this convergence, without a real baby boom occurring and which now offers quite distinct patterns of behaviour. Analysis of current disparities in fertility have the effect of bringing men back into the picture, and our argument supports the view that the differences have to do with variations in the relations between the sexes as they differ from one country to another, in particular between the north and south of Europe.

Table 1.1   Total fertility rate (TFR) in 1903 and 1989 and deviation from mean (%)

Country	1903 TFR	Deviation (%)	1989 TFR	Deviation (%)
Austria	4.93	21	1.50	− 9
Denmark	4.01	− 1	1.67	2
France	2.77	− 62	1.77	8
FRG	4.77	17	1.48	− 10
Italy	4.43	9	1.26	− 23
Netherlands	4.42	9	1.61	− 2
Norway	4.16	2	1.92	17
Sweden	3.84	− 5	2.11	29
Switzerland	3.82	− 6	1.61	− 2
United Kingdom	3.40	− 16	1.84	12

Convergence – an optical illusion

At the beginning of the century, fertility levels in European countries varied considerably, but they all concurred in registering the drop that continued across the periods of war and the economic crisis of 1929. In the aftermath of World War Two, all experienced markedly higher fertility – the baby boom – counting in about 1965 for an average of between 2.5 and 3.0 births per female. This in turn was followed by a sudden fall that over ten years or so brought the average down to well under two births.

It is my intention to show that the degree both in convergence and in the drop have been overestimated: in the first case by the representation used, and in the second by the nature of the TFR indicator, chosen as a base for analysis. Taking the case of convergence first, and the ten countries represented in Table 1.1, it is evident that in 1903 the differences were more marked (from 2.77 per female in France to 4.93 per female in Austria) than in 1989 (between 1.26 in Italy and 2.11 in Sweden). The question may also be put in relative terms: what is the variability in regard to average fertility expressed as a percentage of this fertility figure? Is it 10, 20, 50 per cent? The same table shows that variability has been virtually unchanged over a 90-year period, the standard deviation falling from 14.9 to 14.4 per cent.

It is further noticeable that countries have changed positions. They can be roughly distributed in three groups: those which were below the average and have moved above it (France and Britain); those adopting the opposite pattern (Germany, Austria and Italy, the former 'Axis' nations); and those remaining in the neighbourhood of the average (Denmark, Holland, Sweden and Norway). The fact that the groups are not without some spatial resemblance suggests that the changes that have occurred are less mysterious than one might think. If it is inaccurate to talk of convergence in regard to relative levels of fertility, we need to ask ourselves to what the difference and the changes are due.

How the total fertility rate responds to economic factors and structural change

Logically, the question is meaningless: a cross sectional indicator self-evidently measures what occurs within a given year. But analyses customarily tend to ignore short-term fluctuations and focus on long-term trends: the baby boom lasted for 20 years, the fall in the fertility rate in the 1970s more than ten years and more than 50 years between 1880 and 1940. While the indicator was deliberately intended to point to changes in the situation from one year to the next with a view to revealing short- and medium-term trends, it is in fact used to analyse very long-term trends. In one of its latest reports to the French parliament, the institute of population studies (INED) calculated what would have been the French population had the total fertility rate stayed at its 1805 level until 1945, or, to take another example, the UN and most central statistical offices in their projections set their objectives and the course of fertility in terms of the total fertility rate.

However, its contingency character renders it highly sensitive to contingency variations. To take an extreme case, if every couple suddenly decided to put off having a child for a year, hence rigorously applied contraceptive methods or recourse to abortion during the year in question, the total fertility rate would register zero. Would this imply that reproduction had ceased? Obviously so, momentarily. But the year following, things would get back to normal. In the end, couples would have the same number of children – 'completed fertility' so called – only a year late. Here one needs to be mindful of the conduct of those who did not plan a child during the year in question: either that they looked on that year as 'fallow' or that they adopted the timetable of people who have opted for delay and planned to start their family roughly a year later. In the first instance, demographers speak of 'recovery'. The two world wars provide an illustration: when hostilities ended, unions that had been deferred were finalized and the children thus postponed were born. The younger generations who had no reason to fall behind resumed their pre-war pattern of behaviour and the birth rate peaked to mark a return to normality. The Japanese 'year of the horse and of fire' provides a further illustration. The Japanese seek to avoid having children under this sign because the girls are said to be difficult to marry off, so in 1966, a year in question, births fell by more than a quarter. But in the preceding year and in the years following, births were higher than normal and made up for the 1966 shortfall. Those who would have chosen to have a child during 1966, had it not been 'horse and fire', put off - and sometimes brought forward - doing so; while the remainder simply carried on as before.

The case of falling behind is quite different. Suppose the average age for a woman's first marriage being 22 moved to 23 over five years then became stabilized. There would then be fewer births initially because a growing number of those who might have been expected to marry would have put off doing so; during each of the first five years, an increasing proportion would postpone marrying and so the overall figure for marriages would fall. At the end of the five years, the entire population would have made the adjustment of one year's delay and marriages would have resumed their previous volume. There would not then be recovery, which would imply a return to the initial situation, but the stabilizing of a new timetable for marriage, a year later than before. How is such delay to be seen as distinct from recovery? It is applying the following test: In the case of recovery, the timetable discrepancy is rapidly resolved; in the case of delay it is stabilized. Unions deferred by the 1939–45 war were realized in 1945 and 1946, slightly increasing the average age for marriage, though it fell back in the years following. Hence recovery shows all the characteristics of a contingency occurrence whereas delay signals structural change. And, since the end of the nineteenth century and still more since 1945, the choice of a later time (and an earlier one corresponding to schedules showing a decrease in age) has become more marked. Figure 1.1 plots changes since 1946 in the average age of women in Sweden at the time they were first married, moving down from 25.6 to 23.5 in 1966, then steadily upwards to 27.6 in 1987 before apparently stabilizing. These changes were not contingency-prompted, but a clear indication of a series of strong long-term structural adjustments. Given what has just been said about delaying, such changes have certainly had a repercussion on the observed effect of the total fertility rate. Hence in speaking of fertility trends in terms of the number of children - that is, the size of families - the total fertility rate has to be corrected for structural variations, by estimating what it would have stood at had it not been for

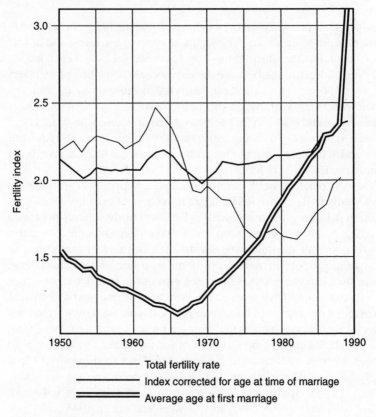

Figure 1.1   Sweden 1950-1990

these fluctuations in schedule, or what it would have stood at all things being equal. Such a correction is possible as a first approximation.

Correction of total fertility rate for the effects of age at the time of marriage

One might begin by taking a hypothetical case. In a given population the women all marry at age X and every generation is identical in number; further, in the course of a given year T, their marrying age rises steadily by a fraction of a year A, becoming by the end of the year X+A and thereafter remaining so. Hence marriage and the average age for marriage for the years T−1, T and T+1 are as follows:

Table 1.2   Distribution of ranked births in 1985

	1st ranking	2nd	3rd	other
France	42	35	14	8
Denmark	46	37	13	4
FRG	48	36	11	5
Netherlands	44	36	14	7
Spain	46	32	13	9
Great Britain	45	35	15	5
Choices	45	35	15	5
Interval in years	1	4	7	10

Year	Marriages	Mean Age at Marriage
$T-1$	M	X
T	$M(1-A)$	$X+A/2$
$T+1$	M	$X+A$
$T+n$	M	$X+A$

This formula remains valid when people of one generation marry at different ages provided the delay in marriage represented by A is the same with each age. If births follow one another and follow marriage on a schedule that is invariable (intervals between births likewise when the age of marriage changes), the marriage discrepancy will produce a similar discrepancy with births, hence an apparent fall in fertility in the ratio $1-A$. However, this discrepancy will not occur at the time of marriage but when the first birth is due. At a given moment T, if the distribution of marriage duration for mothers giving birth is $g(U)$, the overall drop in fertility is thus expressed:

$$\int_0^{35} g(U)(1-A(T-U))dU / \int_0^{35} g(U)dU$$

This expression cannot be calculated directly by means of available data on fertility. However, since variations in the age of marrying develop over longer timespans than the intervals between births, one may consider $A(T-U)$ to be constant for a given birth ranking N and U equal to the mean interval between marriage and the birth ranking in question. In which case, it is sufficient to know the values $g(U)$ (that is, the number of N ranking births in T). There is relatively little variation as is shown by Table 1.2, listing miscellaneous European countries in 1985, which gives the values of g as well as the marriage–N birth-ranking intervals applied. The formula thus becomes far simpler and more readily applicable to current data since it only makes use of variations in the marrying age:

$$1-A^* = 1-(0.45A(T-1)+0.35A(T-4)+0.15A(T-7)+0.05A(T-10))$$

Figure 1.1 makes it clear how the formula corrects the curve described by the Swedish total fertility rate. The term 'correct' is exact. Whereas the indicator fluctuated between 1.6 and 2.5 over the last 50 years, when corrected the values expressed remain in a far narrower band, between 2.05 and 2.25 children per female. This result is not due to its being theoretically dependent on the mean age for a first marriage and the cyclical indicator. Calculation does not assume unvarying consistency in fertility. And so it is of interest in that it produces the result it does. If one discounts the effect produced by the considerable fluctuations in the marrying age on the total fertility indicator in Sweden, it is more or less constant for the whole post-war period. Not only has the baby boom disappeared but also the 'drop' in fertility which put Sweden, along with other western European countries, below the 'reproduction threshold'. How is the remaining fluctuation to be accounted for? A question which appears to be of minor importance for Sweden as shown by Figure 1.1 takes on quite different significance when it comes to Federal Germany where, as Figure 1.2 shows, an identical adjustment has been made.

As in Sweden, though rather later, the marrying age fell then rose again describing the same V-type curve. From being 25 in 1947 it went down to 22.6 at the start of the 1970s, then between 1976 and 1988 rose again to 25.4. This delay, as compared with Sweden, results in a marked fluctuation of the index corrected for the effects of marrying age. Even so, as in the case of Sweden, the final result (1.8) is very close to that for the 1950s and even the 1930s. Such a fluctuation gives the impression of a movement forward followed by a movement back, as if the upper part were counterbalancing the lower that followed it. Referring back to the assumptions on which the model is based, such an effect would not appear unreasonable, giving an unvarying schedule of births following marriage. Further scrutiny is needed.

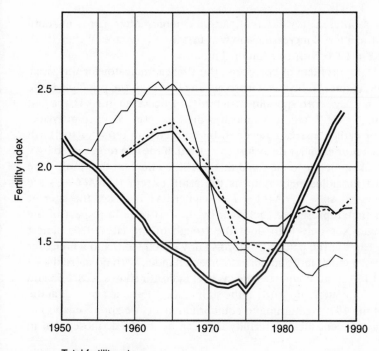

Total fertility rate
Index corrected for age at time of marriage
Index corrected for age at time of marriage and protogenetic interval
Average age at first marriage

Figure 1.2   Federal Germany 1950–1988

Variation in the interval between marriage and birth of the first child

One source, the *Eurostat 1989 Yearbook*, provides information on the mean age for first pregnancies in the Federal Republic, based not on fertility rates but on mothers' ages. Mean ages at the time of the first marriage available via the same source are established in the same way and this makes cross-comparison possible (the slight discrepancy between marriage and first birth nullifies any effect of varying age distribution). If the schedule of births was established after marriage, these should be identical and adjusted in terms of the mean interval between marriage and the first birth. If this interval is then taken as equalling one year and the marriage curve on the abscissa adjusted by twelve months, a very different pattern emerges. After narrowing until 1966, the interval increased slowly at first then very rapidly after 1970, settling in 1976 with 14 additional months.

With the problem of correcting the cyclical indicator for this variation in the interval between marriage and first birth the principle is the same: marriage corresponding to a birth in T occurred in $T - U$; the first birth in $T - U + V$, where V indicates the time elapsed since marriage. Later or earlier marriage needs to be corrected in terms of the birth being later or earlier, a delay just calculated. If the gap represented by V is not taken into account – and this has little effect on the result – the formula for adjustment remains the same except that $A(T - U)$ are replaced by $A(T - U) + A1(T - U + 1)$, where A1 indicates the later or earlier time represented each year by the first birth in respect of the marriage. Not only then does the trough of the late 1970s almost disappear, but the pattern conforms fairly exactly to that obtaining for Sweden: a much more stabilized corrected index with no more than a 1.75/2.15 variation whereas the cyclical indicator shows 1.28/2.55 and the same variation, upwards at the start of the 1960s, downwards at the end of the 1970s, returning to equilibrium in a close approximation to the most recent lifetime fertility that can be assessed (those born in 1955).

Direct use has not been made of mean ages at the time of the first birth. A later time for the first birth begins to appear in 1970, eight years before that for the first marriage. On the face of it, one would attribute this to a straightforward chain of events – later marriage leading to concomitant delay in first birth. In fact, it is the converse that has occurred – a later first birth has produced an impact on the marriage, and delayed it accordingly. Sweden provides an exception in that the gaps between marriage and first birth showed little variation during the 1970s, since evidence of increasing fertility outside marriage disturbed the relation between the two figures. Marriage climbed at the same time as did first births, on which it anyway depended. On the other hand, this concurrence did not yet show, and the pattern of marrying young continued while the tendency to delay a first pregnancy developed. With the gap growing too wide, an adjustment occurred, with marriage following in the wake of the first birth. This brings into focus fertility outside marriage which comes to have significant bearing on the whole question.

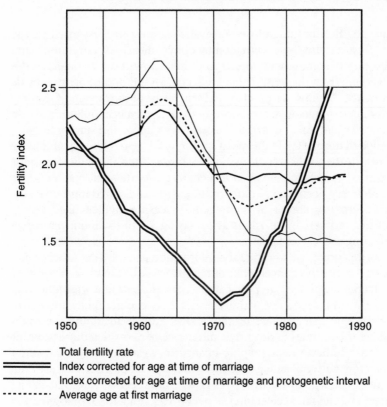

Total fertility rate
Index corrected for age at time of marriage
Index corrected for age at time of marriage and protogenetic interval
Average age at first marriage

Figure 1.3   Switzerland 1950–1990

Generalization of correction

It is tempting to apply the method to all the countries for which we
have an annual series of cyclical indicators and age at the time of first
marriage. Figure 1.3 shows that results obtained in Switzerland corroborate those for Sweden and Germany, with the first and second
corrections giving a similar result to that provided by Germany. Britain,
Denmark and Norway, though not represented here, correspond to the
same trend – that is, not showing a recent drop in fertility on the
corrected index and maintaining a slight fluctuation upwards between
1960 and 1965, and downwards between 1972 and 1980.

In Latin countries, in France and especially in Spain and Italy, a new
pattern emerges as a result of the first correction. Recovery in the 1960s
is slight and the downward trend continues. Further afield, with eastern

Europe, the adjustment loses most of its interest because marriage age drops after the war, with contraceptive measures developing and abortion becoming widespread, and then shows little change. Besides diverging from the west, Poland, Czechoslovakia and Hungary provide evidence of how at precise dates a measure in favour of fertility produces simultaneous response both in the cyclical indicator and in the mean age at first marriage curves. For example, in Hungary in 1973, a sudden drop of 0.3 in the mean age for marriage is followed directly by a rise in the cyclical indicator of 0.3 births, then the indicator drops again as the age picks up. In more general terms, these fairly short bursts of recovery occurring at different moments in each country give substance to the notion of contingency measures which have simply accelerated certain decisions as to having a child without ultimately affecting the size of families.

At this point, we assessed the information given by the total fertility rates. There is no convergence of fertility in European countries, rather a divergence of demographic pattern between east and west following the war, and divergence within the west between the centre and north, on the one hand, where fertility shows little change, and the south where it continues to drop. The difference here is the more significant because hitherto demographic change in western Europe showed a common pattern: falling steadily since the nineteenth century, the gouge produced by the the 1914–18 war, brief recovery in 1920, falling again and the fall accelerating between 1930 and 1935, following the economic crisis, slight recovery in every country on the eve of World War Two, the incision this produced, recovery, then between 1955 and 1965 slightly varying movement in a generally upward direction. Thereafter if southern European countries had followed those in the centre and north in a downward direction until about 1980, the course of fertility would be fairly simple using the corrected indicator, but the continued drop in the south breaks with the long-term trend and poses something of a puzzle; it also provides a clue towards understanding the whole pattern of movement in the post-war period.

Indeed, without the south, the general movement upwards then downwards might be compared with the 1930s situation. The 1929 crisis doubtless accelerated the fall in fertility by lengthening the period between marriage and childbirth and by delaying marriage. After 1935, signs of a return to normality help explain the slight recovery better than does the start of an enigmatic baby boom. Similarly, inflationary trends in 1955–65 led to a higher rate of fertility; then, following the oil shock and a slowdown after 1975 there was a levelling out five years later. Hence there would only remain a very long-term trend towards falling fertility with approximately two children per family, and varying medium-term shifts such as post-war upturns (deep troughs followed by peaking) and major economic transformations (with gentler contours such as the variations produced between the the 1960s and 1980s in Sweden, Switzerland or Germany). These last recall the long-lasting economic fluctuation pointed to by Wrigley and Schofield (1981) over three centuries in England, where the rise and fall in the age of marrying in roughly 50-year periods followed fluctuating wages and economic performance, bringing in its wake variations in fertility and illegitimacy. After the so-called 'transitional' drop, western European countries resumed a fluctuating pattern in line with economic (and employment) conditions and the political situation (wars). On this assumption, all variations in the cyclical indicator are the result of timetable fluctuations and it would be misleading to look for a new transition or wait for the situation to be made good.

Such a conclusion leaves the case of southern Europe open and overlooks the very source that enabled us to correct the total fertility rate. Why have marrying ages in all western countries experienced a downward – then an upward – movement, in so consistent, extensive and similar a way? Changes in fertility are not then to be understood in terms of the baby boom or the fall in the uncorrected total fertility rate but via the study of age at the time of marriage and particularly at the time the first child is born. An initial lead is suggested by the different behaviour pattern in eastern Europe: why after 1965 or 1970 did age at the time of marriage not move upwards in the east as it did in the west?

Differing models in east and west: contraceptive measures and age at the time of marriage

Usually two reasons are provided for early marriage in eastern Europe – the right to an apartment that marriage conferred and a woman's right to work. With marriage conferring the right to an apartment, it becomes the accepted means of achieving independence: leaving home and setting up on one's own are thus synonymous, whereas in the west an interlude has grown between gradual independence and marriage. Female employment, though not implying conditions of equality between both sexes, nevertheless affords a vital channel for aspirations, given expression in the west with the catch-phrase 'first a job, then a

Table 1.3   Number of abortions per 100 births

	1975	1987
Bulgaria	83	103
Czechoslovakia	30	73
Hungary	52	67
Poland	22	20
East Germany	47	42
Romania	86	131
USSR	153	122
Denmark	40	36
France	-	21
Federal Germany	3	14
Italy	-	34
Netherlands	9	10
Sweden	33	32
United Kingdom	18	23
United States	33	42
Japan	35	38

family'. In the east, with a job theoretically provided, the family had no need to wait.

Looking more closely, equal conditions between men and women seemed in fact impossible to achieve, or even activate, in the east for two reasons that complement the above two – the means of birth control and the traditional form of marriage. In regard to the first, the east, as one knows, differed from the west in that, with other more modern methods being little available, contraception tended to mean abortion. In the absence of the pill and the coil, over 80 per cent of couples in eastern Europe used the rhythm method or *coitus interruptus*. When this failed, as it inevitably did, women had recourse to abortion (see Table 1.3). Abortion was of course legal because the jobs undertaken by women, as well as being guaranteed, were necessary in an underachieving economy. Even so, abortion was a policy instrument in the hands of government and wielded as such, notably in Romania in 1967, capable of being prohibited without warning, while more traditional methods are dependent on the will to apply them. In other words, in the east, contraception could not mean that women had control over reproduction, and in no way corresponded to the feminist slogan in the west: 'I shall have a child if and when I want to'.

One may even question whether the fact of marriage conferring the chance of a home was really a conquest of socialism and not rather a reversion to an age-old tradition. Since Hajnal's celebrated article (1965), we are indeed aware of a line from St Petersburg to Trieste separating eastern Europe where marriage takes place early and western Europe where later marriage is favoured. Thus in allowing young couples to set up together, the popular democracies were restoring long-established family traditions. It provided a means to requite opposition to economic reforms; likewise in Algeria, the introduction of state socialism was accompanied by a strengthening of the traditional family. Furthermore, early marriage places the woman in a subordinate position since age difference between marriage partners counts for more at 20 than at 26 or 28, and all in all makes a young couple more dependent on their entourage and outside help than one older having, in the sound Malthusian tradition, acquired resources of their own.

Thus, the availability of abortion, the right for all women to work, and marriage giving access to an apartment, all of which appear to advance equality between the sexes, in all probability reinforced the sexual roles by disallowing women any margin for initiative. Conversely in the west, the decisive moment occurred around 1965 when modern contraceptive methods became legally available. When women have the means of independently deciding whether or not to conceive, their access to equality with men takes on a more concrete, more general, significance. After 1965, contraception provided an answer to unwanted pregnancies, which in a survey carried out by Siebert and Sutter (1963) accounted in France for 20 per cent of all pregnancies. Very soon, however, the demand for equality moved beyond the family to education. The number of girls continuing in education increased rapidly, catching up with and, in some countries, even moving ahead of the number of boys. Employment provided a third sphere for the development of equality. In every country, women came into the labour market in vast numbers after 1965, though the rate decreased about 1970 and in some countries even became stationary. During the same period, surveys show women giving precedence to job access over starting a family. Early in the 1970s the oil crisis and rising unemployment suddenly imperilled these prospects.

Three models of female occupational activity

There are three distinct models characterizing female employment worldwide. In the first, women work in the market sector only before being married or having children. This attitude is found traditionally in

Table 1.4   Young female employment rates in 1960, 1970 and 1990

| | 1960 | | | 1970 | | | 1990 | | |
	15-19	20-24	25-29	15-19	20-24	25-29	15-19	20-24	25-29
Denmark	66.7	58.9	38.7	47.8	67.8	58.7	64.4	81.7	85.1
FRG	78.2	71.9	50.7	64.4	67.1	51.5	34.8	73.4	70.8
Greece	46.8	52.2	43.6	36.5	33.4	31.9	19.7	46.7	55.6
Spain	27.1	28.2	16.6	36.7	39.6	20.8	21.6	58.8	66.7
France	35.7	61.8	45.6	27.0	63.0	55.0	9.4	59.5	80.5
Ireland	59.6	68.2	38.9	47.6	65.5	34.7	23.6	73.3	64.8
Italy	39.3	40.6	30.1	36.7	44.7	36.2	23.0	61.2	65.1
Luxemburg	55.8	49.2	29.4	55.2	53.3	33.5	25.7	71.0	68.3
Netherlands	59.3	52.8	22.5	49.6	55.5	28.2	42.9	76.0	73.0
Portugal	27.3	26.5	19.8	44.8	45.5	33.1	30.0	63.9	79.6
United Kingdom	71.4	62.4	39.9	55.7	60.1	43.0	57.2	72.5	69.7

Europe in cases where women provided a bridal trousseau as in present-day Muslim countries. Employment rates at whatever level are in this instance highest between 15 and 19, and then fall rapidly. In the second model, characterized by its two humps, women go to work on leaving school, give up their jobs in order to raise their children, then go back into the labour market at 35 or so. In the final model, where the sexes face employment on an equal footing, the occupational curves for both sexes more or less coincide. Over the last 30 years, western European countries show various combinations of these three models, frequently moving rapidly from one to the other (see Table 1.4). In 1960, for instance, the first model still applied almost universally. However, northern Europe differed clearly from southern in showing high levels of female employment between 15 and 25, though beyond 25 the fall was general. An upward movement of women into the labour market was reflected in most countries in a growth of the second model after 1970. Divergence came about afterwards.

Denmark is the only country in the European Union where the third model applies, with women virtually equalling men in occupational activity. In the other north-western or central countries of Europe, female employment, though significantly high in late adolescence, decreases a little with motherhood, then rises again, so corresponding to the second model. On the other hand, in France and the south, the rise in female employment tends to shift to ever higher ages. The levels drop before 25 and rise beyond. For the 11 countries in the Union for which we can profile female employment, the typology works without exception. These contrasts remain to be accounted for.

Table 1.5   Population and family indicators in the countries of the European Union

	Out of wedlock births (%) 1991	Difference in fertility 1985–1991	Young people belonging to no association (%)	Young people finding work through family (%)
Belgium	7	0.08	41	28
Denmark	46	0.22	15	19
Federal Germany	10	0.20	41	21
Greece	2	−0.61	74	69
Spain	10	−0.35	67	61
France	30	−0.04	59	35
Ireland	17	−0.32	41	33
Italy	6	−0.15	54	65
Luxemburg	12	0.22	24	27
Netherlands	12	0.10	26	18
Portugal	15	−0.19	76	58
United Kingdom	30	0.04	41	28

In our opinion, the varying situation of women vis-à-vis their family and kin and their immediate entourage accounts for this divergence in levels of employment and accordingly of fertility.

Three models for fertility in western Europe

Table 1.5 considers the reasons that may determine women in choosing this or that occupational profile. It looks at aspects of fertility such as the proportion of births outside marriage, or recovery in the total fertility rate after 1985 which clearly sets out the contrast between north and south, as well as two findings from a European Union survey on young people in 1990 – those between 15 and 24 not belonging to any association and those who found their current job through family or friends.

These two data show a remarkable split between south and north: on the one hand, close dependence on family; on the other, rapid incorporation in a wider social grouping. Leaving aside Ireland, where the demographic transition is still not completed, fertility increases where young people live in the larger community and drops where family pressure is strong. The proportion of births outside marriage makes for a further distinction, very marked in the north and north-west, low in the south and the centre (Benelux and Germany). So pressure from the family and the locality does not tell the whole story.

Let us attempt to piece together these still relatively isolated observations, looking upon them as so many parts of a general movement in women's liberation. In Denmark, Sweden and the UK, parity between the sexes in the labour market is close to being achieved. Certainly women are not yet working at levels equivalent to men, but their role in the community is at least equal if not greater. Family pressure is weak because young people are accorded a greater measure of freedom, perhaps also because the sense of individual rights is more developed. The decision to have children does not involve women in abdicating their quest for equality; they thereby assert their autonomy. They may continue the fight for equality by demanding equal pay, but their continued inequality often takes the form of the higher jobs being denied them or their having to work longer hours. Yet, even if women on average hold less skilled and less well-paid jobs, individually there are numbers of men who are equally poorly paid and with jobs that are equally low-level. This is a grey area as far as sexual discrimination goes, unlike the criterion of employment which is two-fold and particularly clear. More than 95 per cent of males between 25 and 45 are at work in every country considered; hence not to be at work clearly means not to be like men. That one's job may be low-skilled does not have this clear-cut significance. Once women have attained a job-level they can hardly hope to better, their potential for asserting their particularity as women – above all, by childbearing – takes on greater importance.

And it is in these same countries that teenage fertility is the highest in Europe. In Britain, where it is the major demographic preoccupation, it is explained by the desire on the part of young women who feel they have underachieved both at school and at work to affirm their maturity. Besides, the high percentage of births outside marriage is a further expression of individualism. In these countries, the reasons for postponement of a first pregnancy no longer apply, with the result that automatically fertility has risen while the age for starting a family has stabilized. It is noticeable also that in Britain, as in Denmark, the proportion of young women (15 to 19) at work has increased since 1970, signifying that the obstacles in the way of women gaining access to the labour market have largely been removed.

A second group includes central European countries – Belgium, Holland, Luxemburg and Germany, with Switzerland and Austria presenting a similar profile. Female employment is not so high and conforms to the second type – that is, with an interruption while the children are still very young. Another major feature here is the low rate of births outside marriage; further, lifetime fertility has been smaller than elsewhere in Europe over a longer period. Essentially the cultural distinction between these countries and those of the first group has to do with their perception of the mother–child relationship. In all six countries, attitudes inculcated by morality, psychology and sociology emphasize the importance of motherhood in its early phase. This group happens also to be the least well provided for in crèches, child-minders and nursery schools: fewer than 25 per cent of children between 3 and 5 use these resources as against almost 90 per cent in France. The importance attached to the mother–child relationship often compels women to stop working when they have a child (hence employment curves that conform to the second type), to have a husband as a means of financial support (hence the low percentage of births outside marriage), and reduces their desire for any further children in that they feel that this would divert their attention from the firstborn (hence the low level of lifetime fertility).

The third group comprises the four southern countries – Italy, Greece, Spain and Portugal. Both family and local group still maintain their influence over women (the two 'family' indices reach their highest levels here). Liberation and achieving equality with men hence imply eluding this group pressure. The degree of resistance can be measured by extramarital fertility. Women in Spain and Italy have achieved sexual freedom; their first sexual relationships occur ever earlier and outside marriage. They have also won the right to cohabit without being married, but they continue to recognize the barrier of childbirth outside marriage. Acquiring a job is the first condition of their freedom, and their commitment to doing so is the greater for knowing, as they do, that the birth of a child would immediately oblige them to return to their traditional position of inferiority. Motherhood – what differentiates them – can only be accepted insofar as they have achieved equality with men – that is, similarity. This search for equality doubtless explains both the low levels of employment below the age of 20, the high unemployment figure for young women, and the growth of the employment rate beyond 25. We are here faced with the snowball effect which, according to Bourdieu (1984), maintains the demand for continuing education: higher numbers reduce the value of qualifications. In order to obtain the sort of position which a particular qualification previously put one in line for, one is forced to go for a higher qualification which in turn depreciates. Competition between men and women may aggravate the mechanism, explain it even: indeed before the qualification in question depreciates, girls are unable to benefit from it to the same extent as their male fellow students. Hence they carry their studies further so as to compensate by yet higher qualifications for the discrimination they undergo, and men follow so as to maintain their domination. The mechanism is self-sustaining, the role of the family being reinforced because young people remain at home longer to complete their studies and find a job; and the family thereby stokes the desire to get away, expressed by the pursuit of study and the subsequent search for a job. In these conditions, the age at which motherhood occurs should continue to climb, so keeping the cyclical indicator at a low level.

So by a curious paradox, in one part of Europe, the family is stifling fertility, while in another the importance attached to the mother–child relationship, or its institutional replacement, endorses fertility and so pushes the total fertility rate up. France has not yet been allotted to one or other of these groups. One can only say that France is currently experiencing a debate on the family which places it at the centre of these contradictions; and this may have to do with the fact that in France a more complex interlocking process is at work, a relationship linking government to families and families to children, as if by a form of delegation.

Self-perpetuation was the central concern of the traditional European family and, beyond that, of all societies where descent has been held to be important, but in present-day Europe biological reproduction no longer seems to be a family imperative. It is more and more becoming an indirect consequence of arbitration between men and women, or between individuals and institutions in power-sharing and the alloca-tion of their respective rights. The very notion of the reproduction of the family has become highly abstract in a world where geographical and social mobility is on the increase and where the limits of physical and social environment are no longer perceptible on a human scale. The fascination, however ill-conceived, exercise upon the French govern-ment by rates of fertility and the whole question of population renewal very probably represents a transferral to national level of preoccupa-tions which once existed at the level of the family. And this is why the adjustment of the index of fertility that we have here drawn attention to has more than technical application. It undermines a symbol of the perpetuation of the state.

2

FAMILY AND KINSHIP IN ITALY

Marzio Barbagli

Kin relations in Italy

Unlike their colleagues in other Western countries, Italian sociologists have only recently begun to study kin relations in their own country. They have shown that, in Italy as elsewhere, there is still a close, strong network of ties among kin. In addition, those who marry, though following the rules of neolocal residence, maintain a strong relationship with their family of origin and in particular with their parents.

A major survey conducted in 1983 by Istat (Istat, 1985) found that there is a strong exchange of goods and services among households tied to one another by family relations (for example, among households composed by parents and households formed by their married children). Some of these exchanges are made up of continuous flows (like aid for child care), others are exceptional and occur only in crucial moments (marriage, job transition, a death in the family).

An important part of these exchanges is made up of intergenerational patrimonial transfers. In Italy, as in other Western countries, the passage of property from one generation to the next takes place during the entire life-course, not only upon death of parents.

The proportion of Italian families who own the houses in which they live, which has been increasing over the past 40 years, reached 68 per cent in 1990 (Istat, 1993). Intergenerational transfers are a particularly important factor in determining home ownership; 23 per cent of families residing in Italy in 1983 had obtained their home as a gift or as dowry or through inheritance. The percentage is even higher in the South and in smaller towns (Istat, 1985).

Italy and other countries

It is relatively difficult to tell whether or not the strength of kin ties has changed over the last 30 years and whether there are any differences, from this point of view, between the various Western nations – that is, whether intergenerational ties are stronger in some countries than in others. Nevertheless, empirical evidence of different types and drawn from different sources suggest that the strength of kin relations in Italy is greater than elsewhere.

The first piece of evidence concerns the age at which young people cease to reside in their parents' home. The lengthening of children's permanence in their parents' home is a phenomenon common to all Western countries, among which there are, however, important differences. Ninety per cent of all young males aged between 20 and 24 live with their parents in Italy, compared with 50 per cent in France, Great Britain, the United States and the Netherlands, and only 26 per cent in Denmark (De Sandre, 1986).

The second piece of evidence concerns the spatial distance separating parents, adult children, siblings and other relatives and the frequency of contact among them. A survey carried out in 1986 on samples drawn from eight nations shows that the countries in which the frequency of face-to-face contacts with kin was higher were Italy and Hungary, followed by Austria, West Germany and Great Britain. The countries with the lowest frequency of face-to-face contacts were the United States and Australia (Höllinger and Haller, 1990).

A December 1993 Istat survey, performed on a particularly large sample, provides the opportunity for making comparisons on the basis of two indicators: residential proximity and frequency of interaction. According to those findings, 69 per cent of adult children over 25 years of age reside in the same municipality (that is, the same comune, the basic Italian administrative unit) as their parents (see Table 2.1).

Research conducted at the end of the 1970s in Middletown, in the United States (Caplow and others, 1982), revealed that 43 per cent of adult children with living parents resided in the same locality as the latter. In France, according to two other inquiries (Roussel and Bourguignon, 1976; Gokalp, 1978), 35 to 40 per cent of adult children live in the same municipality as their mothers and fathers.

There seems, therefore, to be a notable difference between Italy and other areas of Europe and the United States for which we have comparable data. However, we must take the second indicator into consideration before we can reach sounder conclusions. In the mid-

Table 2.1 Residence of Italian adults (aged 25 or older) with respect to parents (or mother, if father deceased) in 1993, by age group (percentage values)

	25-34	35-44	45-54	55-64	Total
Together	36	12	11	16	21
In another flat in the same building	7	12	10	9	9
In the same municipality	33	44	39	43	39
Different municipality	24	32	40	32	31
Total	100	100	100	100	100
(N)	(8231)	(6741)	(4508)	(1569)	(21049)

1950s in the traditionally working-class districts of London, characterized by extremely close intergenerational ties, 74 per cent of adult children with parents still living saw them at least once a week (Young and Willmott, 1957; Townsend, 1957). Not long afterwards, in another district of London with a strong middle-class presence, about 60 per cent of adult children with living parents met them at least once a week (Young and Wilmott, 1960). According to another inquiry conducted in Swansea, in Wales, the proportion of adult children who saw their fathers and mothers with such frequency was 70 per cent (Rosser and Harris, 1965).

Since then various other inquiries have been conducted, but none of them have revealed a particularly high frequency of interaction between parents and adult children. In Middletown in the 1970s, for example, 48 per cent of adult children saw their parents at least once a week (Caplow and others, 1982). The proportion reached 40 to 45 per cent in Boston in the 1980s (Rossi and Rossi, 1990) and 50 per cent in France in the 1970s (Pitrou, 1977). According to the 1993 Istat study, in Italy the proportion reaches 80 per cent.

Though only partial and in no way satisfying, these data do show that ties between parents and adult children are stronger in Italy than in other Western countries for which we have comparable data.

Regional differences

Many observers and scholars claim that there exist important differences between Italian regions as regards the cohesion of kin relationships. The most famous argument of this kind was put forth by Banfield (1958). Studying a poor village in Lucania, this American anthropologist and political scientist maintained that among the population of this specific village and among the Southern regions in general there prevails the ethos of 'amoral familialism', which leads people to 'maximise immediate material advantage for the nuclear family, on the understanding that others will do the same', and thus deprives them of civic spirit and the capacity to act for the common good. This ethos depends upon three factors: 'A high rate of mortality, particular arrangements governing property, and the existence of an institutionalised extended family.'

According to Banfield, in the South, kin relationships among relatives who do not belong to the same nuclear household are weaker than in Central and Northern Italy. In the Mezzogiorno, in fact 'a man once married considers father, mother, brothers, sisters and close relatives as enemies. ... This conflictual stance protects his new family from demands and pressure on the part of his original family, yet at the same time paralyses any form of family cooperation. Even if a total break is avoided, the link between son and parents is decidedly weakened by marriage of the former. Once he has taken a wife and had children, he is no longer obliged to look after his parents – unless they are dying of hunger.' (Banfield, 1976, p.92, Italian edition)

Banfield's theses have been discussed on various occasions.[1] Some critics and reviewers have claimed the exact opposite – that is, that kin relationships were once and continue to be much stronger in the South than in Central and Northern Italy. However, there has been absolutely no systematic research aimed at ascertaining the existence of important differences in kin relationships among Italian regions.

If one considers relatives (no matter if ascendant or descendant, blood-related or in-law) belonging to the same household, Banfield's thesis is certainly correct. Historical studies have shown that in the past (at least since the fifteenth century), in the cities of both Northern and Southern Italy, a large part of the population engaged in neolocal post-marital residence – that is, set up a nuclear household after marrying. In the countryside, by contrast, there were major differences among areas. In the Central and Northern regions a large part of the agricultural population followed patrilocal norms, and its members lived long periods of their life in households composed of three generations (at times in multiple horizontally extended households, uniting two, three or even four component nuclear family units). In the countryside of the South, on the other hand, a very high proportion of the population practised neolocal post-marital residence and lived in nuclear households.

According to 1951 census data, in Italy three distinct areas were identifiable on the basis of post-marital residence rules and household composition. Extended and multiple households were particularly widespread in regions of the 'Third Italy' (Umbria, Marche, Tuscany, Emilia and Veneto), whereas they were particularly scarce in the South (excepting Abruzzi). The North-western regions (Lombardia, Piemonte and Liguria) occupied an intermediate position as regards the frequency of extended and multiple households.

These differences in household composition in the various rural areas of Italy were due to the prevailing crops, the settlement pattern and the size of agricultural holdings. In the Central and Northern countryside, intensive cultivation systems prevailed, whereas extensive cultivation was typical in the South. In Umbria, Marche, Tuscany, Emilia-Romagna (where the sharecropping system was very widespread) and Veneto, the agricultural population lived scattered across the land in isolated farm households in which people worked all year long. In the South, by contrast, people lived not on their farmland, but in dense small or medium-size settlements. Thus, for them, in contrast to the farmers of the North, place of residence and place of work almost never coincided.

Industrialization in the 1950s and 1960s brought about radical change, in that it dissipated the organization of agriculture that had been the basis for the formation of multiple households in the rural areas of Northern and Central Italy. Yet important differences are still to be found among Italian regions as concerns household structure. Some of the regions of the 'Third Italy' continue to have the highest percentage of extended and multiple households, and Southern regions still have the lowest.

Italian regions also differ as concerns living arrangements of the elderly. There having been no systematic research on the subject, we cannot determine whether there are any differences among Italian regions as regards the moral obligations which adult children may feel they have towards elderly parents. Some anthropological studies, however, reveal that in Southern Italy both younger and older people have a strong desire *not* to live with other kin. The elderly tend to live with other relatives only in three cases: if they are ill and require assistance; if a child or grandchild is widowed and needs help; if the newly formed couple does not have enough resources to buy or rent its own home (Minicuci, 1989, pp.191–193).

What little data we do have show that there are considerable differences among regions in the elderly's living arrangements. Table 2.2

Table 2.2   Percentage of widows, aged 60 or over, who lived alone (A) or in complex (C) households (i.e., multiple and extended) in five Italian regions in 1981, by sex

Males	Lombardia A	Lombardia C	Tuscany A	Tuscany C	Umbria A	Umbria C	Campania A	Campania C	Sicily A	Sicily C
60–64	43	17	46	22	42	34	41	23	42	14
65–69	53	20	54	26	47	36	53	22	58	13
70–74	54	24	50	33	45	45	60	23	65	14
75–79	51	29	45	40	38	53	59	26	66	17
80–84	45	33	41	43	35	57	55	29	64	19
85–89	41	37	38	44	33	59	50	35	58	25
90+	34	42	32	48	29	63	46	39	53	30

Females	Lombardia A	Lombardia C	Tuscany A	Tuscany C	Umbria A	Umbria C	Campania A	Campania C	Sicily A	Sicily C
60–64	53	21	53	23	44	40	43	26	54	16
65–69	59	24	55	29	47	43	54	27	62	18
70–74	58	27	52	34	45	48	57	29	65	19
75–79	54	32	47	38	40	54	55	32	63	23
80–84	46	38	40	43	35	58	49	38	58	28
85–89	38	45	36	46	31	62	42	45	51	35
90+	28	51	28	47	22	69	35	51	44	41

shows the percentage of widowed males and females living alone or in complex (that is, extended and multiple) households in five Italian regions: one in the North (Lombardia), two in Central Italy (Tuscany and Umbria) and two in the South (Campania and Sicily). The percentage of widowed males aged 60 to 64 and who live alone is practically identical in all these regions. This percentage increases in the next highest age groups (in the next two age groups in some regions). The percentage of widowed males living alone then falls in the over-70 or over-80 groups, regardless of the region; and the percentage of widowed males who live with relatives in extended and multiple households increases, but to differing degrees according to region. In Umbria, already at the 75-year threshold widowed males living in extended and multiple households are more numerous than those living alone. In Tuscany this happens at the age of 80, in Lombardia after 90; in Campania and Sicily it never happens at all.

Similar patterns may be observed for widowed females, although those living in extended and multiple households become more numerous than those living alone at a relatively early age compared to males.

Table 2.3 Residence of married Italians with respect to parents (or mother, if father deceased) in 1993, by geographical area (percentage values)

	North-west	North-east	Central	South	Islands
Together	4	7	9	5	4
In another flat in same building	11	11	11	11	9
In same municipality	39	41	47	58	64
Different municipality	46	43	33	26	23
Total	100	100	100	100	100
(N)	(3415)	(3310)	(3134)	(4470)	(1739)

Table 2.4 Three- to five-year-old children residing in Italy who play with their grandparents sometimes or often, in 1989, by geographical area (percentage values)

	%	(N, 000s)
North-west	74.1	(277)
North-east	67.8	(434)
Central	72.9	(321)
South and Islands	76.6	(912)

Source: Istat (1994)

If, however, we do not consider co-residence and focus our attention exclusively on spatial distances, the interregional differences become more complex. If we examine the percentage of married Italians who live in the same municipality as their parents, it is highest in the South, lowest in the North (see Table 2.3). In fact, Italy's Northern population tends to be more mobile, either because it moves from one place to another within the North or because it comes from the South (Istat, 1985, pp.58 and 219; 1993, p.55). For example, in 1993 more married Italians lived together with their parents in North-eastern and Central regions than elsewhere.

On the other hand, Table 2.4 shows that the percentage of children who play with their grandparents is highest in the 'Third Italy' regions, which leads one to think that that is the area in which adult children have the most frequent contacts with their parents after they have married and had offspring.

Table 2.5 Percentage of Bologna residents who live alone (A), in nuclear households (N), in extended and multiple households (EM) and in institutions (I), in 1981 and 1991, by age (percentage values)

	1981				1991			
	A	N	EM	I	A	N	EM	I
60–64	16	66	9	–	13	67	9	–
65–69	21	60	10	1	19	62	8	–
70–74	27	50	12	1	26	55	8	1
75–79	32	36	18	2	32	45	11	1
80–84	34	24	21	5	36	32	15	3
85–89	32	14	26	10	35	17	22	7
90+	24	6	32	13	29	8	25	14

The Ageing of the population and the relationships between parents and adult children

Many factors should lead to a change in the relationships between adult children and elderly parents. One of the most important is the ageing of the population – that is, the increase in the proportion of the population aged 70 or over. This process involves all Western countries, but it has been particularly rapid in Italy, especially in some regions.

From this standpoint, the city of Bologna is an interesting case. It is the regional capital of Emilia-Romagna, a region in which the incidence of multiple and extended households was and remains among the highest. It is also a city with an extremely high ageing rate: today the ratio of residents aged 60 or over to those aged less than 20 is 2.32, versus 0.82 in Italy as a whole and 0.77 in the rest of the European Community (Golini, 1994). The number of people aged 80 or over has gone from 14,869 in 1981 to 21,610 in 1991.

So, the relationships between adult children and elderly parents has also undergone change in Bologna. Table 2.5 shows that the percentage of elderly people that live in extended and multiple households has diminished from 1981 to 1991. The percentage of older people who live in institutions has remained the same, and the percentage of people aged 80 or over who live alone has risen only slightly. There has been a greater increase in the percentage of elderly residents, especially among those aged between 75 and 84, whose spouse is still alive and who therefore live in nuclear households.

Even in the case of widowed females (Table 2.6), the percentage of those living in institutions remains the same from 1981 to 1991. The

Table 2.6   Percentage of female widows in Bologna who live alone (A), in extended and multiple households (EM) and in institutions, in 1981 and 1991, by age (percentage values)

	1981			1991		
	A	EM	I	A	EM	I
60–64	58	13	–	51	7	–
65–69	60	17	–	60	9	–
70–74	60	21	1	65	11	1
75–79	54	25	2	62	15	2
80–84	46	27	5	55	21	4
85–89	37	32	9	42	27	8
90+	23	37	13	29	30	14

percentage of widowed females who live alone, however, has grown significantly.

Gender and lines of kinship

In theory, the nuclear family and bilateral or cognatic kinship systems are dominant in Western nations. This means that those who marry should expect to go and live on their own and give equal importance to both lines of kinship, maintaining, therefore, the same relationship with the husband's relatives as with the wife's.

Research conducted in Great Britain, the United States, Holland, Sweden and Finland has shown, however, that in reality there is a relative dominance of matrilateral patterns – that is, giving priority to relationships with relatives in the female line of kinship. This conclusion has been arrived at by taking various indicators into consideration.

The above-mentioned inquiries have above all revealed that in families in which married couples live with their parents, the parents are more often those of the wife than those of the husband (Sweetser, 1966); in the second place, they demonstrate that couples live closer to the wife's parents than to the husband's; in the third place, they reveal that mothers more often stay in contact with their daughters than with their sons.

Residential proximity, frequency of contact and frequency of interaction are the dimensions of intergenerational relationships taken into consideration by most studies. A more recent inquiry (Rossi and Rossi,

1990), however, arrived at the same conclusions by studying two other aspects of such relationships: the affective importance given to various relations and the moral obligations people feel towards certain kin. The key relationship in this kinship pattern is the one between mother and daughter. According to the results of all inquiries conducted in Great Britain, the United States and other Western nations, the behaviour of mothers seems to be inspired by the old English proverb: 'My son is my son until he's married, my daughter's my daughter for life.' (Young and Willmott, 1957, p.43). Even after her daughter has married and left home, 'a special bond remains between the two' (Willmott and Young, 1960, pp.74-75). When the daughter gives birth the relationship becomes even closer; indeed, the daughter turns above all to her mother for advice and moral support during this phase (Finch, 1989).

Lines of kinship in Italy

All available data suggest that, unlike other Western countries, there was and still exists in Italy (or at least in some regions) a relative dominance of patrilateral kinship patterns. This is demonstrated, firstly, by data concerning aid provided by parents and other relatives to young married adults in Lombardia and Veneto allowing the latter to have their own home. Such aid is forthcoming from the husband's parents (and relatives) more often than from the wife's. The Lombardia data show that this holds true when the home is received as a gift or inherited by children (Tosi, 1991, p.259). The richer Veneto data stress that married children benefit more often, and in a greater variety of ways (see Table 2.7), from the husband's parents than from the wife's.[2]

The relative dominance of patrilateral kinship patterns can be inferred from the findings of a 1992 study on Italy. Table 2.8 shows that in Italy, unlike in other countries, married sons, regardless of age, tend to live closer to their parents (or mothers, if the fathers are deceased) than married daughters. The importance of patrilateral kinship patterns also emerges from the examination of the relationship between parents and sons and daughters who do not marry. Research carried out in Great Britain (Finch, 1989) has shown that it is usually daughters who remain single that tend to be charged with the task of looking after elderly parents, going to live with (or very close to) them or seeing them very often. This does not seem to be the case in Italy, however.

By examining Table 2.8, the reader may compare the situation of men and women who do not marry. Such comparison reveals that unmarried

Table 2.7   Aid to married couples residing in the Veneto region in 1991, by kinship line (percentage values)

Family supplying aid:	Wife's	Husband's	Total	(N)
Live in a house owned by parents or relatives	34	66	100	(118)
Inherited house or received it as gift from parents or relatives	35	65	100	(156)
Were helped by parents or relatives in finding house to rent	41	59	100	(71)
Received loans or financial aid to buy a house	49	51	100	(376)

Source: data supplied by Salvatore La Mendola

sons over the age of 25 live with their mother more often than unmarried daughters. In addition, the former live in the same municipality as their mother much more often than the latter.

Today patrilateral kinship patterns do not have the same importance (nor, most probably, did they in the past) in all Italian regions. Data from the 1993 study (see Table 2.9) show that:

(a) in north-western regions married sons and daughters live roughly at the same distance from their parents;
(b) in the southern and insular regions married sons and daughters tend to live together with their parents in equal proportions, although married sons tend to live in the same municipality as their parents more often than married daughters;
(c) in north-eastern and central regions, married sons live with their parents, or in another flat in the same building or in the same municipality more often than married daughters.

Strong interregional differences emerge once again if we examine the data pertaining to kin with whom married adults live in two very different stages of their life-course: during the early years of matrimony (Table 2.10) and many years later, when they decide to take in a needy, elderly parent (Table 2.11). According to these data, there is a patrilateral preference in Umbria and Tuscany, a matrilateral preference in Sardinia, a bilateral one in Campania, Sicily and Lombardia.

If they are integrated with the findings of the few previous studies (Bugarini and Vicarelli, 1979; Paci, 1980; Barbagli, 1984; La Mendola, 1991a; 1991b; Oppo, 1991) the data allow one to draw the conclusion

Table 2.8   Residence of Italian adults (aged 25 or older) with respect to parents (or mother, if father deceased) in 1993, by marital status, sex and age group (percentage values)

Unwed males	25-34	35-44	45-54	55-64	Total
Together	86	67	65	79	81
In another flat in the same building	3	8	7	4	4
In the same municipality	4	13	15	11	7
Different municipality	7	12	13	6	8
Total	100	100	100	100	100
(N)	(1970)	(465)	(167)	(48)	(2679)

Married males	25-34	35-44	45-54	55-64	Total
Together	5	5	8	12	8
In another flat in the same building	14	15	12	12	14
In the same municipality	52	51	48	46	50
Different municipality	29	29	32	30	28
Total	100	100	100	100	100
(N)	(1965)	(2833)	(1945)	(699)	(7442)

Unwed females	25-34	35-44	45-54	55-64	Total
Together	82	63	56	68	77
In another flat in the same building	2	7	13	10	4
In the same municipality	7	16	18	8	9
Different municipality	9	14	13	14	10
Total	100	100	100	100	100
(N)	(1201)	(274)	(142)	(62)	(1664)

Married females	25-34	35-44	45-54	55-64	Total
Together	3	4	6	11	5
In another flat in the same building	8	8	8	7	8
In the same municipality	48	48	48	45	48
Different municipality	41	40	38	36	39
Total	100	100	100	100	100
(N)	(2848)	(2911)	(1790)	(619)	(8168)

that patrilateral kinships systems are strongest in the regions of the 'Third Italy'. This system's primacy is nevertheless weaker than it once was, say 30 or 40 years ago. It has also all but disappeared in the larger cities (such as Florence and Bologna), where the bilateral system is gaining ground, whereas it remains important in smaller towns.

Table 2.9   Residence of Italian adults with respect to parents (or mother, if father deceased) in 1993, by geographical area and sex (percentage values)

Males	North-east	North-west	Central	South	Islands
Together	4	8	12	5	3
Same building	12	16	14	14	9
Same city	38	42	48	59	67
Different city	46	34	26	22	20
Total	100	100	100	100	100
(N)	(1633)	(1562)	(1469)	(2066)	(801)

Females	North-east	North-west	Central	South	Islands
Together	4	5	7	5	4
Same building	10	6	9	8	8
Same city	39	40	48	56	62
Different city	47	49	36	31	26
Total	100	100	100	100	100
(N)	(1782)	(1748)	(1665)	(2404)	(939)

In the South and on the Islands, there are areas in which the kinship system is patrilateral, others in which it is bilateral, and even some (for example, parts of Sardinia) in which it is matrilateral.

In the North-west a bilateral system prevails, although it will quite probably give way over the next 20 years to a system similar to the mostly matrilateral systems extant in the United States, in Great Britain and in other Western countries.

These interregional differences are basically related to the stronger differences which existed in the past. The patrilateral kinship system was dominant in the regions for centuries. When a woman married she was incorporated into her husband's family, obeyed the patrilocal residence norm and went to live in her husband's parents' (and sometimes married brothers') home. Moreover, after her wedding a woman was expected to dedicate more time and energy to her new relatives than to her blood relations. Her children were expected to be tied more closely to their father's relatives from an affective standpoint (Barbagli, 1984; Solinas, 1987).

A patrilateral system existed in many areas of the South as well (Cives, 1990; Palumbo, 1992): if, after marrying, a farmer went to live on his wife's land (*su parte di donna* or *su terra di donna*, as it was commonly called) he was judged very unfavourably by others, even when such a choice was economically sound, for instance if the wife was her family's only heir. '*Casa di mugliera, Casa di galera*' ('A

Table 2.10.   Married adults who live with their parents and are offspring of the head of household, in Pisa and Bologna countryside in 1841–47 and in selected Italian regions in 1971, 1981 and 1991, by sex

	Males	Females	% Females
Lombardia 1981	17,916	12,689	41.5
Lombardia 1991	17,493	14,870	45.9
Pisa countryside 1841	2,453	51	2.0
Tuscany 1971	56,289	15,994	22.1
Tuscany 1981	34,368	13,790	28.6
Tuscany 1991	30,409	24,115	44.2
Florence 1971	5,861	3,150	34.9
Florence 1981	2,985	2,199	42.4
Florence 1991	2,637	2,747	51.0
Bologna countryside 1847	2,387	18	0.7
Bologna 1981	1,824	1,345	42.4
Bologna 1991	1,911	1,833	48.9
Umbria 1981	10,536	2,571	19.6
Umbria 1991	8,766	3,607	29.1
Campania 1981	16,640	14,175	46.0
Campania 1991	26,252	29,824	53.2
Sicily 1981	11,626	11,192	49.0
Sicily 1991	10,569	12,700	54.6
Sardinia 1981	1,295	2,171	62.6
Sardinia 1991	3,785	4,338	53.4

Table 2.11   Kinship relationship with (male) head of household of widows who live in extended households in Tuscany and Bologna, in 1981 and 1991, by sex

Tuscany	1981				1991			
	Parent	In-law	Total %	Parent	Parent	In-law	Total %	Parent
Males	6093	2963	9056	67	4694	3408	8102	58
Females	38518	19209	57728	67	32902	22884	55786	59

Bologna	1981				1991			
	Parent	In-law	Total %	Parent	Parent	In-law	Total %	Parent
Males	374	280	654	57	233	214	447	52
Females	3001	2289	5290	57	2058	2032	4090	50

woman's house is a penal settlement') says a proverb that disapproves of such choices (Palumbo, 1992).

In Sardinia there was, on the contrary, a matrilateral system. The matrilocal post-marital residence rule was observed, and the husband usually moved to the village or house of the wife. The wife-mother of the agro-pastoral family enjoyed broad areas of decision-making autonomy within the household. In Sardinia, unlike the rest of Italy, there was a community system for property acquired during marriage. In addition, the system of inheritance typical in Sardinia was quite different from the dominant one in the other parts of Italy, where the law stipulated that only male offspring had the right to inherit from fathers, whereas daughters could only hope for a dowry out of the estate. In Sardinia, however, as early as the Middle Ages daughters had the same rights as sons to the parental estate (Oppo, 1990a; 1990b). Recent research has shown that, in some parts of Sardinia in the sixteenth and seventeenth centuries, there operated a surname transmission system through two lines: maternal for females and paternal for males (Murru Corriga, 1993).

Conclusion

In every Western country, the nuclear family functions within a compact network of interchange between relations, such interchange being especially strong where parents and grown-up children are concerned. However inadequate, the evidence available makes it clear that these particular ties are stronger in Italy than elsewhere. In Western countries there exists a cognate or bilateral system of kinship and those who are married are required to maintain ties with both sides of the family. A number of studies have brought out, however, that in the United Kingdom, the United States and other Western countries, there is a tendency towards matrilaterality, in other words for a married couple to maintain closer links with the wife's family and kin rather than with the husband's. But in Italy today still there is a slight inclination towards patrilaterality.

Among Italian regions there are still significant differences to be noted. One is that the links between parents and adult children are stronger in the regions of the 'Third Italy' (Veneto, Emilia-Romagna, Tuscany, Umbria, Marche) than they are in the south. Then, a patrilateral tendency prevails in north and central regions, whereas in some southern regions a bilateral or matrilateral kinship system is dominant. All the evidence we have suggests that differences have become less marked during the second half of the century, whether in terms of the strength of ties between parents and grown-up children or of the dominant role of one or other side of the family.

The strong ties between parents and grown-up children that are still maintained in Italy constitute an important resource wherewith to face the crucial problem of an ageing population, over the next 20 years or so. The drop in fertility, which in the recent past has been more pronounced in Italy than in other Western countries, means that in future the burden of caring for elderly parents will fall on fewer and fewer shoulders and so severely test the traditional system of kinship.

Notes

1. See the essays collected in the 1976 Italian edition of Banfield's volume. We feel that Gribaudi's essays (1993; 1994) are even more important.
2. The same thing appears to happen in France, where the wife's parents, however, tend to supply aid under the form of material services (Segalen, 1996, p.109).

3

THE MISSING LINK: FAMILY MEMORY AND IDENTITY IN GERMANY

Franz Schultheis

In 1991, a German documentary film broadcast on the second national channel at peak time (just after the main news bulletin) presented a mass audience with an astonishing picture of family life in a country at once distant and very close – France. In the course of an hour or so, German viewers witnessed scenes that were clearly of the most commonplace kind if you happened to be French (meals, leisure activities, celebrations). But the testimony provided by Monsieur Dupond or Madame Dupont, though hardly 'sensational' for a French public, seemed exotic in the extreme to Herr Mayer or Frau Maier. Family relations and kinship networks in France are invariably characterized by enormous liveliness and intensity, of a kind frequently envied by Germans. As several of my 'informers' concurred in saying, image after image managed to produce waves of nostalgia made all the more poignant because the world of the family in France as portrayed in the documentary seemed so much and so clearly to contrast with a state of affairs in German society that now seems irreversible and the deep collective malaise that attends it.

One may well wonder whether this is not an instance of exotic romanticism of the kind that feeds on spontaneous sociology to produce stereotypes that are simplistic when set against unfamaliar social realities but this still does not explain why and how such misleading stereotypes catch on and appear plausible. And were it simply collective projection, such a representation of things is likely at the same time to correspond to a need and fulfil a real function. This hypothesis is not without foundation because the representation of family life as it exists in France belongs to a long German tradition and has a direct antecedent in an essay by Hans Magnus Enzensberger published early in the 1980s in *Le Monde dimanche* under the title '*Un bonheur tranquille*'. As a critical observer of life in Germany, Enzensberger takes the image of family life in France as a distancing device in relation to the contemporary German malaise. The message that comes across from this essay on the contrast between the realities of family life – seen as a microscopic universe of complex socio-historical realities – on both sides of the Rhine, is barely less nostalgic than that purveyed by the television documentary; and in essence it says: happy the people who are our neighbours, whose collective identity and memory allow them to live their daily lives easily as families whose members are in accord with each other, generation with generation. This message, it hardly needs saying, has to be read as a radical criticism of intergenerational relationships as they have prevailed in West Germany since the war. And we are reminded that even in the inter-war period, German sociologists – Michels, for instance – drew attention to the fact that family life in France portrayed itself as showing an intensity and a solidarity far above that experienced in Germany. So it is not incorrect to see the cultural representation of the family as forming a particular German tradition, wherein France – rightly or wrongly – affords the ideal image of joyous family life. Such a view is confirmed by other observations. Few young Germans, for instance, when asked about their relations with their father, describe him as someone in whom they can confide (Erni, 1965; Höllinger, 1989). And one is reminded of other surveys that reveal the surprisingly high number of Germans (in particular, compared to French) who admit to being very distant emotionally from their fathers (Noëlle-Neumann and Köcher, 1987).

In the same comparative study, carried out in 1980 and looking at the values of Europeans, Germany again stands out in contrast to France in the matter of how mutual obligations between parents and children are represented. The question 'Should one love and respect one's parents for all their faults, beliefs and attitudes?' elicited positive replies from three-quarters of French respondents and fewer than half the German. And again, the question 'Is it the duty of parents to give their children the best even when this imposes sacrifices on them?' found three-quarters of the French respondents agreeing and only half the German (Noëlle-Neumann, 1983, pp.108–9).

A further point relating to 'sacrifices' to be accepted in intergenerational relations has application to a socio-demographic characteristic which is unknown outside Germany and in general little studied there. The falling birth rate puts western Germany, as opposed to the ex-DDR, in the position of world leader since the 1960s, and in particular there is the question of childless couples: 25 per cent of West German couples, born after 1955, will never have children, as against 10 per cent in France and the ex-DDR, and 10 to 15 per cent in the other industrialised countries.

Further, this German originality seems to be corroborated in comparative studies such as those published by the European Commission in 1979. To the question 'Does giving birth to a child represent an achievement for a man and his wife?' 45 per cent of French respondents, as against 25 per cent German, replied 'Yes', with 18 per cent French and 29 per cent German replying 'No'. Similarly, to the question 'Does giving birth to a child testify to facing the future with confidence?' 41 per cent of French respondents gave affirmative answers, only 23 per cent German; and to the question 'Does having children represent a necessary condition for a woman's happiness?' the figures were 67 per cent French and 30 per cent German.

These differences are accompanied by openly contrasting political views as regards action by government on socio-demographic trends. On the French side there is general acceptance of the need for a policy in favour of the family, in Germany vehement opposition since the domain of the family is presented as purely 'private'.

Furthermore, in regard to dominant educational values, Germany shows itself again different from France in the significance given to the child's self-reliance as the main objective of family upbringing; and this seems to be directly reflected in the propensity for leaving home relatively young. Only one third of young Germans continue to live at home before marriage, whereas in Italy and in Britain (both countries affording comparable statistics) the figures are respectively 90 per cent and 75 per cent (Höllinger, 1989, p.517); in France, 56 per cent of those aged between 20 and 24 lived with their parents in 1990.

Besides, the tendency to leave the parental home as early as possible seems to be sanctioned, if not reinforced, by welfare legislation in Germany with its explicitly individualistic character, which guarantees everybody a basic living wage (income and housing and other allowances) on reaching their full legal age, sometimes before even, and so live apart from the family, whose involvement is discounted. A comparative study conducted in a German welfare bureau and a French family allowance office points to the fact that German welfare legislation is an enabling factor in young people leaving home. One needs only report to the *Sozialamt* specialists that there is strife at home or reluctance to accept paternal authority and the wherewithal for independence is forthcoming. Even when parents agree to provide a child with all that is required so that or she stays at home, they are not party to a decision but merely providers of a living allowance. The welfare system advances the allowance in this case, reclaiming it subsequently from the parents. This type of take-over by government of the attributes and responsibilities proper to family is likely to appear odd and perhaps disturbing, or even revolting, because the relationship between family and communal interdependence springs from a very different legal and political philosophy. French welfare legislation, unlike German, provides for a fairly high minimum age, this being 25 years, before access to income support (*revenu minimum d'insertion*) is granted. In France then, unconditional priority is accorded to intergenerational solidarity within the family and government is precluded from affording replacement. Here then are two types of collective representation of the respective legitimate domains of 'family affairs' and 'affairs of state' that are widely divergent: on the right bank of the Rhine we encounter a fundamental attitude to law that is individualistic; on the left, one that in an ideal sense propounds a 'familial' rationale for regulating political society.

All the signs in Germany are that attitudes towards and within the family are characterized by a degree of detachment on the part of the younger generation in respect of family ties, and this is borne out by other socio-historical idiosyncrasies such as the explicitly and strategically 'anti-paternal' character of the May 1968 eruptions rightly noted by a French observer (Girod de l'Ain, 1983) as being in marked contrast to parallel events as observed at the same time in other European countries, which were directed rather against the bourgeois state and the class system. There were also the belated effects of the movement of May 1968 that found expression in Germany as a radically 'anti-authoritarian' educational philosophy, which has left its mark on the process of socialization across both family and school undergone by young Germans in the course of the last 25 years or so. This needs to be seen in connection with the generally highly critical and negative connotation given to the concept of authority that emerges from opinion polls of the type instanced above, where German views diverge markedly from French. And this rejection of authority goes along with a particularly high educational value put on the principle of autonomy, which seems to dominate the attitude of the older generation in Germany in regard to help and support from their children. As has been shown by Martin Rein (1994, p.21), 40 per cent of old people who receive help from their relatives declare themselves 'very satisfied' as against 61 per cent and 56 per cent of their American and Canadian counterparts. Similarly, only 44 per cent of elderly Germans offering help in the form of minding their grandchildren consider themselves 'very satisfied' with their lot as compared with 71 per cent and 65 per cent in the cases of Canada and America.

In concluding her examination of these few distinctive features of intergenerational relations in Germany, Noëlle-Neumann remarks that in each of the five sectors under survey (attitudes towards religion, morality and sex, social relations and political opinion), the division between the older and younger generations in Federal Germany is distinctly wider than in any other Western country and she speaks of a marked distemper in the relations between generations (Noëlle-Neumann, 1983, p.104); in this she is supported by a French observer of German society, in whose view ' . . . nowhere else is the gulf between generations as deep as it is in the Federal Republic' (Le Gloannec, 1989, p.63).

Hence one might expect German sociologists to have developed out of such fascinating material a theoretical study based on a body of empirical research; this, however, is not the case. We propose to take this very absence of research as a starting point for some critical observations on the sociology of the German family.

Kindred and family perpetuation in Germany: outline of a critical objectivation of the state of sociological research

If one takes the state of scientific research as a more or less accurate reflection of social reality, the proposition that family relationships in the wider sense have already very largely become obsolete in the context of Germany today would seem scarcely exaggerated. Some of the other contributions to this volume speak of the subject as a 'neglected' one; this would seem to be a euphemism in the German context. A significant theoretical current has formed round the 'post-modernist' paradigm of a growing individualization and pluralization of lifestyles, of the notion of a successive 'destructuring' of the forms of modern social life, such as the nuclear family, and has put forward, in the formulation of Ulrich Beck, one of the proponents of this current, that the nuclear family now constitutes no more than a myth nurtured by society and that its strength, itself an anachronism, rests chiefly on its unremitting reproduction by the sociology of the German family itself (Beck and Beck-Gernsheim, 1990). Family relationships and the question of family transmission, faced with the paradigms of individualization and the destructuring of lifestyles, take on a still more obsolete and fusty aspect than in the most reductionist Parsonian perspective imaginable.

Outside this current, more especially since the end of the 1980s, Germany certainly provides evidence of growing interest in the question of forms of family interdependence. Since the wave of major political debate began on the inevitable reform of social insurance and the setting up of a new type of insurance to do with support for those who are elderly and dependent, the question of generational interdependence has struck a timely chord. However, interest in the subject is limited and influenced by the technocratic and instrumentalist viewpoint that takes its stand on who shall accept responsibility and the notion that this primary form of interdependence will in time perhaps come to constitute a vital resource insofar as the social security budget is unlikely to be able to do without it. Such thinking informs the recent study carried out by the Infratest institute (1993) under federal government sponsorship, which seems to envisage intergenerational exchange in a one-way upward direction and disregard the fact that multidirectional forms may coexist.

Apart from this type of study which seems foreign to the field of social sciences research in Germany, there is a dearth of anything like sociological research into the handing down of material possessions within the family (there has been no significant research either on inheritance or settlements) or of symbolic ones (the question of family memory attaching to place or possession is still not given firm acceptance in German sociological discourse; there is no indication of an appropriate interest in the family house or its contents and the significance they hold for family survival, and so on).

How is one to account for the almost total silence on the part of social sciences in Germany in regard to the question of what is passed on within the family and by what means? The hypothesis put forward here points to a complex syndrome of German collective memory in respect of the trauma of totalitarianism and the collective blame linked to the holocaust.

Joint research carried out by a group of German sociologists of Jewish origin who found refuge from the Nazi regime in the United States has to do with the interdependent relationship existing between the 'authoritarian disposition' (manifest as prototype under the Nazi regime) and a particular family model, found in its purest form in the 'stock family', itself also characteristic of the German context. Another study by the psychoanalyst Alexander Mitscherlich was published in post-war Germany under the title 'Auf dem Weg zur vaterlosen Gesellschaft' (Towards a Fatherless Society): it too speaks in theoretical terms of a socio-historical syndrome that is peculiarly characteristic of post-war Germany. We propose then to resite these two texts in their respective socio-historical and cultural contexts. This 'genealogical' or 'archaeological' approach is likely to be of more help in illuminating the circumstance of collective 'lapse of memory' or 'repression'. We shall begin then with the 'classical' period and the sociological discourse surrounding the 'stock family'.

Of the 'authoritarian disposition': elective affinities between family models and political regimes before 1945

In the wake of the comparative analyses between political institutions and social structures in France and America, Alexis de Tocqueville's thesis as to the essential impact of laws of inheritance upon microsociological realities (family relationships) and macro-sociological realities (social stratification) has been returned to again and again. Among his many followers, Frédéric Le Play certainly merits a chosen place because, far from simply using the thesis for an ideological critique of modernity (though this was close to his heart), he devised a scientific process which could identify the degree of affinity between modes of family inheritance and forms of interdependence. In 1855, the very year in which *Les ouvriers européens* appeared, a study that provided scores of detailed family monographs and extremely valuable material on the socio-cultural modes and material conditions of working-class life in various European countries in the middle of the nineteenth century, the third volume of Wilhelm Heinrich Riehl's the Natural History of the German People was published, a work that considers the particularities of family structures in Germany. Le Play and his German *alter ego* reach broadly similar conclusions. For both of them, the German family model, the ideal type of 'stock family' (*Stammfamilie*), that could also be found in other 'Nordic' regions and elsewhere in enclaves in Europe, stood in marked contrast to the type of family that predominated for instance in northern France – that is, the 'unstable' (Le Play's term) or nuclear family. These two family models were distinguishable in particular, according to both authors and many of their successors, by their respective modes of intergenerational inheritance: on one side, the underlying principle being primogeniture, the basis for an unequal and, as Riehl makes plain, 'patriarchal' family order; on the other, the principle being equal sharing accompanied by a non-authoritarian model for family life.

Even if this typology of forms of 'family reproduction' across systems of inheritance was probably originally conceived for the analysis of agrarian societies, hence it may be difficult to transpose to an age, characterized by an *'allgemeine Marktvergesellschaftung'* (a generalized marketing principle) (Weber) and an increasingly widespread wage structure governing populations, Le Play provided repeated evidence of its relevance to the question of the creation and perpetuation of a 'family asset' in an industrial epoch. Since the studies undertaken by Riehl, the notion of an elective affinity between the German model of the stock family and an 'authoritarian'-type collective mentality has been a commonplace of historical and sociological research in regard to family life in Germany.

Many writers have dwelt on the considerable impact of Protestantism in Germany. As the vector of an authoritarian conception of the 'ordered state' (Ball, 1980, p.60) as *Polizeystaat* Lutheranism has contributed in no small way to the development of the myth of the 'father state' (*Vater-Staat*, a somewhat special representation of the state which is at once 'providential' and 'authoritarian') and of the 'omnipotent family father'. According to another approach developed in particular by the sociologist of family, René König (1957, p.112), the pronounced authoritarianism of the German father is to be largely explained in terms of the authoritarianism which is built into the state and the defeat of the German bourgeoisie in the unsuccessful revolution of 1848: being compliant as a subject is not a bar to making the members of one's family comply with a regime of 'family politics' which is no less authoritarian, as has been well shown by Heinrich Mann in his novel *Der Untertan* (*The Subject*) or the literary critic Hugo Ball in a book that first appeared in 1919, *Zur Kritik der deutschen Intelligenz* (*A Critique of German Intellectuals*).

A distinctive German academic institution – the '*Studentenverbindung*' or '*Burschenschaft*' (association of students) – played and to an extent still plays a key role in Germany in the production and reproduction from father to son of an appropriate 'habitus' (Weber's term), inculcating through a complex martial ritual submission to social authority in each new generation (Schultheis, 1990).

With the advent of fascism, the Frankfurt School saw in the concept of the interlinking relationship between social 'character' and 'structure' an exceptionally rich field for research and the work it did on the affinities existing between family structures and social and political attitudes strongly influenced post-war German research, and especially the 'family discourse' of the 1960s and 70s. Here is a characteristic example of such discourse: 'Family life revolves around the figure of the father. He is omnipotent, omniscient and omnipresent, as far as it is possible for a human being to be. He is the source of all the authority, all the security and all the wisdom that his children expect to receive . . . . He is a *Vorbild*, an ideal for them to follow' (Schaffner, 1948, p.15). For a very broad consensus of the German and international scientific community pre-war Germany represented a *Vater-Land*, in the proper sense of the term dominated on one level by a *Landes-Vater*, legitimately representing a *Vater-Staat*, and on the other, micro-social, level by the father, the undisputed head of the family. As will become clear below, this virtually mythical conception of the partriarchal principle as the ground of social and domestic order collapsed in ruins, part and parcel with the Nazi regime, so making way for a complete ideological transformation of the 'discourse on family'.

German methamorphoses: From a patriarchal society to a 'fatherless society'

An examination, however cursory, of post-war literary culture in West Germany cannot fail to leave one with the somewhat disconcerting impression of its appearing to find its centre of gravity in family or rather 'intergenerational' tensions, of a particular kind and that carry within them, in the form of a reduced model, socio-historical factors that relate closely to the nation as a whole. This resort to the family as a microcosm of all the ideological issues of the 'German question' – the *deutscher Sonderweg* – is found as a prototype in Heinrich Böll whose major literary works – *Haus ohne Hüter* (*House without a Master*) (1964), *Billiard um halbzehn* (*Billiards at 9.30*) (1959) or *Ansichten einer Clowns* (*Opinions of a Clown*) (1963), for instance – propose multiple variations all converging on a single theme, namely the explanation demanded of the fathers who belonged to the generation that gave active support or passive sufferance to Nazi totalitarianism and the holocaust by the generation that benefited from what a certain German politician described as the 'grace of having been born late' (*Gnade der späten Geburt*). Already in Alfred Döblin's *Hamlet oder die Nacht nimmt kein Ende* (*Hamlet or the Unending Night*) (1956) the context of a disabled soldier's family serves in some way as a psychosociological laboratory for the truth and the responsibility for historical events. Calling for an explanation, a moral gesture that is made a thousand times over in the narrative yet realist world of Böll's, is a cornerstone too of novels like *Hausmusik (Chamber Music)* (1962) by Reinhard Baumgart or *Deutschstunde (German lesson)* (1968) by Siegfried Lenz; in fact, if one takes into account poetic output (Marie-Louise Kaschnitz *et al.*), theatre (Gerhard Hauptmann *et al.*) and cinema (Rainer-Werner Fassbinder *et al.*) in post-war Germany, the degree of consensus in discourse and praxis – intellectual, political and ethical – expressive of a people and a country that have experienced an exceptional crisis, becomes abundantly clear.

Calling for an explanation from German fathers who did their military service after 1933 (not to mention those who served in the SS or were directly implicated in the machinery of death of the concentration camps) appears between 1945 and 1975 roughly (that is, for one particular socio-historical generation) to have become an exclusive form of critical reflection – both individual and collective – upon German identity and the abiding problem: '*Was ist deutsch?*', a problem that has haunted German political philosophy since the eighteenth century.

Yet if this tension between the fathers' generation and that of the children riven by the crisis of history and of national and family identity seems to pervade, indeed dominate, post-war German literary reflection and production, it is hazy and inexplicit if not strangely absent in German sociological discourse in regard to the family. With one exception: representatives of the Frankfurt School such as Horkheimer and Adorno, who came back from the United States following the defeat of fascism, brought back with them the theory of the 'authoritarian disposition' which found a particularly favourable climate in West Germany in the reverberations of May 1968; added to which there was the work produced by Herbert Marcuse on the repressive nature of the sexual morality which characterized the bourgeois family and the antipsychiatric theories that posed the 'death of the family'. This particular set of circumstances, that gave the events surrounding May 1968 the appearance of a revolt against the father, against the nuclear family and against the 'authoritarian' nature of family upbringing, hence a markedly different stance to the revolt against the state or against imperialism or capitalism associated with the May 1968 movement in America or France, seemed to spring from the relations which those in the front line of the movement maintained with their fathers' generation, a generation that carried the stigma of collective guilt. In other words, it seems clear that the theory of the 'authoritarian disposition' served to legitimize a 'generational conflict' in the true sense of the term and that this conflict took both an individual and collective, a private and a public form.

The paradox would seem to be that family life in West Germany underwent a process of swift and radical modernization in the early 1950s with new legislation. Equality between the sexes and the interests and autonomy of children were enshrined in the 1949 West German constitution and the Constitutional Court kept a close watch on parliamentary legislation in initiating a rapid series of reforms affecting the family that in some cases went far beyond measures attained elsewhere in Europe in the way of making family law more democratic and individualistic. In short, the 1960s revolt against the father figure in West Germany represents an enigma and an anachronism if one limits one's attention to the present position and socio-cultural context of the family, and leaves the historical dimension out of account. It is this dimension which provides the sociology of the German family with the only pertinent clue for a 'socio-analytic' understanding of the cultural significance of the evidence given in our introductory description of family life in Germany. The theory of the 'authoritarian disposition' that was originally developed in and for the context of the 1930s made an inevitably belated appearance in Germany, where it had the impact of a time bomb and served as a symbolic weapon in a type of very violent 'collective family therapy' that was chiefly focused on recent history.

After playing a key part in the rhetoric of the family in and around 1970 the paradigm of the 'authoritarian nature of the family' seems paradoxically to have undergone transformation into its opposite. The notion of a fatherless society put forward by Mitscherlich in 1973 in the form of a general diagnosis of modernity, also seems to find its socio-historical *raison d'être* and its real theoretical pertinence in its original context – post-war Germany – where to all appearances the father had effected a double disappearance: in a concrete sense, with the disappearance of millions of 'soldier-fathers' and the mass phenomenon of lone-parent families; but in a symbolic sense too, the German father had been morally dethroned because of the historic guilt attributed to him. His children's generation had put him on trial at the close of the 1960s and the repercussions of this trial on the values inculcated at home and at school – pronounced anti-authoritarian ideology, normative priority given to the autonomy and rights of the individual, for example – have come to have lasting effect on everyday life in Germany.

While community surveys provide a number of indicators by which to identify the moral and emotional rift affecting generational relations in Germany and enable some specific features of transmission and family memory in a socio-historical context marked by collective pathology to be detected, sociology in Germany has offered little by way of contribution to elucidating the social mechanisms at work behind these descriptive indicators and so make the socio-psychological syndrome that overhangs German family life more transparent.

Nor has the theory of the 'authoritarian disposition', given the place it had in the symbolic battle of the generations, contributed anything worthwhile in devising a more rational approach to the social problem in question. Similarly, the concept of the 'fatherless society', a forerunner of current 'post-modernist' theories, has played little part in the collective task of *Aufklärung* in the face of a collective unconscious and taboos that are still very much alive in family relations in Germany. Instead of contributing to a rationalization of the ongoing relationship with family and national history, post-modernist discourse seems precisely to further entrench the collective unconscious and inhibition (one is reminded of Durkheim's dictum: 'The subconscious itself is history'), while offering the only too welcome illusion that we are now once and for all situated beyond the period of history in question and the stigma that attaches to it.

4

FAMILY, KINSHIP AND RESIDENCE IN URBAN CATALONIA: THE MODERNITY OF 'PAIRALISM'[1]

Joan Bestard Camps and Jesus Contreras Hernández

The character of kinship relations

One of the theoretical advantages in studying kinship in an urban setting consists in the visibility of kinship in a pure state, that means without supposition of an embedded functionality of kinship institutions. We can, as Firth *et al.* (1970, p.121) say, isolate the principle of kinship itself. However, due to this pure state, it is difficult to set up units of analysis that make sense of relations of persons as kin. The meaning of kinship modifies according to the social context and life cycle of individuals.

In social sciences, kinship and family call up community and continuity and appear opposed to the individual dynamic of modern urban societies. They appear as the remains of a past that is still alive in the tissue of modern urban life. However, as Strathern (1922, p.135), has stated, the view that extended kinship is of the domain of tradition comes from the same constellation of ideas that gives sense to the notion that in the course of time societies grow more complex and the world is more full of individuals. In this representation of a world that is more and more complex, kinship is consigned to the domain of the domestic and private. Going from society to kinship means possibly losing the capacity for social identity. Kinship, therefore, either considered as a basic concept for understanding traditional societies or placed in the margins of modern European culture, has become invisible for the analysis of contemporary societies. Of kinship there only remains the 'nuclear family', belonging to the domain of private life, separated from the economic system of modern society.

In this chapter we propose to demonstrate that family and kinship, far from being an exclusive part of tradition, are a central component of modern society, having a basis in the production of individuals creating diversity and social change. The modern idea of kinship is related to the idea of individuality and social plurality. In this sense we propose to analyse what family means as a social category referred to by people in their everyday lives and relate this meaning to the meaning of family as a category of social analysis, since the category of family that we use as an analytical tool and as a category of social classification is a term used either in official documents by the bureaucratic state or in common parlance or by social analysts. It is, as Bourdieu (1993) states, a 'realised category' that is part of the experience of modern societies.

When we speak of 'family', we refer to a group over and above its members. In this sense, it is an analytical unit based on the composition of its members, on the type of its relations and on the form of the group. We can speak also of a family spirit, of a family sentiment and of a family tradition, and we stress the sameness and continuity of the individuals forming the group. From the point of view of social organization, the stress is on the 'social cohesion' of its members and from the point of view of the relation between groups it is on the closeness of each group. However, in its everyday meaning, family is a term defined by the context of the meaning of kinship. Family is a form of expressing affective identity, in opposition to kinship implying moral obligation by the fact of existing relationships. Kinship relations are independent of individual choice. A genealogy is made without the intervention of the individual will, a fact of nature that can be recognized and used as a model. As Jaime[2] says referring to his genealogy, 'I accept the tree, but without structure, without model'. What can be an object of choice is the social recognition of facts of kinship which gives meaning to these relationships. In opposition to kin, family connotes intimacy and identity. The recognition and the meaning of relationships suppose close contact ('*roce*' in Emilio's term). This contact is what makes the family, what produces a diffuse and enduring solidarity as Schneider (1980) says. If interpersonal relationships imply a continuous and close contact, this relationship can be one of familiarity. If there is not any contact, they are only relatives, something given for ever. Relatives are given, as nature is given - it is a question of blood and of genealogy - but family is constructed by contact, as social relations are constructed - it is a question of social affinity. In this sense, family can be transformed into a model of society: as kinship relationship is what is given in society and as family relationship is what is created by social subjects. For this reason, the distinction is constant between relatives with whom there is continuous contact and relatives with whom there is only the known relationship but no contact. Having a family relationship implies creating such a relationship by continuous contact, a way of life in common. In this sense there is opposition to simple consanguinity. As Jaime asserts, 'the important ties are not ones of kinship, they are ones of a life in common'. Family implies living together and sharing common experiences. Ties are based more in elective affinities than in blood: 'I behave more by affinity than by consanguinity' says Anna, denoting that neither nearness nor kinship is enough to create family relationships. They are 'pure relationships' as Giddens (1992) defines intimacy in the contemporary world, that is social relations which are internally referential, without support from external elements. It is not enough to be close kin or living nearby to be real kin: it is necessary to share intimacy and trust. What defines a person as a relative is not 'blood' or 'genealogy' but close contact.

What nature gives by birth – a genealogical link – must be transformed into a social relation which every individual creates. A person is recognized as a relative not only through a genealogical link, he must behave as if he was of the family. Josep, a peasant who is 85 years old, looking at his genealogical chart, in which he had included all persons linked to him by filiation or by affinity, considers the role of social intercourse in order to consider a person as a relative. Speaking of a close relative, he says: 'We were a little bit family, but we only interact a little bit'. Similarly Anna, recalling her family relations during her life, amplifies or reduces her notion of family according to the intensity of the relationship at this or that moment in her life. For Anna, the idea of family varies with the circumstances. She was, as Firth *et al.* (1970) would say, a kin keeper. Her two grandmothers lived with her. That converted her into the centre of family relations: family rituals were celebrated at her home. As she narrates in her story, her home was the *casa pairal*, the ancestral house in Catalan tradition, referring to the stem family. Now the relations with her brother's family are being redefined: Dolors, the grandmother who symbolized the family unity, is no longer there and the children are incorporating new members into the family. Before, Anna had an extensive notion of family: she included all her brothers, husband's brothers and sisters-in-law. Now she has a restricted notion: 'Family is my mother, my husband and my children', she says. She expresses an idea of family characterized by co-operation and the experience of living together. In her narrative the past is full of an extended kinship and the present of a restricted kinship. However, such nuclearization seems more related to her own individual experience.

Family means interaction, living together, and an active participation in relationships: it must remain united and someone must mobilize kin. Escarlata remembers her mother had this role as kin mobilizer, providing information to each member of the family about the others: 'My mother united us, I could go without seeing my siblings or my nephews, because I knew how they all were. With my mother dead, my elder sister now has this role, it's she who unites us and distributes information'.

And mobilization may not only be in terms of the distribution of information between kin, as in the case of Vicenç who has an active role in the residential changes of his siblings, helping them in their move to the city of Tarragona, by looking for an apartment and work and so moving the family centre to a new city. Sibling relationships were extremely strong, with family commanding residence, work and leisure. Hence there was a sense of group membership despite the different individual characters and changes in family life.

Julia's grandmother was also a kin mobilizer: 'At Epiphany we all went together to grandmother's home. That was a great celebration. She prepared a meal .... All the family was there. The elders in the dining room, juniors in the next room .... Other Christmas festivities were celebrated in other homes, but grandmother was never alone'. The Christmas rituals are really kinship rituals, and even today, after grandmother's death, the 30 members of this kindred gather together for a meal in a restaurant.

In all the kindred observed there is a kin keeper. Normally women have this role; however, as we have seen with Vicenç, it can be a man. Women have this role more often because they maintain the family memory and circulate family news between relatives. Also, the differential incidence of mortality between the sexes implies a continuing presence of elderly feminine ancestors who maintain the union of the next generation. Another reason could be that women are specialists in 'care' and in 'help'. Anna's story has this meaning. Over eight years Joan's and Anna's mothers resided with them. At the beginning it was Anna's mother who came to live with them in order to help her daughter with four little children. With her mother's help, she could also help her husband in his work. When her husband's mother fell ill they decided that she must live with them because they considered it their duty to care for her.

Keeping the family united

Keeping the family united was the main motive for change of abode by a couple who, living in a village, had their children in Barcelona, as if it was necessary that someone maintain the union in order to remain a family. 'How exciting it is to gather together as a family', says Lola, who felt very happy on the occasion of a family meal when she could see all the members of her kindred who live in Barcelona together. This meal may be considered as the achievement of her desire for family unity, and a principal motivation on the part of this elderly couple who wanted to keep the family united in spite of migration and social change.

Fifteen years earlier she and her husband had felt it necessary to come and live in Barcelona because her elder son and daughter were living there. 'They were living here and we there; so it was a divided family and we were unable to be on good terms'. Migration to Barcelona was the only solution. Here the 'family question' centred in the need 'to live united' becomes the principal motive for migration, and the economic necessity, the normal motive for moving from village to city in the 1950s, is relegated to second place. In the village, says Felix, 'I had got plenty of work . . . . Had it not been for the children I'd have stayed . . . I'm not here of my own volition'. In his narrative Felix wanted to differentiate his own reason for moving from that of others. He differentiates between 'family' and 'work' as two separate values in his motivation. When he speaks of motives for migration, he emphasizes family; but when he speaks of his past in the village he emphasizes work. For this reason, he relates the intensity of neighbourly relations in his village to the value of work and the intensity of relations in migrating to the value of family. The motives for migration in his children's generation are different from his own. This different motivation imposes a re-evaluation of family considerations as stated by social scientists in the 1960s when migration from the village to the city was a recent phenomenon. Family, it was said, was destructuring and individualizing. The present perspective allows us to affirm that families were not destructured, they were adapting to a different situation and this adaptation involved a long process. Now families once destructured have been united. Today, the nuclear family can be considered as a phase for the construction of a new form of family and we can even say that the extended family tradition has resurfaced. The modern family system based on the ideal of the nuclear family has lost its cultural dominance as Stacey (1990) says, but that does not mean that family as a value has lost its significance.

As a mature couple, Felix and Lola's personal realization is based on the necessity of maintaining their family united, their elder children especially. For this reason they did not question the move to Barcelona, in spite of Felix having to take up a different job, harder, in his view, than farming in his village, and in spite of his wife's difficulty in adapting to the new way of life in the city. Definitive migration is a long process, as if over five years they were testing their relationship with the new place of abode and evaluating their personal determination to help their two elder children. Their first attempt was in 1970: they were 47 years old, and their elder children rented an apartment for the family to live together. However, after six months they returned to the village, with Lola unable to adapt to life in the city: 'she was taken ill with her nerves' and she 'thought she might die'. When their parents returned to the village, their children again stayed with their uncle and aunt. Gradually over five years and regular visiting, their mother adapted to city life. The children rented another apartment where they often received their parents. When the elder daughter married and the elder son was left alone they decided to move to Barcelona. The elder daughter's marriage was the final point in a process of migrating to Barcelona. They then came to live in Barcelona with their other two children 'in order to keep the family united'. Lola became used to life in the city and Felix found work in the municipality as a dustman; work that he now feels is very good compared with his previous agricultural labour in the village. He has work with a definite time schedule as do people in the city, not as with agricultural village work, with different times depending on the agricultural cycle.

In this process there is a 'family need' beyond the obligations of parents to their elder children who are independent, both economically and emotively. It is the need for family union that determines decisions in relation to their children and to the residential arrangements in Barcelona.

If we can say that it is the need to maintain a united family that is at the origin of the decision to migrate, the same need – to be near the family – guides the children's choice of residence. Carmen (who is 37 years old), the elder daughter who married first, sells her apartment to her brother and buys another one closer to her parents' apartment. Felix, the elder son, has his office in the same place, and her younger sister works there and lives not far away. In this way visits and meals in the parents' home are very frequent; some of them informal, but every Friday they meet together for a meal prepared by her mother in a way that recalls the village meals of the past. The mother's domestic activity on that day is intensified, she can express the feeling of union: 'You feel very good when you see all together: they are ... this union, this thing'.

The residential propinquity of their married children – all of them live nearby, we have all of them very near us', says their father – the intensity of relations expressed in a common meal prepared by their mother and the constant and informal visits of their children and grandchildren, make their parents' home the context and very expression of the idea of family union. In spite of independent households for all their married children, relations between them thrive through the parents' home. It is the centre of a localized kindred and the basis for the organization of family exchange. Extended kinship is compatible with nuclear households.

Now that Lola and Felix live alone, a niece has come to live with them, thus reproducing the same situation as with the children who, on coming to Barcelona, lived with their aunt and uncle. The relationship between aunt and niece is not simply one of convenience; common residence implies strong sentimental relations. As Lola says, referring to her niece who has been with them for three years, a link between them has been created and will not be broken without pain. Her niece told her one day, recalls Lola: 'Aunt, when I came here, I came crying, but when I come to leave you, I'll also be crying'. She came from the village to Barcelona when their younger daughter married. She went back to the village but, after a while, she came back to her Aunt's home in Barcelona. Marriages are thus the axes for deciding important choices of residence. Changes in the domestic cycle are very important for introducing new relationships and so extending the idea of family union.

The elderly couple provided support for their children, niece and grandchildren in Barcelona. The mother, Lola, is the 'family centre' and on special occasions she gathers together all her kindred living in Barcelona. She is a 'kin keeper' as Firth *et al.* (1970) would say. Across this role she maintains continuity between the village and the city, because she can evoke the same identity of role in both places: 'There in the village it was the same; there, although the house was very small, I was also the centre'. It is as if her role as kin mobilizer was part of her identity as a person. Her personal identity is defined her active role in the construction of family union. 'There was much union' – this idea seems to govern all important family decisions and it allows one to conceive of three generational changes in terms of continuity preserved by unified family values.

However, when she recalls her village life, this 'unity' refers not to family life, but to friends, neighbourhood and work, that is to say, to different forms of social relation beyond the scope of domestic life. In her narrative, she speaks of children and adolescent games, of first meetings with boys, of 'street meetings with boyfriends' away from the control of parents. She speaks of her group of friends, of exchanges between women in the neighbourhood or when they went to wash linen on the river bank; of dances during pig-killing or after the olive harvest: 'After the olive harvest, there was a good dance, they made rolled wafers, bunches of flowers, and there was this unity, this thing'. All her narrative of her past in the village evokes a world dominated by values of 'union' and 'help' and through these values the social life of the village appears in her mind as an intense life, compared with the present where it seems that people have disappeared and the people remaining in the village are closed in on themselves and in their homes. In their street it was 'union', while 'it is enough to look at the street to confirm how deserted it is now', say Lola and Felix when they contrast the past and the present of the village. An imagined community is the basis for her narrative of the past.

While in the village Lola centres the 'union' on the group of friends, the neighbourhood or the work, that is to say, on social life outside the domestic domain; with urban life the 'union' is centred only on family life, as if what the village had offered could now only be replaced by a family life actively shaped by herself, and the community unity of the village replaced by family unity in the town. The urban life that followed migration is the basis for reinventing a family tradition.

'Being near the family' is an ideal that we found in other cases in spite of differences in regional tradition. For example, in spite of conflicts with her mother, Julia, when she looked for an independent apartment, found it in the same 'four streets' where she had spent all her life. This residential propinquity was not perceived as an inconvenience, but as a 'likely advantage'. Also, Felip, Rosa's husband, on his marriage, did not want to live with Rosa's elder sister, but his wife desired it, and she brought him round to the idea by saying that his earnings were low. Also, Rosa says that they 'had good luck' when their second daughter came to live in a house in front of theirs. Proximity has a double aspect: it is the material condition for making the exchange of services between kin possible, and it constitutes the accomplishment of the desire for members of the family to 'be near', as if spatial propinquity was the expression of the family sentiment and values. For this reason it is not unusual to see the main role of family as trying to find young couples somewhere to live (Iglesias, 1993, pp.345-6).

Life cycle, family obligation and individual autonomy

The meaning of family is ego-centred and it changes with different periods or situations in individual lives: child, adolescent, adult or elderly; single, married, divorced, widowed. Each situation has a specific time span and kin are more present in one period or situation than in another. Thus kinship support is often predetermined. Age difference, capability and social position to a large extent decide which party is provider and which the receiver.

A central element of kinship relations is its character of moral obligation based on reciprocity: previous conduct to a significant degree governs present conduct. Hence the basis of trust assumed by Escarlata when she refers to her family obligations: 'I know I'll receive, because I've given'. Kinship relations create rights and duties which an individual cannot refuse. In every day practices kinship relations are perceived as having a moral obligation and everyone respects an articulated set of rights and duties, obligations and expectations related to her or his position in the family cycle. The character of moral obligation attaching to kinship relations should be understood as a set of prescriptive rules, in terms of the capacity of kinship symbols to give sense to individual conduct. For an individual, kinship is not a system, but a resource in his or her social world. When kinship symbols fail to give sense to shape the social world of individuals, their moral imperative is reduced and may come in conflict with other interests and obligations. 'Personal realization' can become more important than 'family life' and there is then a dichotomy between kinship 'obligations' and 'individual freedom'. In this respect, the most telling of our stories is that concerning Mariano and Julia. Mariano perceives kinship as a 'restriction', as an 'obligation' that one has to fulfil against other ambitions or desires. For this reason, he restricts his stays in his parents' home in his village. When his daughters were young, they and his wife, spent virtually all their holidays there, Mariano only joining them when he was free. For him this house represented the 'fulfilment of obligations to his parents' family'. For her part, Julia expresses in a very explicit way her aspiration to preserve 'her private life' in relation both to her own family and to her husband, Miguel's. Her mother took care of her daughter till she was seven months old, while she and her husband were at work, but they decided to send her to a nursery because she thought that her mother's intervention was excessive – 'she considered herself to have the right to criticize our conduct. I prefer a slightly more distant relationship'. Julia considers, however, that they have a good relationship, since they have a meal every Sunday at her husband's parents' home and they pay visits to her parents. Anyway, she prefers to 'have relations with old friends; when I have free time I prefer to spend Saturday and Sunday with my friends, in spite of the family. It is better with friends; with the family you never get away from family conflicts and family stories. With friends it is different, you have a good time. … With the family there is always a source of conflict'.

The sense of relationship within the family is not neutral, it can be positive or negative. So family, in regard to the individual, may represent support or oppression. It is a support for individual life expressed in constant helping between its members but it can be a constraint on individual development. In this sense, in certain contexts the family can be considered the basis for authoritarian or abusive behaviour, while in others as a support for individuals. The position in the family cycle is very important for the perception of family rights and duties. Julia, being young, perceives the family home as excessively organized by her mother without private space for herself. Being herself implies leaving the parental home. Conflict between generations appears when personal autonomy cannot be assured in the family domain. Nowadays the family is perceived, not as an end in itself, but as a means for the development of individual autonomy. Kinship obligations are understood as caring for the physical, emotive and social needs of its members. Parents behave in relation to their children as a support system to their lives and they are perceived as very important in the development of children as autonomous individuals. When children reach maturity in the family development cycle, parents' obligations change and personal needs are met by society. The family is perceived as a set of resources transmitted to children in order to introduce them to society. Family life provides a means for living: as a cycle of socialization it is considered as an introduction to life, but it is not itself life nor is it society. For this reason, family in the modern world relates to 'private' relations, to obligations that are 'natural', because it is considered as a 'support' or 'apprenticeship' to public life and a means whereby to introduce new autonomous individuals into society. In this sense one can understand the contemporary emphasis on education within the family as a training for life in society. This is perceived as a basic obligation and it is a very different one to the concern in previous generations to pass on a trade or skill or transmit an inheritance. Our evidence bears out that 'a formal education is a fundamental priority for family'. It is understood as professional training, so that children have 'minimal skills for the world of work'.

Our family stories provide evidence of different ways of building family networks. Silvia married in 1979. Since then, she and her husband have a meal every Sunday at her parents' home. And they visit her and sometimes care for their grandchildren. Encarna's brothers and sisters pay frequent visits to each other. At the beginning, their nearness to each other enabled it, but now that they live in different parts of the city, they still maintain the custom in spite of the distance. Apart from ceremonial occasions, such as birthdays, they have a 'fraternal dinner' every two or three months; a dinner that takes place in turn in each conjugal residence. Ana has a holiday home in a town near Barcelona; her brother has another in the mountains and her husband's brother has one also in the country. These three houses are places for family meetings, principally in summer, a time when they pay a lot of visits to their relatives in their holiday places. Rosa and Felip welcome all their children in their house every week: and on Saturdays or Sundays they have some of their married children with their families to a meal at home. In turn, their children, every year at Christmas, make a gift to improve their parents' house: trees for the garden maybe, or an addition to the heating system.

Family migration affords a good example of how kinship becomes a resource for individuals in hard times. The kinship network and the circulation of services is a very important resource for each individual who decides to leave home and settle in Barcelona. The fact of living close to one another reflects reciprocal interaction between family units. And the evidence provides good examples. In the case of Encarna's family, her apartment and that of her uncle provided hospitality to relatives migrating to Barcelona: Encarna's two younger sisters and then, after several visits, her parents. The move was realized, according to Felix, through relatives - 'they followed each other in succession'. Some of them arrived in Barcelona and, when settled, they welcomed others, so forming a kind of chain between village and city, and maintaining a continuity with the community of origin. Such moves, far from causing a community to disappear, maintain links with the place of origin and recreate a community: instead of showing instability in an urban setting, family becomes a very important resource in a network of helping and becomes a symbol of unity and continuity with the place of origin; so maintaining and transmitting cultural identity.

The relationship between *casa* and family

Family refers to 'home', as a place of residence and it expresses a lifestyle. Family and house are related through home. As Schneider (1980, p.45) says, 'a house is where a family lives: the way in which it lives there can make it into a home'. 'Home' unites 'house' with 'family' However, in the cultural context of Catalonia *casa* symbolizes 'family', and there is not a clear differentiation between 'house' and 'home'. One is a member of a *casa* and this cultural category can be used to refer to a family even without any residential connotation.

In a way that is different from other regions in Spain, there is in Catalonia, a long tradition of jurists, historians and ethnologists, who have stressed the cultural peculiarity of '*casa*' as an institution related to the stem family and undivided inheritance. *Casa* is used as a symbol to express the family group in the sense in which it transcends the individuals that make it up and the very foundations of kinship. The lines of family are a function of *casa* or, as Iszaevich (1981) says, kinship is ecocentric. *Casa* has particularity as an institution and, as the historian Vicens Vives (1954) said, 'it is the social basis of the Catalan nation'. There is an ideology of the 'Catalan family' based on '*patralismo*' (the rural house, at once the source of family and tradition) and associated with cultural nationalism. That means that national differences can be expressed in terms of family customs, because the family is related to a particular cultural tradition. In the same way as nation can be expressed as '*casa nostra*', the institution of *casa* is an element of cultural identity and of differentiation with other cultures (Barrera, 1985, p.65).

In this cultural context *casa* is perceived as a means of ensuring the continuity of family identity. To have lived in the same house and to have had the same name for generations is reason for pride and social prestige. *Casa* is a focus of expectation and negotiation among kin due to its capacity to express continuity as a 'family house'. Residence condenses symbols of family identity and continuity and across *casa* symbols of kinship and land are united. We found in our family stories some houses which are considered as a focal family point; where relatives meet frequently and where important family rituals are celebrated. *Casa*, considered as the site of socialization, is perceived as a mediator between the individual and society. In this sense, *casa* is conceived as a system of cultural values, a principle of social solidarity that characterizes its members and gives them a cultural continuity. Relations within the *casa* – where social links are formed and cultural values transmitted – provide a context that gives meaning to individuals with shared experience. Culture becomes immediately identified with family and house. It comes to have spatial expression and so is a metaphor for country. Nation and house become synonymous.

This image of the traditional family intimately related to *casa* or house is little more than a cliché for contemporary people living in an urban setting. Barcelona, proud of its vocation as a great city, has great heterogeneity in terms of cultural traditions and of family customs. There are types of family – single-parent, reconstituted – that correspond neither to the nuclear family, once considered as the type best adapted to urban and industrial life, nor less to the stem family, once considered as characteristic of Catalan tradition (cf. Flaquer, 1992). This family type is considered to belong to the past, to the rural and traditional world, no longer having influence on the present. Furthermore, it is a stereotype that is called into question as much by social anthropologists as by family practice. It can be viewed as the concrete expression of nostalgia for an ordered past and for the thrust of a national culture, yet a kind of nostalgia that sectors of population can use in order to affirm their cultural legitimacy. It is a cultural stereotype not adapted to practice, but like other clichés rethought and restructured in the present, and so like other traditional customs goes to build a Catalan tradition.

In an urban context, *casa* is experienced merely as a resource in family life. It is not a symbol expressing family continuity: it provides the context for representing a certain lifestyle. This explains the importance given to domestic design and the objects one surrounds oneself with that convey a personal style. Changes of furniture are more important than continuing with old family pieces. *Casa* is the symbol of the individual trajectory, expressing individual values, a lifestyle that changes according to the needs of its members.

However, we can consider some urban contexts in which the *casa* tradition is recreated and is transformed into an autonomous focus for cultural ideas related to kinship. In the Catalan tradition the *casa patral* is represented as a common stem to which one always belongs though one may live elsewhere. The house of origin, normally a rural house, symbolizes 'family unity'. In our urban family stories we found references to the *casa patral* as a family symbol. One of the sons in the Valls family, for instance, who did well, acquired a second home in the country and all the family now refer to this as *casa patral*: it bears the family name and also the Catalan emblem and provides a good example of reinventing and condensing symbols of tradition. When a house is a centre for family meetings, it comes to personify the identity of the family stock. Jaime says, referring to his family meetings at home: 'this house, at these times, is something like a *casa pairal*'. Since this cultural category implies thinking of family in past terms, the grandparents' home – when and if reunited with descendants – easily becomes the symbol of family tradition. Enric remembers such meetings at his grandparents: 'There we used to meet all the cousins, all the aunts and uncles. Everybody came. It was the *casa pairal*, you see'.

Insofar as *casa* implies the idea of origin, the function of symbolizing family tradition can be attributed to a village house that has become a holiday home, a second residence. And here the idea of residing independently, as a nuclear family, combines with greater sociability with siblings and their families. So old village houses are divided into different apartments according to the number of married children who use the house; and the traditional notion of·a stem family is realized during holidays, when different related couples and different generations co-reside in the same house.

Hence '*pairalismo*', an ideology particular to the Catalan industrial bourgeoisie relating family, patrimony and undivided inheritance, is transformed into a 'cultural ideal' forming part of a 'Catalan tradition' which can be realized precisely because it is now largely divorced from the former necessary association between family, patrimony and inheritance. It is only when *casa* as patrimony is not central, that it can symbolize and integrate all members of family, both as individuals and as one, there being now no separation between the hereu (eldest and heir) and the cabalers (the younger). So it can be shared by all the siblings and does not give rise to conflict, since each separate part of the family have their place of work and residence.

Among migrant families coming from other areas where there is no identification between house of origin and family, a village house can also now symbolize and represent the 'family house', allowing all those who have left the village to relate to their place of origin. The village house owned by Felix and Lola has been transformed, since they migrated to Barcelona, into a 'family house'. In this sense, they emphasize that it was owned by her father, in spite of his having sold it and they having bought it again. In fact a house can only now really express family continuity when it is built or arranged anew. The old house is redolent of the narrowness of domestic life in the past and relations with the village neighbours as they were then. So the old house was made more spacious with two flats where all their married children and grandchildren can stay in the holidays. This new house expresses the value of family unity that is a consequence of their migration to

Barcelona. And it is this completely new house which has come to represent their family tradition in the village. A type of multiple household including different conjugal units – a residential form completely alien to any kinship tradition in the village – now has the power to express lines of continuity between generations, and the house representing as it does family unity is a link between family life in Barcelona and the village of their origin. *Casa* is again the symbol that joins kinship and land, and modernity (wage employment, holidays, for example) is what recreates tradition.

Conclusion

Our aim has been to show that kinship and family values are key factors in the social experience of contemporary Catalan families who have moved from villages to the city. Far from being a static entity that belongs essentially to the past, kinship relations are constantly recreated. And it is this active element, whereby the significant role is taken on by this or that family member, which enables the vitality of family identity to be maintained. There may, however, be conflict with the principle of individual automony, when it comes to the place of each individual in the family life cycle, which accounts for the family appearing to be more a bulwark for its members than an active principle in itself. Common residence is a central element in the elaboration of family identity the *casa* takes on symbolic force as representing family continuity. Whereas in the context of the married couple, a lodging, an apartment, provides for the family and expresses a distinctive lifestyle, *casa* appears to transcend the separate family units. The notion that *casa* symbolizes family continuity is considered as a distinctive historical feature of Catalan Culture, representing in the stem family rooted in the continuing customs and practices of rural society. Even so, as a notion it is not exclusively linked to the past and to tradition: it lives on as a social category that unites the fragmented family and ensures its collective survival: having shed the image of its rural origins, it has become a factor of identity in the present-day construction of kindred relations within the city.

Notes

1. *Casa pairal* is the Catalan term for the house where the stem family has lived without a break.
2. First names in this chapter are those of 'actors' in the various family histories assembled.

5

HOUSES AND LEGENDS: FAMILY AS COMMUNITY OF PRACTICE IN URBAN PORTUGAL

João de Pina-Cabral

Introduction

All community is based on actual shared experience (that is, some sort of intersubjectivity) and, at the same time, all community leads over time to some conscience of itself, thus it leads to the production of an identity, a conceived community. Between the experienced community and the conceived community there is the arena of social relations (the community of practice) that shapes the experience and allows for the intersubjectivity. In this chapter I will explore the interplay between identity, the sharing of a common set of references, and the participation in a community of practice, in order to capture the process through which families exist in time and across generations. Furthermore, it is my concern to show that personal identity and familial identity imply each other and are jointly reproduced.

In Portuguese urban contexts, the main unit of social reproduction (the 'primary social unit' – cf. Pina-Cabral, 1989b) is the group formed around a conjugal couple and its children. This is the principal unit of residence and of property. Thus, it can be argued that the model of reproduction of the primary social unit is a syncopated model (cf. Pina-Cabral, 1992a): at each generation, a new unit is formed by two members coming from different units of the earlier generation; these two older units, in time, are expected to disappear with the death of their founders. When there is some joint property between primary social units, it is usually temporary and it has a weaker force of allegiance.

However, the study of actual family histories shows that such a model is no more than the basic frame of reference within which a large amount of variation can be observed and around which a whole network of extradomestic family relations is created. Much as most residential situations may correspond to neolocal, nuclear families, such a description leads one astray. On the one hand, it is normative, because out of all the actions that people undertake, it concentrates exclusively on those gestures that conform to a preconceived model. On the other hand, it casts a shadow over a series of strategies to which people take recourse in dealing with their lives.

In particular, it does not provide for the understanding of what are called in Portugal *famílias*. A 'family' is an open-ended group of people who feel that they are associated with each other because, in the past, they participated jointly in the process of social reproduction. It is very much a polythetic category, as one cannot usually ascertain the precise number of people who belong to a family, neither can one say that they all share the same definition of what is that family.

The process of growing up as members of the same primary social unit is a major source of identification. 'Selves' are socially constructed (Viegas, 1994). One's sense of inner identity is deeply marked by those in the company of whom, and by reference to whom, it is created. The feelings of identification which growing up together creates are carried on by these people and, in turn, by those with whom they associate in new moments of social reproduction (be they children or spouses). I call these ever-fading links, 'continued identities': these are the identities derived from the joint association to earlier moments of the cycle of social reproduction (that is, to primary social units now extinct or in the process of extinction).

These links of identification are perhaps one of the major tools to which people take recourse in attempting to cope with the insecurity resulting from the mobility of urban living. At the risk of simplifying, one can identify two major familial dispositions: members of families collaborate either in order to hold on to an earlier position of prestige and/or wealth, or in order to create a certain amount of security where it was formerly absent. Thus, this chapter will be divided into two parts. Firstly, I will deal specifically with upper middle-class and aristocratic families. My concern will be to show that the representations given of the ancestors function as horizons within which persons construct reflexively their own images of self.

Secondly, I will present residential histories of lower middle-class and working-class urban families, to show how the association with a particular house assumes major importance as a marker of individual identity and family belonging in these more insecure urban contexts. These houses are 'anchors in the city', which function as means to create identity in an urban environment that is perceived as unstable and conducive to the erosion of social links and of personal identity.

Of course it may be argued that upper class mansions are also anchoring devices and that middle-class and working-class families also have family legends. This is no doubt true. However, in families with considerable patrimony to transmit across generations the emphasis on a lineal perpetuation of identity is more clearly perceived, whilst in families with a lesser investment in transmitted patrimony, lateral relations marked by reference to a common arena of family interrelation are more visible.

The eight case histories examined below have been collected as part of a long-standing project on the study of the family in Portugal[1]. They have been chosen not because they are thought to be statistically representative, but because they contrast interestingly, bringing out the similarities and the differences in the strategies followed.

Family legends and the production of persons

In this section, I will present examples of upper middle-class and aristocratic families with the aim of eliciting the process of mutual production of families and persons. I will start by showing that continued identities in these families tend to be visibly objectified both in items of shared property (namely mansions) and in prestigious names. It will then be argued that 'family legends' are one of the central processes through which these processes are integrated.

In these families, a considerable amount of property is usually devoluted from generation to generation. Often the division of property-units of symbolical or economic significance (homes, businesses, factories or farms) would entail a serious loss in terms of prestige and in terms of their economic profitability. In some extreme cases, an effort continues to be made to favour the male first-born with the control over these property items or over the items of greater symbolical significance. Legally, however, this is not permitted.

The solution most often found to this quandary is the family society. It is important to stress, however, that this is not a permanent solution. Thus, it does not imply the existence of lineages or descent groups. Sooner or later, it will be necessary to divide the property, but this strategy manages to delay the moment of partition, maximizing in the meantime profit and prestige. The example I will now present is an extreme one, in that this strategy was taken further than is commonly the case.

Case 1

The Marquis of P shared the inheritance of his manor house with his celibate sister. Until his father died, he lived and worked in the city of Oporto. After that he moved to the manor, as head of a considerable agricultural enterprise from which he earns his living. The property has been turned into a family society, where each of the two siblings owns 50 per cent of the shares. In practice, however, the Marquis and his six children treat the property as their own, with the exception of a set of rooms (two bedrooms, two sitting rooms, a bathroom and a kitchen) which are kept apart for the sister's sporadic use (as she lives in Oporto).

The eldest son is a lawyer in Oporto. He is married and it is expected that he will be the main heir. The two youngest sons live in the manor house, one is a zoo technical engineer and the other is finishing a degree in agronomy. The two sisters are married, living away from home in Lisbon.

An attempt is being made on the part of the sons to have the house and farm declared national patrimony. The purpose of this move (which runs counter to the normal attitude of owners of such houses) is to prevent the property from being divided. As it stands at present, the property is owned integrally by the family society. Should, however, at a later moment, a majority of shareholders decide to terminate the society, the assets could then be divided between them and the property would disintegrate. If they succeed in turning it into national patrimony, the property will become indivisible. This means that it will lose much in market value, but it also means that whoever controls most shares will remain in practice sole owner of the property.

In this example, the strong personality of the Marquis and the prestige of his line, as well as the certainty that none of the children will ever accumulate sufficient capital to recreate anything like the bulk of property that presently exists, mean that a strong agnatic line is preserved and fought for. This, of course, implies that the younger brothers have to contemplate a future as bachelors (which, according to them, is precisely what they plan to do) and that the sisters' heirs can expect little benefit from the society – apart from a largely symbolic share in the society's annual profits.

It must be understood, however, that this example is uncharacteristic because of the strong emphasis placed on agnatic succession. The symbolic capital associated with the one titled line completely over-shadows the other possible family identities. But, as one of the daughters put it, 'my family has two branches, my father's and my mother's.' In fact, the mother's family is a military family of prestige, and the children's extra-domestic kinship links distinctly favour the mother's relatives – as is so characteristic of family life in Northern Portugal. This same daughter married into a military family that has long been close associates of the mother's family. When we interviewed her, we observed that, as far as depth into the past is concerned, her genealogical memory is much richer on the aristocratic side (where it goes as far back as the first Marquis, FFFF[2], her great-great-grandfather). But her knowledge of living kin is far more detailed and broader on the maternal side.

Indeed, for the majority of such families, the choice of a source of familial identity is broad and complex. Although each marriage forms a new primary social unit, the feelings of unity and shared interests which are associated with having been raised within a primary social unit are prolonged at later moments of the cycle of reproduction, giving rise to extra-domestic forms of familial association – 'continued identities'.

The research I have been carrying out into genealogical memory indicates that the typical depth of the kinship universe of an informant is his grandparental generation, rarely going beyond the generation of the great-grandparents. Of course, in aristocratic families and older upper middle-class families it may go considerably beyond that. When that is the case, however, informants only remember particularly salient figures of national historical relevance and the line's originator. For example, in Case 4 below, the original ancestor (a royal bastard who was a bishop in the sixteenth century) is 15 generations earlier (he is FFFFFFMMFFFFFFF). Nonetheless, even in this case, personalized, broader information does not really go beyond the great-grandparental generation, extending only along the principal titled lines.

What this means is that continued identities may derive from the two households of origin of the informant's parents, the four households of origin of the informant's grandparents, or more rarely the eight house-holds of origin of the informant's great-grandparents. In practical terms, none of the families we have studied uses anything approaching these eight lines as active sources of identity for the purposes of family reunion.

In a markedly cognatic and bilateral system of kinship reckoning such as this one, perpetuation of family identity depends on choice. Some identities are perpetuated, some are denied perpetuation. Furthermore, although some continued identities are perpetuated, it is important to understand that what is transferred to the filial generation, is a continued identity that has been worked upon and recreated by the parental generation.

Broadly speaking it can be said that these continued identities have implications at three levels. Firstly, they are the basis for the creation and maintenance of extra-domestic familial networks of social relations. As has been pointed out, these tend to have a strong uxorilateral leaning and play a major role in terms of child raising. Regular child-minding, holiday activities and annual festivities (as well as birthdays) focus very heavily on these networks. The result is that strong links are created between cousins which function as the basis of reproduction of the continued identity for yet another generation.

The joint ownership of assets of economic relevance is another important factor. Businesses, farms and factories are often jointly owned by the family and function as a common source of interest, drawing people together, on the one hand, and pulling them apart, on the other. Conflicts over control both of management and of profits are exceedingly common. Whichever of these situations prevails, however, the end result is the creation of strong feelings of association.

Finally, continued identities are reproduced through the sharing of names, tombs and memorabilia such as photographs, small decorative objects, and sets of furniture the pieces of which are divided among the heirs.

One item, however, to which I have not yet referred, is of utmost importance, as it encompasses all of these: the country home. Most of these aristocratic and upper middle-class families have a country seat, usually attached to an agricultural enterprise, which performs a central role as far as the three aspects referred to above. The following example will show how this functions.

Case 2

Mrs N is the sole descendant of an aristocratic, military family, some of whose members played important roles in colonial Brazil and, later on, in the colonies of Africa and the Far East. Following the masculine line, her genealogical memory goes as far back as her great-grandfather's great-grandfather (FFFFFF), but she has no specific knowledge of any other relatives of these genealogical levels. (There are records, however, and the correspondence of some of the ancestors has survived; but this is not information which she can readily recall.) It is only at her grandparents' generation that she starts to have a clearer picture of other members. At that genealogical level her memory is equally rich on the father's side as on the father's mother's, mother's father's, husband's father's and husband's mother's sides. Furthermore, her detailed knowledge encompasses all of the descendants of these families.

Her husband was an engineer. Like her ancestors, she too lived for a long time in the Portuguese African colonies. In turn, her children have also been very mobile geographically. For this reason, the casa de N *assumes a central role in the family's self-representation. As she puts it, 'we were all born in the nearby city, but we all say that we are from N'. In her Lisbon apartment, on a central wall, she displays in vertical order, five photographs of the five generations of army officers ending with her father. Beside these she has a photograph of her mother, of the house in N and a reproduction of her family's coat-of-arms.*

The house was not inherited from her distinguished military and aristocratic ancestors, however. These lost all of the property they once owned. It was built by her mother's father's father in 1840 and restored late in life by her own father, for his personal use. At present, it is a focus of solidarity of central importance to her children and grandchildren as well as to her husband's siblings' children and grandchildren. Here Mrs N rules supreme, having inherited from her mother-in-law the role of family integrator. She has taken over the major celebrations of her mother-in-law's house and she has buried her mother-in-law as well as her own husband in a plot of land belonging to the house of N – but not in the family mausoleum, for that was her husband's wish.

The interesting aspect about this example is how Mrs N picked on the different continued identities which converged on her in order to create an integrated familial universe. The house of N is a construct built with the name, title and prestige of her father's line, with the property of her mother's line and with the network of kinship links created by her mother-in-law. With all of this she has attempted to create an integrated family legend – that is, a mythically coherent narrative of family identity. Her own children and grandchildren share the continued identity which she has created and are, in turn, fashioned by it.

Continued identities are created and reproduced by means of props, such as houses, names, titles, photographs, books and, not least, income-bearing property. Their essence, however, is far more elusive. What integrates them is a sense of joint identity, of shared fate. This, in turn, depends on the creation of a narrative of family identity. I call these narratives 'family legends' because they tend to attain a level of coherence through people's more or less explicit elaboration, assuming a mythical aspect (cf. Pina-Cabral, 1991, pp.210–12).

These family legends comprise two aspects: on the one hand, generalized statements of familial characteristics; on the other hand, personalized legendary accounts of specific ancestors. They are not necessarily positive. For example, it is as common to hear comments of the type, 'the Xs are good husbands' or 'the Xs have always been very artistic', as 'the Xs are stingy and small-minded' or 'the Xs are reckless'. Similarly, the personalized accounts too need not be bland, whitewashed biographical sketches, although admittedly there is a tendency for positive, exotic, or outstanding aspects to be stressed.

These personalized legends often correspond to men or women who are at the grandparental or great-grandparental level and who are seen either as the originators of the family's fortunes or, in the case of the older aristocratic families, as relevant reproducers. Often they were people who came from abroad or from another milieu, starting a new family project. Their strong personalities left a deep imprint in their descendants after their death.

These family legends function as descriptive practices within the context of normal family life. People constantly classify each other's behaviour in terms of this stock of standard legends. Comments of the type, 'One can see you are an X', need have no further specification, for the whole audience (the remaining sharers of that continued identity) know precisely to which particular proclivity the speaker is referring. Families, like all communities of practice, are an 'activity system about which participants share understandings concerning what they are doing and what that means in their lives and for their communities'

(Lave and Wenger, 1991, p.98).

This tendency constantly to interpret a family member's actions in terms of a shared stock of family legends is enshrined in a whole set of proverbs and proverbial locutions. One often hears the proverb '*Quem sai aos seus não degenera*'. This is not easy to translate, as in fact people commonly use it in a broader sense than it initially had, simply to indicate that a certain agent's behaviour is clearly recognizable in terms of his or her family background. It means something like, 'If you really are one of us, you cannot go wrong'.

A similar use is given to the proverb, '*tal pai tal filho*' (like father, like son) and to the proverbial locution '*a voz do sangue*' (the voice of blood), which is supposed to be heard when someone behaves in a way that is uncannily similar to one of his ancestors. The use of these forms of classifying implies the existence of a common stock of knowledge. These are forms of stating identity and, at the same time, they are means of reproducing the familial relations which underlie both the knowledge and the identity. As Lave and Wenger have pointed out, 'identity, knowing and social membership entail one another' (1991, p.53).

Indeed, it is worth noting that even the expression of conflict, disagreement or aggression is most commonly couched in terms of family legends. There are positive and negative legends. A group of siblings or cousins, or a couple, always has recourse to more than one continued identity. Even though they prefer to identify themselves by some of these, the others are kept hidden, emerging at such moments. It is then that people attack each other with comments of the genre: 'You are like Granny X, you cannot tell a truth from a lie', or 'You will land up like Aunt Y' (who was insane, or alcoholic, or promiscuous, or any other stigmatized identity).

This practice, which could be read as demeaning the family identity, destroying its integrity, in fact is no such thing. By sharing their vocabulary of shame, people define a common ground. After all, '*quem sai aos seus não degenera*' and the speaker may well turn out to have inherited the same undesirable proclivity as he or she is imputing to the victim. Furthermore, this kind of negative evaluation functions as a means of debating and creating a family project – in the sense that all communities of practice imply the constant negotiation of future action (cf. Pina-Cabral, 1994). Thus, in a system such as this one, continued identities are a field of difference. They are constantly coming together, merging, combining, and submerging one another; but they are also inevitably going to be split asunder. The following example shows this clearly.

Case 3

*This is how the informant explained her upper middle-class family:
'When one is homely, responsible, when one pays one's TV tax, one is
an X. No fantasy there, no imagination, no capacity to break with
everyday tasks. When one is a bad character, envious, small minded,
one is completely Y. But when one is more creative, when one chooses
to do things on the side of light, when one has something to fight for,
one is Z. It's funny because Z was a title attributed at the time of the
Reconquista against the Moors, it comes from the fourteenth century
or even earlier. This is essential because people's behaviour can be
one way or another. There are a lot of people who, when they were
adolescent were Z, but then grew up and became X.'*

There is still a fourth important reference, the Ws - they are the
main source of the family's wealth. Their original ancestor, the
informant's great-great-grandfather (FMFF), was a Dutchman who
came to a provincial Portuguese town and founded an important
line of business.

All of these legends concerning personality types are associated
with specific figures. Thus, Z, the only aristocratic name in the
ancestry, is associated with the fascinating life history of mother's
mother. Z, however, is not this lady's father's or her husband's name,
but her mother's father's name. Thus the informant singles out the
prestigious MMM name and family legend, completely casting into
oblivion MMF's memory. Indeed, this being a favourite legend, there
are still relatives whose family name she reports as being Z, even
although the transfer of the name in the male line was interrupted
with MMM, and it should have disappeared.

X is this intellectual great-aunt's lower-class, younger husband
(MF). He comes, however, from a family with an intellectual, commu-
nist, atheistic tradition and he committed suicide after the death of
his two sons. As such, although no one uses his name, he continues to
be a positively valued legend.

Finally, the Ys - who inherited the property of the Ws, having
become one of the most important families in that provincial region
- are the surviving line. The informant has a decidedly negative view
of her father's father, a powerful business man. But her negative
description hides the fact that she chooses to call herself Y, as well as
all of her siblings and that his house is the point of reunion and the
family space of reference for a whole group of highly mobile kinsmen,
whose professional lives have taken them all over the world.

This example clearly indicates how familial identity is constructed out of a terrain of charted differences. Each person can refer his behaviour and that of his closer family members to a series of family legends. It is these family legends that carry the continued identities. They are altered, manipulated, stressed or effaced in order to suit each person's and each generation's perceived interests. Some personalities survive, functioning as a source of identity between descendants, others disappear. Out of all of her 16 great-great-grandparents, the informant registered only one. Out of her 8 great-grandparents she only referred distinctly to one – W's enterprising daughter.

Class and status group belonging play an important role in the reproduction of family legends. In rapidly mobile families, the break with past identities and social networks may lead to a loss of family legends or to a form of more or less conscious amnesia. In upper middle-class and aristocratic families which, on the whole, tend to be downwardly mobile, there is a reinforced emphasis on these legends, for they are an important resource in the fight against downward mobility and perceived loss of prestige. The only case where family legends are specifically repressed would seem to be when they correspond to a past of extreme poverty or of a stigmatized social group (such as, for example, gypsies).

The game of identification which the informant in Case 3 engaged in, is a major form of family activity. From the very moment the baby is out of the womb, one is expected to find similarities. These are publicly discussed and dotingly searched for at all family meetings. At first these similarities are merely physical but soon enough people start identifying stereotyped behaviour patterns: if it is a smiling baby 'it comes after' (*sai a*) aunt so-and-so; if it has an angry look 'it comes after' grandfather so-and-so.

There is a constant preoccupation to root the baby's identity in the familial past. One need not 'come after' only one person – it is thought to be acceptable to say, for example, that in her intelligence the child comes after relative X, but in her vigour she comes after relative Y. Moreover, one can 'come after' close non-lineal relatives, particularly godparents (especially if they are also relatives) and uncles and aunts.

There are naming practices which reinforce this form of identification. The choice of new, fancy, fashionable or politically meaningful first names for one's children is a characteristically lower middle-class phenomenon in Portugal. Among the type of families we have been observing, conservatism in the attribution of first names is absolutely *de rigueur*. One may find, for example, a man who has the same name[3] as his father, his grandfather and his great-grandfather. Yet another system is the one practised by the Ys in Case 3, where each male descendant receives not only the double-barrelled family name but also the first name Francisco prefaced by another more personal first name. In Case 2, it is the custom to give a male child his grandfather's name.

The fact that family names are supposed to pass on the masculine line, means that these practices of conservatism are more visible with males, but they are by no means limited to them. Girls too are named after their mothers, aunts and grandmothers (particularly when the latter are also godmothers). The names attributed to the children are most often those of members of the grandparental generation and they may be associated with any one of the continued identities.

Case 4

The Ms are a very prestigious titled family. As was said earlier on, the first M was a royal bastard in the fifteenth century. The family's principal title which is still used today was awarded to his great-grandson. At the turn of last century, they intermarried with the Ps, one of the wealthiest families of the then no longer recent liberal aristocracy. The present generation's mother originates from the Os, an aristocratic family of foreign origin with a considerable commercial and industrial fortune.

In terms of family legends, these three main continued identities involve different behaviour expectations. The Ms are more grandiose, less concerned with money, more rooted in the land; the Os are united and mutually co-operative, serious merchants and businessmen. The O women are 'bossy', whilst the O men are supposed to be good tempered and easy going.

In this family, first name conservatism is taken very far. There is a stock of about five names for women and six names for men which are repeated endlessly from generation to generation and laterally across the different lines of cousins. Sometimes the desire to graft new children into the past is so extreme, that it is possible to have one daughter called Maria Teresa de Jesus and another Maria de Jesus Teresa.

This is accompanied by a relatively high rate of marriage between close cousins. Whilst, on the one hand, these marriages do prevent the patrimony from dividing up, on the other hand, they tend to be the result of a rather closed-in social world. They reinforce highly valued continued identities which, otherwise, may have been diluted in the process of out-marriage.

In sum, when a baby is born it is integrated into the family as a socially constructed person. In fact, in the majority of cases, the biological production of the baby is already planned in terms of a future social reproduction of the family – that is why the parents are ideally married before conceiving the child. Children are thus fashioned into persons. The constant game of identification which we have been describing is one of the main forms of producing familial persons – people who will continue the identity. The person, as he or she forms his or her personality in the family, is repeatedly and systematically encased, pushed into, made to fit into the familial legends.

It is, therefore, not surprising that these family legends are often objectively confirmed. For example, if the X family is supposed to be artistically gifted, then it is probable that a considerable capital in books and art objects will have been accumulated. This is transmitted to the younger generations along with a 'name' that, in turn, favours the bearer's entry into artistic circles. When he or she comes of age, the younger member of family X has a considerable head start over other potential artists. The same could be said for families where, for example, women are supposed to be good cooks, or men are supposed to be womanizers, or where an enterprising spirit is the rule.

During childhood and adolescence a person is peripheral to the family situation, in that he or she is not in a situation of authority, but his or her presence is fully legitimate. Furthermore, the process of reproduction of these familial identities, as was pointed out earlier on, is a process where there is a combination of different continued identities carrying a number of family legends. The child is peripheral but not passive.[4] Thus, I have chosen to use Lave and Wenger's concept of 'legitimate peripheral participation' (1991, pp.14, 32) to describe this process through which each person constructs his or her own life project within a process of reflexive interaction between self-identity and family identity. The child is, on the one hand, learning his or her social roles and, on the other hand, actively engaged in reproducing and modifying the expectations about these roles.

Finally, each group of siblings is the receiver and transmitter of a series of continued identities, some are altered and reproduced, some are simply dropped into oblivion. What gives body to these continued identities is the notion that they correspond to some sort of common substance. Typically, this superpersonal substance is talked of by reference to 'blood', but these days one is starting to hear references to 'genes' used in much the same manner.

Moreover, as could be expected of a European cultural environment, notions of a superpersonal identity are not limited to a corporal, 'physical' dimension. There is an elaboration of a supposed mystical link between close kin, that would manifest itself in moments of grave danger and, particularly, at the moment of death. Stories are told of daughters who are living far from home and who, at the moment of the mother's death, have a distinct premonition of it, or of fathers or mothers instinctively sensing their children's pain or death. The role played by the family legends in the production of persons, and in the person's self-image, is what gives objective reality to these stories and to the lived experience of identity that unites the members of a family. This identity is incorporated, producing the family's body as well as the family's spirit.

An anchor in the city

In the cities,[5] lower middle-class and working-class family belonging is affected by the lack of endurable markers of long-term identification. Urban insecurity and mobility tend to prevent the sense of historical rootedness that is characteristic of the families discussed above. However, we have no evidence that familial identity is any less important.

In the next section of this chapter, I will identify one of the major processes through which such identities are reproduced. Case 5 has been chosen in order to create a link with the earlier ones. It corresponds to an upper middle-class family that is undergoing a rapid process of downward mobility. Case 6 corresponds to a situation where a similar process has already been accomplished. The final two cases represent typical working-class situations.

Urban living is marked by mobility of various types. Firstly, residential mobility: it is common for people to move house frequently, both because they live in temporary, rented accommodation and because they change home and neighbourhood whenever their economic conditions alter.

Secondly, socio-economic mobility: in the cities, as opposed to rural environments, people's socio-economic condition can change with relative speed. Thirdly, professional mobility. There are many types of jobs which force people to move from city to city or even from country to country – in Portugal, for the working classes, emigration played this role and, for the middle classes, the colonies played a similar role. Fourthly, conjugal mobility: divorce, separation and remarriage are common phenomena. All mobility is, of necessity, a source of insecurity – a challenge to the individual.

The American myth of the rootless, urban conjugal family aims at responding to these challenges. Whatever its value in other social contexts, in Portugal, such a notion fails to describe the central processes to which people take recourse in attempting to cope with their urban lives. In the case of the working-class and middle-class urban families which we will now discuss, the mode, process and distance of the entry into the city seem to be of the greatest importance in order to understand their residential arrangements. Furthermore, choice of neighbourhood has to do with familial proximity. For that I use the notion of 'vicinality' (Pina-Cabral, 1991). Here, I intend to speak of the actual use of houses over prolonged periods of time.

Case 5

Natércia Sousa Coelho de Andrade[6] (born in 1920 in the house where she now lives) is a housewife and has High School attendance. The apical ancestor of her family is Bento Sousa (1854–1923). He came from poor rural extraction to work in the city as a grocer shop assistant. Eventually, he bought the shop, which was situated in the upper class suburb of Foz (he adopted the former owner's name as a nickname – Ramos). He went on to become a wealthy, Republican capitalist in the first two decades of the century. Ego's father followed a similar trajectory: he also came from a rural area to work in the same grocer shop and eventually became its owner. He married Bento Sousa's daughter and again inherited the nickname Ramos. The shop was on the ground floor of the 'mother-house' ('casa-mãe', as they call it) where Natércia now lives.

The links which characterize the attempt to reproduce Bento Sousa's prestige, wealth, house and names are strongly uxorilateral. So much so that the family is known locally as 'Bento Sousa' or as 'Ramos' (in the feminine). One of his daughters remained in the house and two other children set up home nearby. Subsequently, with the exception of those who stayed in the original house, they moved to new prestigious neighbourhoods. The residential choices of these members are largely representative of the changing urban patterns of prestige in Oporto – a city which, after all, remains sufficiently small for the distance not to prevent intense family life. At roughly each new generation, a different quarter is associated with new prestige housing. This being a middle-class family, they tend to follow these patterns. But, apart from the original house, no one now lives in Foz.

Of all the daughters of Bento Sousa, it is the one who married the man with capacity to reproduce the status and economic standing of Bento Sousa, who functioned as the focal point of family life until the time of her death. She is Natércia's MZ. The 'family' met at her house every week, we are told. She did not live in Foz. Under her husband's leadership, the brothers-in-law formed a series of commercial societies that were very successful. But her subsequent divorce put a violent halt to this situation of social promotion, originating a tendency, which is marked among Natércia's generation and her children's generation, for rapid downward mobility. This divorce had other implications: the *quinta* (country home) that had been inherited from Bento Sousa and functioned as a holiday get-together, stayed with the husband. The whole process was very painful for the family, lasting 20 years in court. The whole family came to suffer from it, as this man was the drive behind all their joint ventures. The role of this MZ as family integrator, however, does not seem to have been affected by the divorce – even after that, she was still the wealthiest member of the family by far.

Of the eight members of Natércia's generation, only two opted for neolocality after marriage. This choice of residing with the parents corresponds to an attempt to preserve familial prestige in the course of a process of downward mobility.

Only in the 1970s did all the cousins start to spend Christmas together in the old house. This too can be seen as a further attempt to preserve the prestige of the old family ties. By the 1980s, however, even that had stopped. Nevertheless, when the relatives from Brazil come to visit, it is still to this house that they direct themselves, staying there for more or less prolonged periods.

The old house is, in fact, two houses back to back, with two upper floors. They were built over and behind the grocer shop founded by Bento Sousa, each one facing one of two parallel streets. The following is an edited version of Natércia's description of her residential history, where people's names have been substituted by indication of their kinship relation to Natércia.

'When my mother married she occupied the first floor of the house at the back. She had a completely independent house: dining room, sitting room, bedrooms, two bathrooms and kitchen. We got to grandparents' home through the steps that led to the second floor. We often went there. In that house lived my grandparents, MFB, MMZ and my aunts.

'The first change in residence was when I was eight, after the death of my grandmother. My grandfather had died five years before, and my mother and aunts decided to divide the property. My parents stayed with grandfather's house and Aunt Bibi with the *quinta* (she then lost it as a result of her divorce). My parents rented out the first floor to the Postmaster (the house at the back has a post office in the ground floor). They also rented part of the second floor – it was a temporary situation. My only aunt that was still single lived with her sisters, she often slept with me.

'When I married, I occupied the remainder of the second floor, but it was very tight. I only had three rooms. It was no good. My daughter shared our room until she was nine years old, at which time the rest of the floor was left free and we had three bedrooms and an office. We lived in common: the meals were prepared and eaten together, we shared the living rooms of my mother's house, we were not independent . . . . My brother and my parents lived in the other house, and he still occupies a room in that area. Nothing changed with my children's rooms after my parents' death.'

During her whole life, she only stayed away from this house for six months, at a time the husband was sent to the countryside by the doctor to undergo a cure for tuberculosis. They paid a nominal rent to her parents before their death. Apart from her and her husband, the house is occupied by her two single daughters (in their thirties) and her bachelor brother. Her son and grandson come for lunch every weekday. They could only afford an apartment in the outskirts of the city.

Having been instituted at the time of entry into the city, the house at Foz marks this family's course of upward and subsequent downward mobility, constituting a major source of physical and social security but also a primary marker of identity. It represents a last claim to prestige in terms of an association to an upper middle-class status that is not being reproduced. In the following case, this process has gone much further.

Case 6

Renato António Cunha Soares (born in 1913) is a childless widower who retired from the Colonial Customs Service where he had officer status. He has secondary schooling. He now lives in an old age home. Renato belongs to a middle-class, professional family of the city of Braga, with many links to the colonial bureaucracy. In his childhood

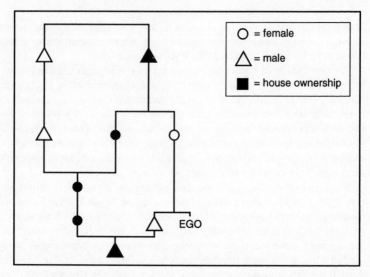

Figure 5.1   The succession to ownership of the Casa do Largo de São F.

he had many homes (he cannot count them all - of his ten siblings, four were born in Matosinhos, each one in a different home, and in Braga the family lived in five different places). In between, they often spent short periods in the Casa do Largo de São F. - his maternal grandfather's home. This uncharacteristic mobility was due to his father, a Radical Republican politician, sometime bureaucrat and journalist. He was an unstable man who squandered the inheritance he received from his own father. His early death left Renato's mother in a difficult economic situation.

She was the daughter of a banking agent in Braga who had acquired some means in Brazil. This man is Renato's apical ancestor - his main reference for prestige and identity. It was in the latter's home that Renato, his mother and his siblings took refuge at the father's death, when Renato was 13. In this side of Renato's family there are many marriages between close kin. (In Figure 5.1, I indicate only those which are necessary to understand Renato's links to the heirs to the house.)

When asked whether he has any kinsmen living nearby, Renato immediately refers the house in the Largo de São F. This house was his main point of reference during his whole life. After his mother's death, at the age of 21, he had to leave to earn his living in the colonial administration. In Africa, where he eventually married, he lived in many Government houses, never being in any one of them for very long. On his periodic returns to Portugal, he always went back to his grandfather's house – always maintaining his relationship with the various kinsmen who inherited it. For a while, one of his own brothers was married to an heiress to the house.

When, in 1975 (at 62 years of age), Renato had to flee from the newly independent Mozambique, it was to this house that he retired with his wife. Later, they managed to reorganize their life and find an apartment. After she died, he moved to the old age home. But he visits the house as often as he can. It grieves him to know that he may not die before it is sold. It has become too large for present day standards of domestic comfort and too valuable not to be sold, as it is placed in the centre of Braga. Renato's BS (also MZDDS) is arranging to sell it.

It should be noted that, as in the other instances presented in this section, we are not dealing with a type of residential attachment that has a cyclical, recurrent renewal. On the contrary, it would seem that, once a house assumes this role of social anchor, it continues to play it for a very prolonged period. Its disappearance is an irreparable loss for those who continue to depend on it for their familial identity. If it disappears, however, it is also because the continued identities it transmits no longer have enough cohesive power. As will be seen from the next two cases, their disappearance signifies that the process of entry into the city has been accomplished.

Case 7

Arminda (born in 1931) is married with two children (both married). She is the porter of a residential building, but she also works as a seamstress. Her husband is a factory worker. Both have primary schooling (hers completed at 13 years of age, his completed when he was already married).

In this case, we will not delve into Arminda's present residential arrangements. She lives in the porter's flat of a building in Barreiro, a working-class suburb of Lisbon. We will deal with the home of her maternal grandparents in Alfama – an old quarter close to the centre of Lisbon. It is a quarter about which much has been written, as it shows interesting sociological features. It is an area of reception into the city, mostly for poor people coming from the central area of the country, but it is also a traditional quarter, as these people integrate themselves quickly into a working-class urban sub-culture which depends on income opportunities offered by the port (as this particular family's history demonstrates) and on other more marginal activities such as prostitution and all types of clandestine dealing.

In 1903, Arminda's mother's parents moved to Alfama from Almada – which at the time was a rural area – and occupied a small flat. They had nine children – Arminda's mother went back to Almada, another to Brazil, two others got married and found houses nearby (in Graça), three died as babies and another girl died before marrying age. Only a son remained with the parents. In 1923 he got married and the following year had a child. At the same time, a young boy – the orphan of one of the sons who in the meantime had died – came to live with the grandparents.

In 1938, this couple moved to Graça, having managed to find a house. This meant that Arminda's mother and her husband could come back to her parents' home, as they had not succeeded in finding a permanent dwelling. This was also convenient, as the mother had become a paralytic and needed looking after. By then Arminda and her three brothers had already been born (she was seven years of age).

In 1940, within a month, both grandparents died, so Arminda's parents and siblings remained in the house, continuing to look after their orphaned nephew. In 1946, Arminda's brother married and brought his wife and subsequent child to live with the parents. Arminda wanted to get married, so her parents insisted with her brother that he should move out. He did so in 1949, taking with him the orphaned nephew. In 1950 (when she was 20 years of age), Arminda got married, so the household was now composed of the young couple, the old couple and a bachelor brother. She subsequently gave birth to two children.

In 1968 her father died and her younger brother got married, moving to his mother-in-law's apartment nearby. Eventually he found a home in the same square as the parental house. With her two children, she now considered that the house had become too small for them. (Notice the rise in living standards: in 1903 the house had been enough for a couple and nine children, in 1938 for two couples and five children, in 1946 for two couples and four children.) She found her present job as a porter in Barreiro and moved out.

Her mother remained alone in the house for a few months, but soon a married granddaughter came to live with her. Within a year this granddaughter and her husband found a house in Almada. But in 1971, another granddaughter, her husband and their son, came back from Cape Verde. They resided with the grandmother until such time as their marriage fell apart. Then the wife moved into her own mother's home with her child. During 1976, the grandmother lived alone again, but in 1977 a grandson, his wife and child moved in. In 1979, the grandson divorced his wife, who remained in the house looking after the old lady. In 1986, the grandmother died and, to this day, the house is occupied by the grandson's ex-wife and child. It is worth stating that Arminda, as well as most of the relatives that lived in the house, keep a close connection with it, visiting it regularly. Finally, the flat does not belong to this family. During their 83 years of occupation it was always rented.

This case confirms that what gives these houses their importance is not any logic of patrimonial transfer. On the contrary, whether the house is owned or rented may turn out to be irrelevant. Furthermore, the house defines no kinship group of any sort; its transfer follows no pre-set system of rules. The centrality of this house in the lives of Arminda and her relatives is its role as an arena of familial interrelation and of personal definition. The house marks a type of belonging to the city.

The type of family belonging, furthermore, is affected by the environment in which the *família* is created as a community of practice. In this case, as indeed in the next one, in contrast to the earlier cases, we can observe that, there being less patrimonial interests, there is correspondingly less emphasis on the formality of family belonging. Biological and legal definitions of kinship are less significant where state-imposed rights to inheritance of patrimony are less important, due to the lack of such patrimony. The boundaries between friends and relatives become less clearly demarcated.

Case 8

Eva da Assunção Oliveira was born in 1921 in the mountains of central Portugal. She married locally and emigrated to Lisbon already with two children. Her husband died in 1984. She lives in a flat with her daughter and son-in-law, her grandchildren and her son-in-law's father.

When they came to Lisbon (she followed the husband after a year) they went to the house in the Travessa das Freiras where they stayed for eight years. (This is the house of which Eva most often talked to the interviewer and the history of which we will briefly outline.) They left this house in order to find a house of their own, but the rent was high and they needed to have guests – they were not happy with that and moved out after a year to a smaller house in Almada.

Eva worked as a charwoman before going to Almada, but there she found no work. After a while, her husband was fired from his job, so she decided to go back to the countryside with the children until such time as he found work. As it turned out, she discovered that she could not leave him alone in the city; he was prone to being unfaithful and did not look for a job. She had to come back. Their only alternative was to go back to the house at Travessa das Freiras. Although she was quick to find jobs for them, they remained there until he died, at which time she moved in with the daughter and her husband.

The house in Travessa das Freiras was the place through which most of her relatives entered the city from their village. There they lived until they found a job and a house, and they returned there whenever their lives took a turn for the worse. As she put it:

> 'To come to Lisbon was our solution for a better life so as to raise our children better. Here I could treat them better as there was more money than back there in the mountains. They could study and live a better life. So, following my father and his brothers, who had come to the house of Tio Adelino, myself and my husband also came to the house of Tia Assunção [she is speaking of the same house at Travessa das Freiras]. That house is a tradition, many friends died and were born there. They were simple but good people. They were very helpful to my father, my brothers and my whole family.'

Father's brother Adelino was the first to come to the city. He got a job in the transportation system and called his wife, Rosa, to come to live with him. They rented the house in the Travessa. Eva's father came after, in order to make a living so his family could live back home. The father was still in the house when Adelino's other brother – César – also came. He brought his second wife to live in the house. Adelino's brother-in-law also came, but he found a house nearby before he called his wife and children to the city. At this time Eva's father died, and Eva's brother and sister, Felisbela, had to come to the city in order to earn a living. They also lived there. The sister did not stay for long, as the uncles were shocked with her sexual behaviour and evicted her.

Adelino then had a stroke and retired into the countryside. The house passed to Assunção, his sister. Nevertheless, she always paid

*him some money for the house (this was in fact a clandestine sub-
letting). It was at this time that Eva and her husband arrived.
Assunção lived there, together with Eva, her husband and three
children, as well as uncle César and brother José. Later her sister
Felisbela joined the house again. Her husband beat her up and she
left home, so she came back there. The brother left, after a few
years.*

*Then sister Alzira came and got married. They also lived there. They
were soon followed by sister Felisbela's daughter and Felisbela's new
husband. Then Alzira left as well as César – who went back home to
retire. Later Eva left to go back to the countryside [see above]. After a
while, however, poverty forced her and her husband to come back.*

*Nine years later they finally found a house of their own, taking
with her her brother José's son. The brother married again and
returned to the house with his new wife for a while. José's daughter
stayed on a little longer, as she also married and brought the husband
to the house.*

*At about this time, Assunção retired and Isaura, her daughter,
moved in with her husband and children – she was now the 'boss'. She
eventually found a better home and handed the house back to the
landlord. This was the end of the house.*

Unfortunately Eva has no notion of the years in which these movements occurred and we have no precise idea of the time gap involved.
However, we can safely presume that it was over six decades, as the
house was already being occupied by Adelino when Eva was born in
1921 and the handing over of the house took place in the mid-1980s.

Finally, it should be clear that we are by no means capable of making
a list of all the people who lived in this house, as apart from the 'boss'
and his or her conjugal family, and the other more permanent members
(such as Eva always was), the house was a point of entry into the city for
most of the relatives and some of the neighbours from their village of
origin. There was a permanent flow of young men to whom rooms were
sub-let for short periods.

What I think justifies bringing these four examples together is that
they show how urban mobility (in its various manifestations) leads to
strategies of residential anchoring. These houses are 'anchors' in the
city. They are reference points and thus they assume a major importance as markers of individual identity and family belonging. The house
is like a switchboard into the city. It is instituted both at the time of
entry into the city and, concomitantly, at the time of entry into a class

niche within that city (that is important for, together with the house, goes a whole network of relations and, most particularly, in all of the four cases above, distinct types of work openings).

Again, whether the house is owned or rented, the time of occupation is very prolonged – only in this way can the house assume its slightly depersonalized character that distinguishes it from the normal conjugal family flat or house. Once a house is instituted in this way, it continues to play this role for a prolonged period.

Another central feature is the structure of authority within the house that permits its functioning. In all of these cases we have found that there is a formal 'owner' of the house and that the owner yields a considerable amount of authority over the other occupants, to the point where she can evict them. I say 'she' advisedly, for it would seem that we are dealing with a form of familial relation that is predominantly matrifocal. It is through women that men have access to these homes and the relationship between women is often stronger than the links of kinship (as in the situation exemplified in Case 7, where the grandson divorces the wife and is forced to leave, so that the 'ownership'[7] of the house passes to the hands of the wife from the ex-husband's mother).

The houses which we have been identifying are characteristically arenas for the creation of familial identity. The shared experience which they imply is very strongly felt by the participants, for there is a very intense co-operation between the members. Even if I only see my cousin once every five years when I come back to Portugal on long leave (as in Case 6); or if I only cohabit with him or her during a period of particular economic crisis (as in Cases 7 and 8), the fact that I sleep, eat and live together with him or her during that period creates a deep bond between us; a bond which may well be stronger than that which I share with a sibling whom I only see sporadically every few years.

Conclusion

I have argued that, in a system of reproduction of the primary social unit such as the one studied here (what I call a syncopated system), where central emphasis is placed on conjugality, extra-domestic family links depend on the perpetuation of *continued identities*. This process of reproduction of family identity is not independent of the very production of the family members as persons. The family is a project (Gubrium, 1988); that is, there is a constant negotiation of a future between the members of this community of practice. This negotiation involves not only decisions concerning what activities to undertake jointly, but also the production of the persons who will undertake them. This process is visible both in wealthier families and in working-class families.

In the latter instances, instead of an emphasis on remembering the past and reliving it, we find a greater reliance on lateral links in order to find a niche in the city. The two cases presented of working-class families show in particular how important it can be for a person's actual survival to rely on familial links such as those that are reproduced through these houses. These 'anchors in the city' are creators and reproducers of familial identity, performing much the same role as country mansions for aristocratic and upper middle-class families. It is around houses such as these that things like family legends are created and transmitted. However, as we descend the socio-economic gradient, we tend to find lesser emphasis placed on 'families' as reified entities – with a presumed atemporal existence and with distinguishing symbols, such as names, titles, coats-of-arms, legends, named ancestors. Moreover, legally defined proximity (in terms of the state-enforced idiom of biology) assumes less formal significance in determining actual bonds of familiarity. Rather, as we approach the insecurity of working-class contexts, the family as a community of practice tends to be produced around the experience of cohabitation and of co-operation between laterally related people.

Notes

1. This involves asking students to study exhaustively the familial universe of one ego, drawing out a genealogical map (and list of relatives) and identifying the major themes which they feel are at play in their ego's view of his or her family. The material accumulated over the years has proved to be invaluable in providing us with rich empirical testing of the sorts of problems that we discuss with them in the classroom. Furthermore, the project has proved pedagogically extremely valuable, as students have invariably been drawn into a fascination with the hidden implications of a material which, normally, they would overlook.

    I am very grateful for the collaboration of Maria Antónia Pedroso de Lima in developing this project. Most of the cases presented were collected by third year students of Social Anthropology at the Instituto Superior de Ciências do Trabalho e da Empresa (ISCTE), Lisbon. The two first cases of the second part were collected by MA students of the University of Minho. These cases, however, are merely a few examples. For the development of the argument, I have relied on a vast collection of such cases collected since 1987. Interesting though her book is concerning the relation between English kinship and the genealogical method, Mary Bouquet's assessment of our Portuguese students' incapacity to grasp this method is based on a radical misunderstanding (cf. Bouquet, 1993).

2. Indicating generations, (F) female, (M) male.

3. I refer here, of course, only to the first name and surname, because the intermediary names (other first names and other surnames, maternal or paternal) usually vary. For example, the father may be called João Mendes Costa Leal, the son, João António Guedes Costa Leal, and the grandson João Pereira Guedes Costa Leal.

4. Much as I have not opted for the 'tragic mode', I agree with Mark Poster that 'Family members must be studied as subjects who internalize structures, but not necessarily in a passive way. Family structures have been oppressive in varying degrees; they have always involved domination. The history of these structures must be written in a tragic mode. It has had its share of brutalities, sacrifices and repressions. But the story also has its moments of conflict. Women and children have not always internalized their roles quietly and obediently. One can assume that, in dealing with human subjects, when there is domination there is also resistance' (Poster, 1978, p.165)

5. It must be stressed that, of course, this argument does not apply to rural families, particularly in peasant or post-peasant contexts.

6. Pseudonym, as are all the personal names and initials used to refer to informants in this paper.

7. The expression used is to be *dono/a da casa* – master or owner of the house.

6

URBAN CLANNISHNESS AND THE NUCLEAR KIN: TRENDS IN SWEDISH FAMILY LIFE

David Gaunt

A young boy, Alexander Ekdahl, wanders through a splendid turn-of-the-century home. The wood shines darkly, the plush chairs and sofas open wide as if to embrace, the chandeliers glisten. There is a close intimacy as if in a small theatre. The boy is alone. He calls out – 'Fanny! Mamma! ... Siri! ... Maj! ... Grandma!' His sister, his mother, the servants, his grandmother. All women. No one comes. Finally he lies down under a table, folds his hands as if to pray and begins to dream in symbols of life and death.

So runs one of the scenes from the beginning of Ingmar Bergman's film *Fanny and Alexander* (1982). It is a well-known film which won many awards. A longer five-part version has been shown on Swedish Television. *Fanny and Alexander* is a romantic allegory about kinship, sexual reproduction and socialization. As so often before in his work, Bergman treats the family – but does it in a new way. Many of his previous films dealt with married couples in crisis or mother–daughter and father–son conflicts. This film deals with friendship, loyalty, solidarity and continuity over three generations. The perspective is that of a child and the central figure is the grandmother who comes to Alexander as he wakes up from the dream.

Fanny and Alexander was made at the precise moment fertility in Sweden underwent a dramatic change. Throughout the 1960s and 1970s the country had one of the lowest rates of childbirth in the world. Until 1983 the trend was continually in decline. Thereafter, the trend unexpectedly changed and Sweden experienced a baby-boom which now places it among the nations with highest fertility in western Europe. Only in Iceland and Ireland are the rates now higher.

When the film was made, the low fertility and high divorce rate of Swedish families was a matter of great debate. What would happen to the Swedish nation, will it die out? asked the conservatives. Will there be enough workers in the future to pay old-age pensions? asked the social-democrats. Will there be enough workers to take care of the growing number of old people? asked welfare officials. A series of commissions and investigations tried to explain the low fertility. Why were families limiting themselves to one or two children? Was there too little public daycare for children? Had family life dissolved? Why were young people not marrying? Why was there so much divorce? What was the effect on children of having step-parents? Was society in general hostile towards children?

Ingvar Carlsson, then vice-premier responsible for future studies, saw the low fertility as a sign of dissatisfaction with modern life in general. In a commissioned work on the conditions of childhood, he wrote in the preface:

> When people in our part of the world choose of their own accord not to have children, this must be seen as a signal that something is not right. That the pattern of production and life does not sufficiently concern itself with basic human needs such as creating and caring for new life. That modern society in some manner is experienced as hostile to children. (Carlsson, 1983, p.5)

Let us turn from the great complexity of these big questions to the film. As Bergman usually does, he inserts many levels of allusion – in this case to Swedish history, to Shakespeare's *Hamlet* and to Ibsen's *The Wild Duck*.

The time is specified in the prologue: it is 1907. All the men have the names of contemporary kings, princes or emperors: Oscar, Gustav Adolf, Carl, Edward and Alexander. They may have the names of the mighty, but all of the males are flawed and unsuccessful – in the film represented by impotence or delicate health. The women are quite different. They are strong, able and successful. The contrast of weak males against strong females is Bergman's hallmark. Grandmother and Alexander's mother overcome the impotence of the husbands through extramarital affairs, which are known by all but still called 'discreet' anyway. The family theatre only goes well when in the hands of a merry widow. The children of the mothers may or may not be the biological children of the husbands. But no one cares. The children are accepted openly.

The final scene in the film is a party for the baptism of two baby girls.

At the same time it is their introduction into the circle of kin. Helena Victoria, born outside wedlock, is the daughter of Gustav Adolf and the young housemaid Maj. Aurora is the daughter of the widow Emilie, now returned to the family after a terrifying marriage to a bishop. The party is set at an enormous round table. There are 24 persons – all the household including some servants. There is an image of harmonious, equal mixture of sexes and ages. My children, your children, our children are all blended together. The circular form of the table gives an added touch of endless community and solidarity (Törnqvist, 1993, pp.110–25).

The oldest male, Gustav Adolf, speaks for all assembled – the Ekdahl clan. 'We shall live in the small – in the little world. We shall keep at it, cultivate it and make the most of it. Death strikes suddenly; suddenly the abyss opens up; storms may rage and catastrophes come in our way. We all know that. But we don't want to think of those unpleasantries.' Here kinship is used as a protection, as security from the outside. It is, in the words of the American cultural critic Christopher Lasch, a 'haven in a heartless world'.

But films are always illusions. Remember the family name Ekdahl. It has been used before in nordic literature by Ibsen in his play *The Wild Duck*. Ibsen's Ekdahls represented a family who refused to see reality, who lived in a world of fantasy and lies. Ibsen called this flight from reality the 'life-lie' necessary for the average person to experience happiness. Transported to Bergman's film, this would mean that the life of the little world, the life in the intimate circle of kin, is a 'life-lie'.

The 'life-lie' can here be many things. For instance:

- patriarchal power
- biological parenthood
- kinship as community
- solidarity between generations
- reproduction of mankind
- family as security.

The Ekdahls are portrayed as if they were a tribe in a jungle. Using anthropological terms one can discover a patrilinear system of inheritance and a patrilocal placement of the household. Within this scheme there is a matriarchy in which widows have great power. They are free to have sexual relations with men who are not their husbands and the children of these unions are recognized as full members of the family. The situation resembles that of the women in the well-studied Nayar caste on the Malabar coast of India. These women, however, did not live with their husbands, but could have sexual unions with other men. The children would be recognized by the husband as his.

Fanny and Alexander is a film and as such is admittedly an illusion. Bergman goes to great pains to make clear that it is not reality. But maybe he is fooling. Maybe it is an illusion which is not an illusion. The issues he deals with are definitely part of a contemporary debate. Not long after the film, a group (led by sociologist Hans Zetterberg) close to the conservative party proposed an ideological programme based on the distinction between the 'little world' of the family and the 'big world' of politics. And this distinction is still used in ideological debate.

Within the realm of family and kinship the great illusion, which I will illustrate throughout this chapter, is the cultural solidarity which is assumed to come through seeking 'roots' and building semi-ritualized relationships upon genealogy.

I shall in the following pages assemble evidence about the changing reality for family life in Sweden. I shall try to relate this evidence back to Bergman's illusion of kinship as community. I will show that the evidence is ambivalent. Contacts with a wider group of kin – the extended kin – exist and are highly valued, but they tend to be formalized and kept emotionally neutral. However, a core of kin outside the household are central and important for friendship, company and support. This core can be termed the 'nuclear kin' as a parallel to the concept of the nuclear family. The nuclear kin is like a matriarchy in being oriented on mothers, grandmothers and their siblings. It seems that the emergence of the nuclear kin is a recent phenomenon.

Concepts of kinship

The Swedish language is rich in words denoting specific ties of kinship. The large number is the result of distinguishing relatives on the mother's side from those on the father's side. Thus the matrilinear uncles are distinguished from the patrilinear uncles. Similar distinctions are made for aunts and for grandparents.

In the generation of grandparents there is *farfar* (father's father), *farmor* (father's mother), *morfar* (mother's father) and *mormor* (mother's mother). There is no generic term covering all the grandparents, but in local dialects *oldföräldrar* (old-parent) exists. The normal distinction is between *farföräldrar* (father's parents) and *morföräldrar* (mother's parents). Aunts and uncles are distinguished as *farbror* (father's brother), *faster* (father's sister), *morbror* (mother's brother) and *moster* (mother's sister). There are no general terms covering all uncles and all aunts, but in some families *tant* can be used for aunt. Both *tant* and *farbror* have been used by children when addressing older strangers. Because of this the terms now have a quaint or humorous meaning. Nieces and nephews are distinguished as *systerdotter* (sister's daughter), *brorsdotter* (brother's daughter), *systerson* (sister's son) and *brorsson* (brother's son). A general term does exist to cover all nieces and nephews – *syskonbarn* (sibling-children). A grandparent can choose between saying *barnbarn* (grandchild, literally child-child) and distinguishing *sonson* (son-son), *sondotter* (son-daughter), *dotterson* (daughter-son) and *dotterdotter* (daughter-daughter). Similar distinctions are available for a great-grandparent in talking about great-grandchildren. And, of course the great-grandchild can term a maternal great-grandmother *mormorsmor* (mother's-mother's mother).

The term for sibling is *syskon* and this is a word which is used in common conversation. *Kusin* is used to denote first cousins. *Syssling* and *tremänning* (third-men) denote second cousins. *Brylling, pyssling* and *fyrmänning* (fourth-men) denote third cousins, but one hardly ever hears of such relationships being recognized except in rural areas. The etymology of *syssling* and *brylling* is sister-child and brother-child, which therefore originally denoted a closer relationship than second cousins. There is some popular confusion about what terms are applicable to distant cousins because there are so many terms from which to choose. It is possible to talk of fifth-men, sixth-men and so on for even more distant relations, but this requires detailed genealogical knowledge which most people lack.

'*Familj*' is a word of latin origin which began to be used in the Swedish upper classes in the seventeenth century. At that time it stood for a household and would sometimes include the servants. During the nineteenth century *familj* became more narrowly defined and began to exclude the servants. Modern usage of *familj* refers to the nuclear family as long as it lives in the same household. The wider family including those outside the immediate household is denoted by the term '*släkt*' which is similar to the English word kin, but is used much more often in daily conversation. Etymologically the word *släkt* entered into Swedish from German in the Middle Ages; it replaced the older term '*frände*', which now is seldom used. The word for genealogy is *släktforskning* (family research). Normally the *släkt* relationship includes cousins, aunts and uncles, grandparents, great-grandparents. A relative can be presented as a *släkting* if the presenter does not wish to specify how they are related. In-laws and their relatives are often termed *släkt i släkten* (relatives of relatives) or *släkt med släkt* (relatives to relatives).

The Swedish system of kin terminology is that of a double-descent system. It insists on keeping separate matrilineal and patrilineal relatives. Rules for terminology are symmetrical and well-balanced between the two lines and between genders. Traditionally Swedish farm families did not have surnames. Thus there was no identifying surname in the patriline with which to identify. In modern times the various lines of descent appear as interchangeable, none has precedence over the others. In anthropological terms it is a matter of undifferentiated filiation.

This system creates a large group of potential relationships. Individuals are then free to choose whatever kin they wish to associate with. A common distinction is between *familj*, which is almost always the nuclear family household, *nära släkt*, which are near relatives, and finally *avlägsen släkt* which are distant relatives. One female informant born in 1933 states: 'I distinguish near *släkt* and distant. Near *släkt* is *far, mor, syskon* with their partners and children, paternal and maternal grandparents with children, children's partners and grandchildren. *Avlägsen släkting* or *släkt i släkten* are the *släkt* of in-laws, children of cousins and so on' (KU 9595. This is the file registration number in the archives of the Nordic Museum in Stockholm.).

A word that sometimes crops up when Swedes talk about relatives is '*klan*', which obviously is connected to the idea of the Gaelic 'clann', but it has little to do with the original 'clann' or clan of Scotland. Martine Segalen (1986, p.55) traces the origin of the clans. Swedish usage of *klan* indicates a kin-group which departs from the norm through being extraordinarily close and intensive and which does as much as possible together. A 55-year-old mechanic interviewed in 1972 said the following about the family his son had married into: 'Our boy's in-laws and their married children, we call them the Pettersson-*klan*. They stick together enormously much. Sometimes we invite our boy to us in the country. Yes, they say, if her *syskon* (siblings) and their partners can come along too.... They always hang about with their relatives' (quoted in Hanssen, 1978, p.225). A farmer's wife, born in 1944, says, 'I remember how unbelievably surprised I was, when I understood that it was completely clear that we should participate in celebrating a man who was married to a cousin of my mother-in-law. Now I have fully understood that they do so in [my husband's] *släkt*, so it is now natural even for me. In my *släkt* we don't have that type of celebration' (KU 7758). This exaggerated kin solidarity is seen as something strange and unnecessary.

'*Klan*' thus refers to intimate, tight, continuous, almost exclusive relationships between a group of kin. *Klan* is a word about the use of kinship with a negative connotation. In order to distinguish this phenomenon from the Gaelic 'clann', I will use 'clannish' and 'clannishness' to indicate the overly idealized extended kin-based emotional bonding and the identity work involved in performing such a lifestyle.

A unique source

The Nordic Museum, which is the national Swedish museum for ethnology, contacted in December 1980 its group of corresponding informants. They received a list of questions about their family and kin (*Släkt och familj*, Question list number 207) and were encouraged to reply. Since that time hundreds of answers have been registered. Most of them take 10 to 20 pages to discuss the definition of family and relatives, to describe the way their family keeps contact, to give opinions about the importance of being part of a kin-group and so on. Some of the replies are very frank about problems within the family, and a number of these are still confidential.

As is natural when dealing with voluntary answers to a questionnaire there is no possibility of judging the representativity of the correspondents for all other Swedes. Probably the most one can hope for is that they are typical for the sort of people who think that the issue of kin and family is so important that they will put great effort into writing answers about it. The correspondents are paid a symbolic sum or receive books.

The answers are probably somewhat biased in giving disproportionate space to spectacular occasions like family reunions and in giving less space to daily life within the kin-group. The spectacular use of kinship seems to be connected with a type of search for personal identity involving 'seeking roots' and are different from the everyday use of kinship which have more to do with friendship and companionship. The vast majority (76 per cent, see Table 6.1) of the correspondents are women and most of these are above the age of 50 and have grandchildren. It may be that kinship is primarily a woman's issue, but male interest does appear to grow in old age. Perhaps this

Table 6.1   Correspondents on family and kin, by year of birth and sex

Year of birth	Women	Men	Total
1890–1909	33	28	65
1910–1929	109	37	146
1930–1949	73	11	84
1950–	40	3	43
	255	79	334

Source: Nordic Museum, Cultural–historical investigation archive, Question list 207

increased male interest in old age is connected with the social-psychological shift called 'gero-transcendence' which conceives of a change from the materialistic interests of young adulthood to existential interests in old age (Tornstam, 1989).

The answers represent upper, middle and lower class families and a geographical spread. The tendency is that the middle and upper class families are more elaborate about relationships than the lower class families. The upper class families tend to be robust and maintain contact with kin even after divorce and widowhood; lower class families tend (at least in this material) to be fragile and often report that relationships have been broken by divorce and remarriage.

Kinship expressed in this material is dominated by contacts maintained and mobilized by women. The contacts are planned, organized, executed and discussed by women. Women even take over the management of kinship for their husbands. The male contributions are passive – being the central figure of a birthday celebration or being the distant ancestor. One man, born in 1910 in a poor rural village, writes, 'kinship in real meaning is not as strong a tie as work or profession' (KU 7721). Another man, born in 1915 in a fishing village, grew up with grandparents. 'Months could go by without me being in the home of my parents, despite it lying only one kilometer away' (KU 7718). Such comments are usual among elder men with a lower class background.

Whatever has caused the modern change of thinking about, and using, kinship, it probably is connected with modernization of the life courses of women. This modernization leads to life courses for women which more and more resemble those for men. Long education, wage employment outside the home, an income and pension, less time for home care – all these and much more are part of an ongoing process. The state and governments of Sweden can be seen as women-friendly in the sense of supporting the modernization of women through legislation and various public welfare services for, among other things, care for children and the elderly.

How do Swedish women see the family?

Seventy-six per cent of the correspondents are women. Many men write that kinship is not especially important. Other men who write about kin only give details about single relationships such as the grandfather to his first grandchild. Women, on the other hand, describe entire constellations of relationships and try not to leave anyone out. Even if a relationship is not very good, it will probably be mentioned.

A 30-year-old middle-class woman from southern Sweden gives the following practical definition of family. She has recently married and has no children.

> 'The *familj* is for me my husband and I. It is we who live together and share the sun and rain of daily life. My parents are not really my *familj* now that I don't live at home any longer, but they are not *släkt* either, they are Mamma and Papa.
>
> 'My own *släkt* are papa's sister, his brother and wife; and my three cousins, my mother's cousins, *tant* Aina, *farbror* Sten (I don't know who his new wife is), *farbror* Axel with wife – *tant* Astrid. I think of them as *tant* and *farbror* because I have not met them since 10 to 15 years back. My cousins' wives and children I hardly know. OK, we are *släkt* but I don't feel for them.
>
> 'My husband's *släkt* – I only feel them as partially mine – is mother-in-law, his two brothers with families (these are closest to me), his *moster*, *morbror* with wife, *fastrar* with husbands, *farbröder* both with and without wives. I am totally indifferent to his cousins.' (KU 9431)

This is a very minimal description of a family. The smallness is probably caused by the fact that she is newly married, relatively young and without children. However, she does mention a large number of relatives, some of whom she hardly knows. Her closest relationships are to her sisters-in-law. Only a few aunts and uncles are mentioned by name. Relatives through marriage are mentioned, but she admits to having no feeling.

Another woman, this time a bit older, in her forties, and living in Stockholm, reflects about what she has written about kin relationships. She does give her own occupation but her immediate kin are waitresses, cleaners, plumbers and metalworkers – solid working-class.

'Note that I write most about [the kin on] mamma's side. I have thought about this often. Is it a rule that you relate mostly with her *släkt*? For my cousins on my father's side I see more seldom than my mother's brother's families. And my husband's siblings we almost never see – although we are not at all unfriendly . . . . The leading person is to a great extent my *mormor*. Since she remained on the farm, we all came to her on holidays, vacations, Christmases etc. We wanted to meet each other for her sake' (KU 9500). The farm of the grandmother was in the far north and visiting her involved travelling long distances. Keeping contact with distant kin is very typical of modern Swedish families. Although Swedish kinship allows the ego to relate with both patrilines, matrilines and in-laws, the usual pattern is through mother–daughter–grandchild triads.

There is an element of choice in kin relationships, especially with distant kin. The same woman, as just quoted above, describes her choices. 'The *familj* is made up of me and my husband. I count as *släkt* my mother, and all my mother's brothers with families, my mother's cousins and their children – my *tremänningar*, since I am acquainted with most of them. Then we have the more *avlägsna* [distant] in my mother's village of birth (where she and I are *släkt* with most – at a distance). I count them in for sentimental reasons. Most of them I neither know nor are acquainted with. But my mother's partner's sister, with family, I do count as *släkt* since we actually "go together" [share a common ancestor] in the middle of the 1700s. I also count as *släkt* a number of those from Västerbotten who I got to learn of by accident and who I LIKE (*sic*), for instance one of my co-workers who is *åttonmänning* [seventh-cousin]. Then I stick to my kin' (KU 9500).

One woman, born in 1942, reports that she was introduced into her husband's kin by the women. It was expected of her as a woman to maintain the contacts instead of her husband. 'My husband's *släkt* expresses great solidarity and I think the women have done much to keep in touch. Lennart's mother has seen to it that I continually meet with most of them. Now it happens that I take care of the future contacts instead of my husband because "he is not up to it"' (KU 7851).

Some of the older women say that their interest in family and relatives increased as they aged. At the same time they mention that their interest in neighbours declined. One Stockholm woman, born in 1915, says: 'The older one gets, the more urgent it is to look backwards and see where the tracks lead . . . . After retirement I intend to spend part of my time on this. I have registered for a course in genealogy which starts in

October . . . . [Kinship] gives stability and meaning and gives the individual a feeling of fixed community. It is in any case so for me' (KU 7989).
Another Stockholm woman, born in 1926, tells of the decreased interest
in friends and neighbours. 'When we were younger and the children
were small, we often had parties which mixed friends, neighbours and
släkt . . . . Now, family and *släkt* contacts make up the main part of free
time, and other relationships are limited more or less to birthday
congratulations' (KU 9458).

These women's descriptions contain many themes. One is that
keeping kin contacts is women's work. Another is that the older the
woman gets the more effort is concentrated on maintaining and developing relationships within the kin. The women envisage kinship to be
a network made up of active and dormant contacts.

The grandmother to grandchild relationship emerges as something
very special in these reports. The grandmothers take care to fill their
contacts with high emotional quality. Some believe that they are
pioneering a new type of relationship over the generations. The new-
ness lies in elements of intimacy, informality and friendliness, which
they perceive to have been lacking before. One middle-class grandmother, born in 1920, lives in the provincial capital of Jönköping.
'Nowadays age does not play such a great role in relations. We and our
older *släkt*, our children and grandchildren get along on equal terms, as
friendly as can be. But I remember my own grandmother, stern and
Schartauan [a puritanic branch of the Swedish Church] religious. I
cannot remember if we ever talked with each other, even less that she
ever gave us children a hug. We always hug each other when we meet.
Grandmother came often and visited us, when we lived in Malmö in the
1930s, but we only thought it was a bother. You couldn't do this, you
couldn't do that, everything was a sin' (KU 9564).

One Stockholm grandmother, born in 1915, makes special rituals
involving all the grandchildren: 'After New Year's Day I treat the
grandchildren to something fun, which they themselves can choose'
(KU 7989). A grandmother born in 1899, living in the small town of
Mariestad, describes relationships with her grandchildren which are
very different from during her own childhood. She especially notes that
the formality of address between the generations has disappeared. 'I
correspond by letter with two of the grandchildren, girls 12 and 15 . . . .
It is very rewarding to hear them talk about their school and their
friends and their grades. And to partake of their language and slang.
They say "*Hej*" [Hi, instead of formal greetings] and "*Du*" [the informal
you]. We are like *kamrater* [comrades]. It is a great pleasure for me to

visit my children's homes in the summers. Usually, I am 14 days in their homes. Sometimes it is several times a year, since one family doesn't live further away than Trollhättan. To Skåne I normally only come once in a year. You get accustomed to the way the grandchildren live' (KU 7794). It is unlikely that grandmothers previously felt themselves or wanted to be comrades with their grandchildren. Until recently rules of etiquette did not even allow children to say 'Du' to their parents (Gaunt, 1991, p.62).

Divorce and remarriage is now common in Sweden. This creates special problems for maintaining contact and can set the status of grandmother at risk (Hagestad, 1988). Several older women comment on how divorce impinges on their possibilities of meeting grand-children. This problem is relatively small for maternal grandmothers. Greater difficulties come when sons separate and the children remain with a former daughter-in-law. Ordinarily Swedish grandmothers have contacts with the grandchildren at the initiative of the children's mothers (Hammarström, 1989).

Divorce breaks the normal chain of relationships over the daughter-in-law. A well situated Stockholm widow, born in 1903, relates: 'One of my sons is married for the third time. The first marriage was very "young" and was entered into because of the expected child. I had and have all the time had good relations with both mother and son . . . . It is natural for me to retain this contact' (KU 8031). Another grandmother, born in 1920, has a more problematic relationship since her contact with the grandchildren and her former daughter-in-law irritates Olle, her son. The divorce is 'something we old people have difficulty in getting over. Almost immediately he moved in with his present partner and after that contact with them, unfortunately, is all too seldom . . . . With Olle's children, 15 and 14 years old, we have contact about every other month. It is most often I who calls. We congratulate on birthdays and namedays. At Christmas they come together with Olle and his partner. We try to lure them [the grandchildren] to us for a weekend or a free day, but it is difficult for two extrovert teenagers to find time. But we don't give up, we "push" ourselves onto them, so that they don't forget their grandparents. With our former daughter-in-law we have telephone contact once a month. We talk about her work and the children. (Our son is not so happy about this contact, we have under-stood)' (KU 9436).

Few of the correspondents see kinship as an important source of personal identity. On the contrary, some take great pains to distance themselves in case there are well-known persons in their kin-group.

Few claim 'pride' – this was one of the questions raised in the list – over belonging to their kin-group. Instead they might say something like the following: 'I have not felt pride over the *släkt*, however I do feel admiration and respect for my grandmother' (KU 7989). This practical attitude fits in well with a view of kin as a web of relationships. The 'pride' in belonging to a kin-group is part of a view of kin as an organic superhuman entity and this view is weakly represented among the correspondents.

The women seldom mention the functions of kinship which sociologists identify as important. Few women talk of how they try to bring up the children to identify with or to learn specific things connected with their family and kin. Some, however, describe personal feelings of other-worldliness, spirituality and well-being through finding roots through genealogical information. 'It feels good to know who came before me, hear about their fates and thoughts and characters. It feels like a root, like a solid ground to stand on', says a 40-year-old Stockholm woman (KU 7851).

Keeping in touch

The main use of the family seems to be for friendship, company and as witnesses of changes of personal status among the kin. It is important to mobilize the kin-group for important birthdays, for family reunions and for common vacations. Very intensive kin-groups will do all of these things during the course of a year.

Celebrating birthdays is a classic form of family festivity. Most important are the fiftieth, sixtieth, seventieth and so on birthdays, which are assumed to involve change of personal status. Birthdays are a natural point of celebration for a family since they celebrate birth, reproduction and continuity through the life course. Families do not appear to mobilize the kin-group to celebrate status changes like a new job, graduation or retirement. These are left to peer-groups.

Some families commemorate the hundredth anniversaries of certain ancestors. 'My husband's *morfar* was born in 1874 and to celebrate the hundredth anniversary of this, my husband's cousins came together in 1974. His *morbror* Frans, honoured his father with a speech and we placed a wreath on his grave', writes a farmer's wife who was born in 1927 (KU 8635). An upper-class Stockholm widow, born in 1903, reports: 'When my mother-in-law would have been one hundred years we invited everyone from that *släkt* and both of my siblings. Not everyone could come, but we were some sixtyish from different ages who had a happy evening together. There were many who had not seen each other for many years – some had never before met' (KU 8031).

More usual festivities are those in which the subject is alive and becoming 60 or 70 years old. Even 65 and 75 can be celebrated. 'We gathered our common relations to a large *släkt* supper in the summer of 1984. My husband had "nilled" [70 years old] and my brother had "fived" [75 years old]. These gentlemen were the hosts for a party, to which all branches of *släkt* were invited. We had the party at a country inn, where we ordered dinner and refreshments and lodging for the far off relatives. It was a bit uneasy at first considering that some relatives had never met . . . . Four generations were assembled . . . the oldest was 82 years old and the youngest seven years old' (KU 9436).

There is great pride in reporting the assembling of large groups of kin. Most end with the standard phrase that many relatives had never before met. This means that the organizer of the celebration has mobilized relationships which were previously dormant.

Family reunions

In some extreme cases feelings of kinship represent themselves in the large family reunion called the *släktträff* (kin-meeting), the formal family association called the *släktförening* (kin-association) and genealogical societies. Family reunions can be more or less spontaeous one-time-only meetings. But if they strike the right chord they can become institutionalized in the form of a kin association with regular meetings.

A spontaneous family reunion needs a forceful kin-keeper in order to come about. The following is a description of a *släktträff* in the North Swedish countryside written from the perspective of a 26-year-old woman who travelled from the city of Gothenburg to participate. The Lindberg family mentioned here is not well-known. The jobs they have are low-paid public service: post office cashier, customs official, nurse's aide. Many relatives had migrated to the cities in the 1950s in order to search for work. '*Moster* Anna is one of the oldest of the Lindberg siblings. Still she is the one who many times sees to it that we meet. The summer of 1980 is typical. Anna began to talk about wanting us to try to meet *everyone*! A family reunion for Nils Erik Lindberg's children, grandchildren, great-grandchildren, etc., with husbands and wives or cohabitants. This caused a long period of preparation. Anna was the one who put in most work in contacting everyone. Fixing a place to be, food and such . . . . It was decided that we would meet the last weekend in June. We were 80 persons. Maybe eight or ten persons could not . . . come the long way to Lindberg's childhood home . . . . The reunion lasted two days. On Saturday we all assembled in the community hall which was rented for the weekend' (KU 7869). On Saturday evening a banquet, with dance, was held. Mass was celebrated in church on Sunday, flowers were placed on the family grave and church coffee was served in the childhood home.

Sometimes a family reunion is followed by regular meetings. One woman correspondent, born in 1948, began such a mobilization of relatives when she as newly-wed celebrated the refurbishing of a farmhouse. 'Since we bought my father's parents' house, *Baggarbo* . . . we thought we had the duty to assemble the *släkt*, when we had it repaired ten years ago. We had a family reunion for my father's siblings, sibling's children and sibling's grandchildren. Most of us live in the county, but a few live in other parts of the country. We had open house and morning coffee at *Baggarbo*. Then we had hired the community hall, where we ate lunch talked and had some activities. I had previously done genealogical research and talked a bit about what I found out about the *släkt*. Everyone received a compendium with excerpts from this plus a list with all the names, dates of birth, addresses and telephone numbers of the relatives. The reunion was appreciated and was repeated five years later. This year it is time again' (KU 9457).

Organizing these family reunions can be a heavy undertaking for the acknowledged head of the kin-group. A perception of dutiful burden can lead to the building of official family associations for the formal management of these affairs. One purpose of such associations is to distribute the burden of organizing contacts over a larger part of the kin-group. These associations can establish committees for planning reunions and outings, can have membership dues and publish newsletters and genealogical works for the members. One woman, born in 1926 and living in Stockholm, explains that she 'played for a long time with the idea of a kin association to keep tabs on all the siblings and cousins on my husband's side. And for some years now this association is a fact. Among the reasons was the purpose to "rationalize" family reunions. The tradition of meeting during Christmas holidays had become more and more demanding of both effort and space. Difficulties in drawing a line [between kin] began to develop. Now everyone has the possibility of meeting all together once in the year, and thereby it is possible for smaller groups of siblings and cousins to meet on other occasions without anyone else feeling left out.... Almost all get-togethers with kin are planned and connected with meals.... We are always many, use a buffet system and have free placement at table. In August 1985 we made, within the framework of the kin association, an outing "to our roots" with a rented bus driven by one of my sons. About 30 persons followed, aged between 2 and 73 years. Every family had its own picnic' (KU 9458).

The family associations are relatively new. Few go further back than the Second World War and most are much more recent. According to the definitive Dictionary of the Swedish Academy, the first printed usage of the word *släktförening* (kin-association) was in an article from 1940 in the major national newspaper *Svenska Dagbladet* about an association which had just held its fifth annual meeting. Many seem to have been formed as a response to the great migration from the countryside to industrial areas in the 1950s and 1960s. This movement went from communities with small farms and forest work to expanding communities needing industrial and building workers. Thus the family associations which began to develop were different from the kinship socialization of the aristocracy and upper bourgeoisie. The new family associations were formed on the model of voluntary organizations like the temperance leagues, trade unions and so on. They had working committees, division of responsibilities, membership lists, regular general meetings and formal channels for spreading information. A committee meant there was no single 'head' of the family, but rather an appointed governing board.

One example is the 'Ekeremma *släkt* association' which a female correspondent describes in her answer. It has about 600 members in Sweden, USA, Finland and Norway. This association is formed by the decendants of a certain Håkan who lived on the farm of Ekeremma in south-western Sweden in the seventeenth century. Neither the farm of Ekeremma, nor Håkan the ancestor, have any historical importance. The association was founded in 1961 and prints a bulletin several times each year. It has published genealogies showing how the members are related to each other. The association is the social manifestation of modern archival studies the members are those who by biological accident trace back to a common ancestor. Of Håkan little is known: 'Of course no one knows any longer where the ancestor's grave is in the cemetery. But a stone has been placed there in honour of the ancestors, and wreaths are placed there at family reunions', reports a woman who was born in 1927 (KU 8635).

Another corporate group built on modern genealogy is the 'Skunke descendants association'. This is also oriented on a common ancestor and has international membership. The Swedish association is linked with similar associations in Denmark and Norway. 'We have an annual meeting each July in Håkas [a rural parish in the north]. This *släkt* is one of the most thoroughly researched and has been traced all the way to the fourteenth century, primarily by Herje Skunce of Norrköping, who died a few years ago. The *släkt* association is only ten years old [founded in the mid-1970s] and is more like a construction since it is descendants of different branches who are especially interested in "seeking their roots" – so popular in our rootless existence.' This description was part of the response a Stockholm woman, born in 1921, sent in (KU 9475). The family associations attempt to create solidarity on the basis of common ancestry and geographical origin. They organize themselves to promote cultural solidarity (Marshall *et al.*, 1993, pp.56–7).

The reunions can be so formalized that they border on being rituals. They can be seen as symbolic connections between the past and the future of the family. It is unlikely that everyone who is entitled to membership will join or be active in such associations. Not all attempts to build a kin association are successful. The main purpose of the association is to organize large reunions, but some people may not want to meet up. The awkwardness of the occasion is ameliorated by meals, the laying of wreaths, going to church, listening to speeches. Creating a kin association which continues to exist over a long period of time depends on creating a network of like-minded individuals. This may not be possible in every kin-group, especially if there is a split over political ideology or religious affiliation. This may be especially difficult in families in which social mobility has been strong. Many correspondents report that they must avoid discussing politics and religion within the wider kin. Preserving kin relationships receives priority over ideological controversy. Segalen (1986, p.85) reports similar priorities in French families. North American researchers report on the considerable tension which surrounds large family meetings. 'There is a wide area of the unknown and unpredictable in the visits. There are things one does not wish to tell and the lurking possibility that one will hear things that one does not wish to hear' (Moss and Moss, 1988, p.662).

There is a paradox surrounding the family reunion and kin association phenomena. Everyone who talks about them mentions that they are a recent invention. Those who are engaged in them talk of finding their 'roots', tracing relationships backward in time. But the family reunion is a short episode – a weekend once a year, once every five years, every Christmas and so on. The shortness of the reunion, the long distances travelled, the large numbers of near strangers (hitherto unknown biological relations) and the party atmosphere prevent the development of deep relationships. One can liken going to the family reunion to a pilgrimage in search of an illusory Holy Grail in the form of 'roots'.

Socializing with the quasi-anonymous extended kin-group causes a need for 'rationalization', as one correspondent expressed it. This means sharing space, sharing responsibility. It may be that keeping the reunion short, planning in detail and avoiding controversial topics of conversation are part of reducing tension. Most reunions are held at distant places to which most of those gathered do not have a daily attachment. If 'seeking roots' is why people attend reunions, then they see the others who attend as informants rather than as potential friends.

One of the reasons for organizing kin meetings is to be able to close the account by saying: 'Many who came had never met before'. This is the opposite of creating a few deep relationships. Instead it involves masses of instant relationships – there is pride in the volume of contact. A woman living in the countryside and born in 1934 relates: 'Some years ago I organized a meeting of cousins on both father's and mother's sides. It was much appreciated and we were about 50 who maybe never had even seen each other' (KU 8506). This is a way of meeting which satisfies curiosity without needing to lead further. Many of these cousins may never meet again.

One woman, born in 1938, maximizes short but very public contacts by congratulating on the local radio. 'On local radio there is a programme, where you can send greetings for different occasions. During 1985, I succeeded 15 times in placing greetings and congratulations to kin and friends' (KU 9513).

The summer place

The collectivity of kin at summer cottages has somewhat longer duration and are more regular than the family reunion. They encompass a tighter kernel of relatives and none of them are strangers to each other. Considerable intimacy and informality characterize these collectives. As mentioned earlier, one can call them the 'nuclear kin' in analogy with the 'nuclear family'.

One of the few male correspondents is a farmer born in 1921. His relatives return to the farm during vacation. 'Summertime is more of meetings with dear släkt. Then comes Mårten [brother of wife and civil engineer] with wife for a week. Ingrid's [his wife's] cousin Kjell Anders [a civil engineer] and his family land up every vacation in the summer cottage which they own together with his brother Karl Erik. We meet almost every day and have a pleasant time.' Note that it is kin to *his* wife.

The summer place is the main theatre for kin interaction. It is often owned and maintained by relatives collectively. The summer place can be a farm which has been inherited over the generations. But it can also be recently built houses in attractive leisure areas. As free time, especially vacations, become longer (Swedes now have five weeks of vacation and certain occupations have even longer) it is possible to use summer places which are distant, and kin from all over can gather there.

Many gerontologists have found that contacts between generations within families are characterized by 'intimacy at a distance'. The inventor of this phrase is said to be the Austrian sociologist Leopold Rosenmayer. They find that extended families of several generations rarely live in the same household. However, it is common that kin from different generations live close by in the same neighbourhood and have frequent contacts – thus intimacy but with a distance.

The summer place is the opposite of 'intimacy at a distance'. It is usual for several generations to live together in primitive conditions, sharing the same roof, kitchen, bathroom (if there is one) and eating table. Informality and lightness of dress contrast to the old-fashioned formality of dress on other occasions, like Christmas parties and birthday celebrations, when the kin is brought together. The summer place is where the deeper relationships can develop within the nuclear kin.

A Stockholm woman, mother of three children, born in 1942, describes the kin-group assembled about her family summer place which is a farm. This place is owned in common and has been in the family for many generations. It is about 150 kilometres from Stockholm. 'We grew up in Stockholm, but spent our summers in Tällberg, where they had made a cottage from my mother's *släkts* chalet, which we use as a summer cottage, now with an addition.' Nearby live father's sisters, Anna and Klara, and brother Edvin. Anna had worked in a jewellery shop in Stockholm, but moved back to take care of aged parents. Edvin had moved back after his retirement from work.

This summer place is so popular, she reports, that it has become necessary to split its use between two branches of the kin. One branch comes from her *farfar* and the other are the decendants of his brother.

'Summer months are the most attractive. Use is shared on a monthly basis by the two branches.... Some relatives we only meet when we and they are on vacation simultaneously in Dalecarlia, since distance within Stockholm makes it difficult to meet. Often it seems to be the women who take initiatives to contact, even with in-laws' (KU 7851). Socially this correspondent belongs to the upper middle classes, she is a teacher and her husband is an engineer. Gathering at a summer place is typical for urban clans in big city environments.

Life at the summer place is idyllic and often rustic. It is a modern paradise in the sense of an abundance of otherwise scarce commodities such as time and nearness. Life at the summer place represents a luxury of immaterial qualities which more than balances the humbleness of the dwelling.

A grandmother born in 1920 describes her family's summer place as a collection point for children, grandchildren and in-laws. 'At midsummer we have our largest family party. Our children, with their children, and their respective parents-in-law and my sister – all in all we are usually 20 to 22 people in the country with us. All participate in celebrating midsummer.' This summer place was inherited through the woman's family. The grandmother sees to it that her daughters come with their families to the summer place. 'This summer cottage . . . which we all love and go to as often as we can, began being built in 1935 by my parents. Papa bought a prefabricated house with two rooms, kitchen and hall, plus a big veranda. The lot lies on a hill beside a lake. After a while another house was built, a small cottage with one large room and a little workshop, to which the privy was attached. Sven and I went there with our children every summer. Eventually the big house was rebuilt and our children got rooms there. Sven and Per [son] with the help of our sons-in-law built another small house in 1974–75.... All summer long we have children and grandchildren out there. Vacations are spent one week at a time, and sometimes when the parents want to travel abroad they leave their children in our care' (KU 9564).

Among the correspondents the summer place is clearly the most valued and normal form of common property within kinship groups. Use can lead to problems with sharing, which is sometimes solved by rotating occupation. A woman living in Malmö and born in 1933 states: 'We siblings inherited a summer cottage from our parents. It is 25 kilometres from Malmö. We spent all our summers while growing up in it, even certain holidays.... It is not large enough for many families to live there at the same time. In a summer vacation of ten weeks it is shared by five households for two weeks each' (KU 9930).

A widow living in Stockholm and born in 1914 writes about her summer place on the western coast. 'After the inheritance from my husband [a top bureaucrat] had been distributed, my children and I agreed that the old farmhouse, which my husband and I used as a summer house, shall now be our common summer house. The proposal came from the children and made me very happy, because alone I can neither manage nor afford to keep it. We have together drawn up a contract, which means that we together shall maintain and live in it.'

Meeting at the summer place is not limited to wealthy and middle class families. The whole tradition probably grew out of the need to find inexpensive recreation, and relatives in the countryside were not hard to find. A nurse's aide from Gothenburg writes about her experiences: 'Mostly we meet relatives in the summer during vacation time. We usually live in Mamma's childhood home. My *morbror* Harry, who is now dead, took over the farm after *morfar*. Now his wife Olga and her children, Kerstin and Jan-Erik, run the farm . . . . Everyone is welcome to Olga. It has become a gathering point for all of us, since it is "everyone's" home. But since it is such a long time between meetings it becomes a matter of driving around to the rest of mother's siblings . . . . Dinner one day with one, coffee next day with another. Therefore these vacation weeks can be a real chore' (KU 7869).

The findings

The material assembled by the Nordic Museum from its correspondents indicates some clear trends on how kinship functions. The material is probably not typical for all Swedes. However, it seems reasonable to say that when kinship is talked about or used by Swedes it is done in the way these informants indicate. The material covers all social classes and both rural and urban families.

1. Discourse on kinship is predominantly a female discourse. They talk about it, they construct the limits and define the character of kinship.
2. Women are the managers and organizers of the kinship network. They are expected to do this even for their husband's kin-group. The success of kinship management is the ability to gather together as many relatives as possible and to be able to say 'many had never met before'.
3. Kinship develops in two forms. The one is expansive and superficial in the form of family reunions and kin associations which tend

to be 'rationalized', formal, well-planned and are used for pilgrimages to 'roots'. They are close to what has sometimes been called secular rituals. The other form is close, intimate and intensive nuclear kinship with a group formed about mothers, grandmothers and grandchildren. The nuclear kin meet during long vacations in summer houses which are often owned in common.

Other research

How do these findings fit in with what other observers of the Swedish family have found?

By the start of the 1990s most academic researchers on the Swedish family agreed that the family was strong and that the previously widely held view of the decline of the family had been misconstrued. Michael Gähler of the Institute for Social Research concludes in 1994: 'the Swedish family is still a very strong institution' (1994, p.84). Rune Åberg, writing for the prestigious Power Investigation states: 'The families we have studied are in general solidly integrated with the community, without strong internal tension and with family life as the central part of living' (Åberg, 1990, p.421). Another researcher in the Power Investigation concludes: 'The kin-group has obviously still great importance for the social life of people .... It is easier to get help from kin than from other friends' (Moqvist, 1990, pp.161–2). What in the early 1980s looked like chaos in the family when studied through traditional statistics turned out, when studied from the perspective of the individual, to be simply a new domestic lifestyle.

Swedish sociologist Jan Trost writes from a symbolic-interventionist approach. He foresees individuals going through a pluralistic series of family forms: 'cohabiting, separating, marrying, divorcing, living together, apart, cohabiting again, having children with different partners, having an abortion, living in a step-family, being a grandparent. Seen from the outside this can seem complicated, but it doesn't need to be so' seen from the individual's point of view (Trost, 1993, p.153).

Trost's view is almost a copy of the view of the family in *Fanny and Alexander*. But what of kinship and contacts over generations? These can probably be best studied from the situation of the very old.

Average length of life in Sweden is long: 74 years for males and 80 years for females. Just under 20 per cent of the population is older than 65 years, the official age of retirement. Kin-groups with four or five generations alive are relatively common.

In preparation for the European Community 'Year of the Elderly and Solidarity between Generations' a Eurobarometer study of old people was done. This was duplicated in 1993 in Sweden. One of the questions concerned the contacts of old people (defined as over 60 years old) with young people (undefined). Sweden was the country with the highest percentage of old people saying that they had a lot of contact with young people (Andersson, 1993, p.20).

Older Swedes say that they have many contacts with the younger generation. About 30 per cent of elderly Swedes said they had daily contact with their family. Sociologist Erik Allardt compared the standard of welfare in the Nordic countries in the early 1970s. He found that 50 per cent of the Swedes met with relatives at least once each week. This figure was much higher than in Denmark (40 per cent) and Finland (39 per cent) (Allardt, 1975, pp.104–5). Many studies of care for the aged show that relatives do most of the caring. A recent bestseller entitled *Mamma to My Mamma* took up the problems of the many middle-aged daughters caring for their aged parents.

These are in a way surprising results. Within social gerontology there is a theory of modernization which posits that the more 'modern' a country becomes, the less respect and concern is given to older people. Sweden is in all aspects a 'modern' country: the level of industrialization is high, the level of education is advanced, health care and welfare programmes are well developed and so on. Old people – when asked – say that their conditions are good and that contacts over generations are satisfactory.

This probably represents an improvement over the situation in the past. Swedish households have seldom included three generations. On the farms the old people moved out to live in separate cabins on the farm land, when their children took over (Gaunt, 1983). Birgitta Odén has ascertained that violence to old parents by grown sons and daughters was increasing throughout the nineteenth century (Odén, 1993).

The ideology of kinship in the past was limited to certain classes. The widely read proletarian writer Ivar Lo-Johansson (born 1901), who was the child of poor agricultural labourers, made the following observation when an academic published the Lo-Johansson family tree: 'Before I had not known any more about my kin than some unimportant details I had heard tell of from my nearest ancestors. I never had any feeling for kin . . . . In the place I grew up only the nobility and the big farmers had kin . . . . We never thought of kin as a unit' (*Pubertet*, 1978, p.5). In contrast Agnes von Krusenstjerna (born 1894 in a family of aristocrats and politicians) had a childhood immersed in kinship ideology. In one of her autobiographical novels she wrote: 'the feeling which ties together the members of a *släkt* like ours, are in general so strong that anyone, who doesn't bear the mark of blood, despite being ever so closely allied with the family, will always be treated as an outsider' (*Tony växer upp*, 1922). In the twentieth century the sense of kinship, family and even clan has become democratized and spread throughout society.

The ethnologist and sociologist Börje Hanssen sees the spreading of the idea of kinship from the upper to the lower classes as a response to the anonymity of the modern big city. He studied families who had moved to Stockholm and settled in the newly built planned suburbs. He found them to be suspicious of the neighbours and reluctant to socialize with them. Instead the kinship network was activated for socialization and help. Telephones and modern transport helped to maintain contacts. Holidays were used for serious visiting and the celebration of kinship.

A clan mentality, previously the privilege of the upper classes, spread to the middle and lower classes. Hanssen interviewed the same families in 1957 and 1972 and discovered what he termed 'Big city clans'. He described them thus:

> Big city clans are another side of anonymity and neighbour hostility found in societies with advanced communications systems. One can assume that if the possibility exists of moving over long distance, technical aids will certainly be used by people (to maintain contact). That is probably biologically conditioned. By clan I mean a group of nuclear families and solitary people who live split up over an area – for instance a residential area – and socialize mutually and often use the terms of kinship to mark mutual identification . . . . The care of the clan is composed typically of persons who have lived in the same family. It is not important that real biological kinship exists. (Hanssen, 1978, pp.283-4).

Hanssen found that these urban clans were matriarchal: 'women are in the center and the men who marry in adjust and – to a certain extent – abandon their own parents and siblings' (p.284). Within the clan there was an obligation to socialize only within the kinship group. This was especially felt at the time of religious and national holidays.

Bergman's illusion in *Fanny and Alexander* is thus only partly an illusion. It, however, gives adequate symbolic representation to the strong feeling of kinship which has developed side by side with modern urban welfare society. It would be wrong to see this clannishness as a folkloristic remnant of previous times, since in historical times only the upper classes had a concept of kinship and utilized kinship to organize their social lives. It is probably even wrong to think of the new clannishness in the form of family reunions and family associations as a renaissance of long neglected social patterns.

Nuclear kin and urban clannishness – on the increase?

It is very hard to determine whether the use of kinship as described above is increasing or decreasing. However, there are a number of changes to the situation of women which probably have the accumulated effect of increasing the likelihood of kin contacts. These are:

1. *Demography*. Swedish women now have an average life expectancy of 80 years and Swedish men 74 years. Many, of course, live much longer. Close to 20 per cent of the population is over 65, the official age of retirement. Most geriatric surveys of health have found that the vast majority of older people are free from major health problems up to the age of 75 to 80. The extension of length of life and the growth of active, healthy grandmothers and great-grandmothers has occurred primarily in the second half of the twentieth century. Having active grandmothers seems part of developing modern kinship contacts since they take on the role of kin-keepers.

2. *Modernization of the life course*. The female life course is in the process of modernization in the sense of becoming more like that for men. Women work for wages outside the home, they have long education, an independent income and pension, they are somewhat less engaged in the care of children and the home than before. Sweden is one of the countries where the modernization of the life course of women has progressed furthest. One consequence is that women have less time to meet as neighbours. It is conceivable that kin are mobilized for friendship as one way of compensating for the disappearance of the company of neighbouring women.

3. *Leisure*. Leisure time free from work has increased for both men and women since vacations were first introduced in the 1930s. The first vacations were four days; since 1978 they last five weeks. The length of the working week and the working day have both decreased. The official age of retirement was lowered from 67 years to 65 in the 1970s and the actual average age of retirement is close to 60 years of age. This means that free time to associate within the family has increased. It also enables the long collective stays at the summer place which so many describe. It gives the retired grandparents time to maintain contacts with grandchildren.

4. *Family symmetry*. In the 1950s Elisabeth Bott found that in an increasing number of families (belonging to the middle class) male and female roles had begun to change. With fewer contacts with networks outside the household, husbands and wives had begun to share activities, friendships and to become more like comrades. Previously husbands and wives had separate social networks. The development of symmetry between husbands and wives leads possibly to a symmetry of interest in the nuclear kin and the development of a network of friendship and intimacy with children and grandchildren. In some ways retirement creates a renaissance for the husband–wife dyad which can spill over into a heightened interest in progeny. A special change involves the role of grand-parent which appears to have become more friendly towards the grandchildren than in the past.

5. *Public welfare*. The public programmes for child care and old-age care developed in the period after 1950. Many of these services relieve families of the burden and tension of care, health and economic support within the family. Economic transfers still exist between the generations, but are no longer a matter of life or death. Families still do give much care to close relatives, but this caring is now supported by public services. The welfare society thus gives greater space for friendship and comradeship within the family. Affectional solidarity has in some ways replaced the duty of filial solidarity.

There are probably more factors than these which increase the probability of mobilizing kinship relations. However, these are probably enough to indicate that it is highly likely that the growth of urban clannishness and nuclear kinship is a new and important part of modern society.

7

INDIVIDUALITY AND ADAPTABILITY IN ENGLISH KINSHIP

Janet Finch

Introduction

This chapter is about contemporary English kinship and takes a partic-ular angle on that rather complex subject. The angle from which I shall address it is inheritance, long regarded by anthropologists as a crucial facet of life in which the social meaning of kinship is displayed, but frequently overlooked in my own discipline of sociology. Partly in order to redress this balance, my own present empirical work focuses on the ways in which contemporary English families handle questions of inheritance[1]

In this chapter, I am going to link general issues of inheritance and generational transmission with specific questions which arise in recon-stituted families, where there has been a history of divorce and remarriage. Much higher rates of divorce and remarriage since 1970 are introducing a greater degree of complexity for many more families. In relation to inheritance, that complexity necessarily disrupts the assumption that each individual will have a maximum of one surviving spouse and that the identification of descendants normally will be a simple matter of tracing down the direct blood line. So how does inheritance work in families where the deceased person may have two or three surviving spouses and ex-spouses, children from several differ-ent marriages, and step-children who are the children of one or more spouse from a previous marriage?

The case of reconstituted families enables us to understand facets of cultural expectations about inheritance which might remain more concealed in families without a history of divorce and remarriage. It also may help us to see a little way into the future and to understand how cultural expectations of inheritance are changing. In turn, this particular dimension of inheritance enables us to understand something of the contemporary meaning of kinship.

English kinship: the context

In order to develop my analysis I need to sketch in the background context in respect of three issues: the historical context of English kinship; the changing significance of inheritance in English families; and the distinctive nature of English law related to inheritance. Without this background, the force of some of my subsequent points will not be apparent.

Traditionally English kinship structure has been regarded as weak, relative to most other European countries. I am referring here specifically to English kinship, rather than British, since somewhat different traditions have prevailed in the other parts of the United Kingdom. I am also aware that, in the context of a multiracial society, there is now a variety of cultural traditions represented in the United Kingdom, each of which historically has embodied a different understanding of the meaning of kinship; in that sense my discussion is confined to the tradition of 'white' English kinship.

The most important point about the English context is that the nuclear family household has predominated for at least six centuries as the key feature of the kinship system. The English apparently have long expected that each nuclear family would live in a relatively high degree of independence from other kin, in respect both of living arrangements and of economic ties. Any historical account of this owes much to Macfarlane's (1978) very influential work in which he traces back at least to the thirteenth century the distinctive patterns of English kinship – the independence of children from their parents, kinship ties which are relatively weak and not normally linked to a common economy, the contractual nature of inheritance.

The concept used by Macfarlane to describe this phenomenon is 'individualism', in a discussion which links the analysis of kinship with a much broader interest in the distinctiveness of social, economic and legal systems in England since the thirteenth century. Macfarlane's work represents a fundamental challenge to writers who see an inextricable link between those economic changes which produced modern societies and an individualistic ideology which emphasizes the equality of persons in the social structure (Dumont, 1986). In relation to kinship specifically, the links between individualistic ideologies, the growth of capitalism and the stress on the nuclear rather than the extended family simply do not work in the case of England where the priority of the nuclear family, and to an extent individualistic ideologies, substantially pre-date the development of capitalism and of modern technological society. Though this is not the place to develop the historical arguments, an understanding of the distinctive background is important for an analysis of contemporary kin relationships. Recently Marilyn Strathern (1992) has confirmed the continuing importance of individualism in her own theoretical and empirical work on English kinship. Indeed she describes the individuality of persons as 'the first fact of English kinship' (ibid. p.14), emphasizing that people are treated as unique persons rather than occupants of positions in a kinship universe. The corollary is a strong emphasis on choice in kin relationships and therefore on the diversity of forms which kin relationships legitimately can take.

These points will be familiar to sociologists and anthropologists who know the research literature. However, it is important to understand precisely what is implied by saying that English society has long had a 'weak' kinship structure. It does not necessarily mean that kinship ties are of minimal significance to people's lives. Indeed the study which I conducted with my colleague Jennifer Mason demonstrated in fact that kinship ties outside the nuclear family household do remain significant at some level and to most people (Finch and Mason, 1993). There is, however, wide variation in what that means in practice. We found that – almost without exception – our interviewees from all age groups and a wide variety of backgrounds presented themselves as belonging to a family (in the sense of kin group) which 'works'. For some people this means very regular contact and many examples of exchanges of mutual aid. For others both the contacts and the exchanges are much less extensive. But even in the latter cases people emphasized that kin *can* be called upon if they are needed, and were keen to give us practical examples of where this had occurred.

The second aspect of the background context for my discussion concerns in particular how inheritance fits into this overall picture of English kinship and how this is changing. Inheritance is only of significance in the context of kinship if there is something valuable to pass on from one generation to the next. Leaving aside for the moment the symbolic significance of passing on objects with little intrinsic value (a point to which I shall return), for the most part this has meant land, property, or money in its various forms. Given the pattern of land

ownership which has been concentrated rather than dispersed historically, this has made questions of inheritance either unimportant or
irrelevant to the great majority of families. Concerns about inheritance
tended to be confined to a small minority of wealthy families, in a way
which would not really be paralleled in many other parts of Europe.
This is linked to – though possibly does not fully account for – the fact
that English inheritance customs have tended to favour primogeniture
as a key principle. Certainly amongst landed families in England, traditionally partible inheritance was strongly disapproved of because it
would break up the estate. (Goody, Thirsk and Thompson, 1976;
Anderson, 1980; Smith, 1984).

The creation of a new bourgeoisie in the nineteenth century, whose
wealth was based on industrial capital rather than on land, served to
extend the number of families for whom inheritance was a relevant
issue. It also led to the development of a more diverse set of bequeathing practices, in which the new middle classes were much more likely
than the aristocracy to divide property between all their children, and
also to leave some control in the hands of widows, as the fascinating
study by Davidoff and Hall (1987) shows.

Nonetheless the number of families who have something valuable to
pass down the generations has remained small, into the later part of the
twentieth century. However, this has been changing in the past 30 years
as the number of households who own the house in which they live has
risen from around one-third in 1960 to around two-thirds in the mid-
1980s (*Social Trends*, 1993). Consequently, there is now a greatly
increased number of families for whom inheritance has real relevance.

This leads me to my third contextualizing point – the way in which
inheritance is dealt with in the English legal system. The key point here
is the fundamental significance of the principle of testamentary freedom which, in its purest form, means that each testator can decide
precisely how his or her property will be disposed of, with no restric-
tions. There is of course a sense in which this is entirely consistent with
the openness of English kinship structure. Though there have been
considerable historical variations in the extent to which it has been
applied in English law, testamentary freedom remains a key principle
underlying the law on inheritance. There are at present some limitations on complete freedom to bequeath, especially to exclude bequests
to close kin. A spouse, child, step-child, or any person who was
economically dependent on the deceased, can challenge a will on
grounds that the provision made for him or herself is not 'reasonable'. It

is then for the courts to decide whether the will was reasonable or not (Mellows, 1983). In practice rather few cases are brought to court, though clearly the possibility of challenge does represent a limitation on the absolute freedom of the testator. Meanwhile it remains the case that English law does not *require* bequests to any named persons. This approach to inheritance may seem very puzzling to people familiar with inheritance systems based on principles enshrined in the Civil Code – as many European systems are – where named kin, usually children, have legal rights to specified portions of the estate.

In summary what I hope to have shown in this discussion of the background context is that English kinship has long been characterized by limited economic ties between kin, by a weak structure of legal regulation and by an emphasis on individuality, thus leaving open possibilities for wide variation in the ways kinship operates in practice. These are characteristics of kinship in general, and inheritance practices in particular. Against this background, it makes sense to ask the questions: How do people actually handle kin relationships and inheritance in this very open context? How do they handle it in particular when the complexities of divorce and remarriage are introduced?

Inheritance and kinship: the broad picture

It is beyond my scope in this chapter to give a full account of how questions of kinship are handled in contemporary families. Rather I shall concentrate on documenting how people actually treat two categories of close kin, namely spouses and children, whose position may be thrown into question in reconstituted families. I shall do this by drawing on data which come from a random sample of 800 wills, which formed part of an empirical study which I and my colleagues have been conducting. These were wills made by people who died in the years 1959, 1969, 1979 and 1989.[2] The data from these wills represent *outcome* data on the bequeathing decisions made by a randomly selected group of people who have exercised the freedom to bequeath which English law allows (for more detailed discussion, see Finch *et al.*, 1996).

A striking feature of the wills data is that people do appear to treat the claims of spouses and children as stronger than all others. I use the word 'appear' rather cautiously since one of the limitations of using data from wills is that we can never know if, for example, a particular testator has children who are not mentioned in the will at all and therefore receive nothing. However, where either children or spouses are mentioned in the will, typically they receive major portions of the estate.

A typical bequest to a spouse is all or part of the total estate. The phrase 'total estate' refers to wills in which no items are mentioned specifically, but all the testator's possessions are added together and passed on as a single entity. Of the 294 spouses mentioned in our wills (that is 37 per cent of all wills), 68 per cent were bequeathed a whole or a part of the total estate and a further 22 per cent were given a whole or a part of the residue. The phrase 'residue' refers to those wills in which the testator does mention specific items – usually personal possessions or small amounts of money – which are given as gifts to named individuals. What is left of the estate once these gifts have been removed is known as the residue. Most spouses do in fact receive all the total estate or the residue, with only a minority sharing it with other beneficiaries. A different way of looking at this is that, of all men who are married at the time of making their last will, 69 per cent bequeathed everything to their spouse, as did 58 per cent of married women. More women than men included gifts, often small gifts of money or personal items, to beneficiaries other than their spouse (for further discussion see Finch and Hayes, 1995).

Spouses therefore typically take all or most of the estate if they are the survivor of a couple. It is only where a spouse is not mentioned in the will that we find children taking the major part of the estate. Around half of all bequests where spouse is not mentioned give the major portion (total estate or residue) to a child or children. Other beneficiaries are likely to receive these 'major' bequests only if neither spouse nor children is present in the will.

So our outcome data suggest that most people do regard their children as having the major claim on their estate. However, this really comes into effect once both parents have died. It is widows and widowers who bequeath the major portions of their estate to their children. People who die whilst their spouse is still alive are much more likely to pass their estate to the survivor of the couple, leaving that person to secure the transmission to the next generation.

In relation to bequests to children, the predominant pattern is to divide assets equally between them, except that it is also common to bequeath a specific personal item to each individual child. Though about 10 per cent of our wills introduce some variation into bequests to different children, in most cases this simply means that different children are being given different personal items which – in so far as one can determine this from the wills – appear to be roughly equal in value.

Only a very small minority of wills (12 out of 800, 1.5 per cent) leave children different proportions of the same type of gift.

Thus we see three basic patterns in our wills, which show us the outcome of people's bequeathing decisions as far as spouses and children are concerned, at least as far as we can determine this from wills. First, a surviving spouse takes all or most of the estate. Second, once both parents have died, most or all of the estate is likely to pass to children. Third, if there is more than one child, there is a strong tendency to equal treatment.

These patterns raise interesting questions in reconstituted families, where the surviving spouse may not be the mother, or father, of all the testator's children, and where the children between whom the assets are to be divided may be a mixture of full siblings, half siblings and 'quasi' siblings. I use the latter term to describe people linked by the fact that the father or mother of one is the stepfather or stepmother of the other.

I shall explore these issues by following through these three patterns and the principles which underpin them. They are principles which can be applied quite straightforwardly, and are compatible with each other, in situations where there has been no second marriage for either partner. However, they all become tricky, and potentially incompatible with each other, where a second marriage has occurred following divorce, or indeed following widowhood. I shall discuss each in turn, drawing in this section on data from our interview study, which enable me to explore how people try to work out what to do in practice. Our interviews were conducted with 98 adults, whose ages ranged from 18 to 89, with a wide range of social backgrounds. In a number of cases we interviewed several members of the same family.[3]

Pattern 1: The claims of a surviving spouse take priority

As I have indicated earlier in this chapter, there is a strong presumption that property will pass to a surviving spouse in the first instance. Our data from the wills study, and indeed from our interview study, support the increasing emphasis in the law on the rights of spouses. Underlying all this is the belief in joint ownership of property between spouses, which has characterized a number of social policy changes in Britain in the second half of the twentieth century, and which itself is related to securing the economic rights of married women (Holcombe, 1983; Eekelaar and Maclean, 1986).

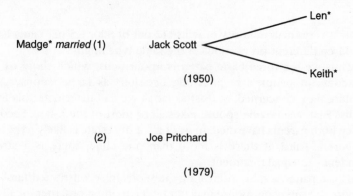

Figure 7.1 members of Madge Pritchard's family

Figure 7.1   Members of Madge Pritchard's family

The fundamental problem which divorce and remarriage creates is that there may well be more than one surviving spouse. Though in most instances the law will have ensured that there is a property settlement at the time of the divorce, so that the first wife does not have a major claim on the estate, this does not necessarily remove all potential problems. Situations can arise where a first spouse feels that she or he is entitled, on the death of the ex-spouse, to have returned any property which she deems to be part of the *first* marriage. Such property may consist of items whose value is symbolic rather than economic but this does not mean that it is insignificant.

In one of the families in our interview study, such an incident did occur and it was charged potently with symbolism about the continuing rights of the ex-wife to matrimonial property. The central character in this saga is Madge Pritchard, living in retirement when we interviewed her and twice divorced. The full set of characters is shown in Figure 7.1. When Madge's first husband eventually died Madge tried, unsuccessfully, to get his second wife to return a painting of Lake Windermere. This had been given originally to Madge and her husband as a wedding present from his parents. Madge herself presented this as a very reasonable request:

> 'I wrote a letter after my husband died – if she wouldn't consider giving it back to me. But the letter was never answered.'

Her son Keith's account makes the request sound somewhat less polite. He says that his mother wrote to his stepmother, Anne, and asked for the painting 'because, she said, it's my painting, not yours'. The question of the painting had undoubtedly become *a cause célèbre* in this family. Madge and her sons, Len and Keith, all mentioned it spontaneously in their interviews, with Len introducing the topic by referring to 'this famous painting'. Neither son was particularly sympathetic to his mother's point of view.

However, the point that I want to draw out here is not so much about personal antagonisms, but about the different views on the issue of *possession* of the painting. These different views offer, in effect, different interpretations about the consequences of the joint ownership of matrimonial property. We actually have three different versions of the rights of possession in the interviews related to this topic.

1. From Madge's point of view, the painting belonged to her because it was given jointly to her and her husband as a wedding present. Though he had the right to keep possession of it during his lifetime, it clearly should revert to her after his death, following the principle that the surviving spouse takes possession of joint property.

2. Using the same principle, but drawing a different conclusion, Anne (the second wife) also claimed possession. We learned of her views indirectly through our interviews with Madge's two sons, who were on good terms with their stepmother. Keith said that she was distressed by the request to return the painting to Madge because 'it is about the one and only thing that she's got from my dad, that really belonged to my dad' (that is, it was amongst the very few items which he had brought into the second marriage). Thus Anne saw the painting as part of *her* marital property, and particularly symbolic of her deceased husband and – using the same logic as Madge – she thought that she should keep possession.

3. The sons were sympathetic to their stepmother's claims to the painting, but both of them introduced an additional piece of reasoning about possession. They said that the painting had *really* been their father's and *not* their mother's since it was originally a gift from *his* parents. Thus they introduced the additional principle of the claims of the blood line to settle – at least to their own satisfaction – the otherwise rather finely balanced dispute between their mother and their stepmother.

Thus in this particular example we have three versions of who owns the painting: that it belongs to the wife in the first marriage because it was given jointly to her; that it belongs to the wife in the second marriage because her husband brought it into that marriage and it then became a joint possession; that it does not belong to the wife from the first marriage because it was given by the husband's family, not hers, and therefore the second wife has the stronger claims. Lying behind these competing accounts is a sense that different people are constructing slightly different models of kinship to reflect perceived interests and to provide a way of settling claims. Though the models are slightly different, each party is constructing a model using principles which the others would recognize.

Pattern 2: Children can expect to inherit eventually

In families which have not been complicated by divorce or remarriage, the emphasis on the prior claims of spouses does not ultimately overrule the claims of children to inherit. It simply postpones the date on which they will do so, since it is assumed that the surviving parent will bequeath the major part of his or her estate (which will include property owned jointly with the deceased spouse) to the children of the marriage. Thus the claims of spouses and the claims of children are perfectly compatible. Divorce and particularly remarriage disrupt all that because they give prior claims to whichever spouse is still married to the testator at the time of his or her death. In second and subsequent marriages, this will not be a natural parent of the children from the first marriage.

Thus remarriage opens up the possibility that the claims of children to inherit from their parents will be superseded rather than postponed, and in these circumstances the claims of spouses and of children are not compatible. English law on inheritance serves to exacerbate this situation in two ways. First, by its emphasis on testamentary freedom it places no restraint on how the second spouse can dispose of his or her property, and certainly no obligation to bequeath to stepchildren. Second, the law does not allow (though in the past this was possible) one testator to tie up property through several bequests. So it is not possible, say, for a man who has remarried to leave property to his wife and then to require that she leaves it to his children in her own will. Such a man may, of course, make an informal request that his second wife does this, but the formality of the law cannot be adduced to require her to comply.

Thus remarriage, whether or not there are children from a second marriage, opens up the real possibility that the children from the first marriage will receive nothing, with their parent's property passing out of their blood line, to that of his or her second spouse. This is a situation which many of our interviewees talked about, usually indicating that they saw it as highly problematic and often telling us stories about people whom they knew who had been in this situation, and where the children were disinherited. Some people's feelings were very strong on this subject and a quote from Tony Lewis, one of our interviewees, would be fairly representative:

> 'I know someone who's remarried and they have children, he has children with his second marriage. And he has children from the first marriage. Now what do you do in circumstances like that, if you was going to make a will out, do you leave money to both children? . . . . I could never just discard my own children from a first marriage . . . . I'd leave some money, if I had money, possessions. I'd divide it somehow between – I'd make sure both children, both sets of children, got something.'

We can see this as an issue in practice in the case which we considered above of Madge Pritchard and her two sons by her first marriage. This case is not complicated by children in the second marriage, but the fact remains that Len and Keith Scott did not receive anything when their father died, and that now his second wife Anne has control over his property. In their interviews, both expressed the expectation that they would be the major beneficiaries of Anne's estate. However, they were very hazy about the grounds for this expectation. Both indicated that they thought their father had sorted it out in his will, but then they also acknowledged that Anne would have the right to decide.

The way in which Len and Keith approach this situation underscores the highly ambiguous status of stepchildren, as far as making inheritance claims is concerned. The fact that Anne has no direct descendants clearly bolsters their expectation that they will eventually inherit. But neither is really certain that he will. Keith indicates that he is maintaining a good relationship with Anne which – whether intentionally or not – can be seen as a kind of insurance policy.

> Keith: I presume that when his wife dies then it's down in his will, or whatever he left with her and the solicitors, that the house . . . will come to me and my brother. Because there's nobody else on her side at all.
> Interviewer: So is this something that you've been told, or something that . . .
> Keith: Er, yes, I think my dad mentioned it. But I'm not particularly worried. To tell you the truth, I'm sure that it will. Because I maintain, I mean I always have done, a very good and a very healthy relationship with Anne, my father's widow. Always got on well, and she's got nobody else to leave it to. I mean I presume in the course of events it'll just automatically come to us. And I'm sure there is, I'm sure it's all written down somewhere.

In essence, the only claim which the sons have on their stepmother's estate is an indirect one, related to their father's expressed wishes. As Len puts it:

> 'On the assumption that she doesn't change the wishes my father had for his estate, the money will eventually come into my family and my brother's family.'

And even here there is some ambiguity. Towards the end of this section of his interview, Len begins to question whether really there are any moral claims on his stepmother's estate, on the grounds that all the equity was built up during the second marriage, since his father left the first marriage with practically no possessions. Len therefore has an 'underlying' feeling that he is not really entitled to inherit from Anne:

> 'Perhaps I think – I've not really thought of it before – but perhaps I think underlying it all is almost a sense of it not being an inheritance necessarily due to us.'

This case brings out very clearly the point that the claims of stepchildren are ambiguous at best, on three grounds. First, because they are not blood kin of the step-parent their claims can only ever be indirect. Second, given the acceptance that the surviving spouse has the right to control property, the strongest ground for a claim by stepchildren is the argument that the wishes of their deceased parent should be respected. Third, there is a sense in which the stepchildren may really feel entitled only to a share of wealth generated during the time when their own parents were married to each other, and a corresponding lack of legitimacy to inherit anything to which the step-parent contributed.

Drawing a more general message about kinship from this example, it becomes clear that in a situation where there is real uncertainty about the status of step-kin as kin, and indeed whether they are kin at all, individuals construct relationships with each other in a way which enables them to work for their own family. In the example I have used, it was evident that Len and Keith not only had constructed a good relationship with their stepmother in general terms but also they had talked to her about the incident concerning the painting in particular. The burden of these conversations seemed to be, as one of them put it, that whatever happened to the painting she 'didn't want it to cause a rift in the family'. Thus the dispute became an occasion for renegotiating relationships with step-kin, defining these relationships as both valuable and as part of 'the family'. The individualistic character of English kinship enabled them to do this.

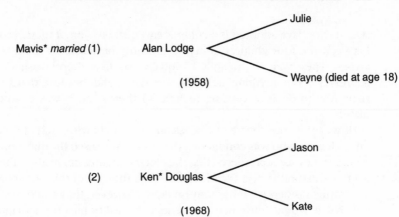

* Interviewed as part of inheritance study

Figure 7.2   Members of Mavis and Ken Douglas's family

Pattern 3: Children tend to be treated equally

As I have indicated, our wills data suggested that there is a strong
tendency to ensure that all children receive bequests of equal value.
This is also confirmed generally by our interview data. That position is
quite consistent with studies on other aspects of family life, which
indicate that equal treatment of children is always a strong theme (Allatt
and Yeandle, 1986; Finch and Mason, 1993). That applies also to
families where there are stepchildren, where parents strive particularly
to ensure that none feels treated unfairly or unequally (Burgoyne and
Clark, 1984).

Thus the basic principle about treating children equally in inheritance is very clear. The problem posed by divorce and remarriage is how
to put that principle into practice, especially in families where there are
various children with different combinations of parents. In order to
explore this, I shall use a different case, that of the Douglas family,
whose relationships are set out in Figure 7.2. Ken and Mavis Douglas
brought up four children together, two of their own, and two older
ones from Mavis's first marriage. One of Mavis's older children was
killed in a car accident at the age of eighteen; all the others are now
grown up, the youngest being aged twenty at the time of our interviews.

Mavis and Ken both have made wills, and indeed they first did so
many years ago when the four children were young. The principle

which they have adopted is a completely equal division of their estates between the four children initially, and now between the three survivors. They wanted to split it equally 'so that there wasn't any animosity about anything' according to Mavis, and 'because that's the right way to do it' according to Ken. In their eyes, it was a simple matter.

However, in the course of discussion (separately with each of them) my colleague who was conducting the interviews raised the question of whether they had considered that the eldest daughter might also inherit from her natural father. Clearly neither had thought of this possibility, and both considered it inherently unlikely. However, they could readily see that it would introduce a potential inequality into the situation, which they had carefully constructed on the basis of treating all their children equally, in that their elder daughter could end up on balance with a larger inheritance than the other two.

It is instructive to see how Mavis and Ken each reacted to this, thinking on their feet in the course of the interview. Mavis's reaction was to stick firmly to the principle that her own estate would be divided on the basis of strict equality between all her children,

> Interviewer: If you thought that they would inherit some money from their father, do you think that would have altered how you wrote your will?
> Mavis: No. No. Not at all. It didn't have any bearing on it at all. But I don't think there's any danger of that (*laughs*).
> Interviewer: Right. Why wouldn't you take it into consideration then?
> Mavis: Because Julie and Wayne are just as much mine as Jason and Kate. So I would think they would be entitled to as much of mine as they. And they were. No I don't think – I just wouldn't alter it at all.

Ken was obviously very thrown by the suggestion that his stepdaughter might inherit from her natural father, and kept saying, 'Gosh, I've never even thought of that. What a thought!' His reaction does suggest that he saw this as creating a real potential problem for the principle of equal treatment which he was trying to adopt. Though he, like Mavis, said that he would not change the division of his own estate he did also try to reason through what the consequences might be, and threw the onus onto his daughter to ensure that she would not be unduly advantaged over her siblings,

> Interviewer: Do you think, if you were to expect Julie to have some money from her father, you would take that into consideration?
> Ken: No.
> Interviewer: No. You'd still write the same will?

Ken: Right. Because hopefully she would, if there was anything like that, I'm sure she would do the right thing by the others anyway. I would have thought. That is something I've never seriously contemplated.
Interviewer: In the sense of giving a bit more back to them, do you mean, to do the right thing?
Ken: No. That Julie would perhaps pass on some to the others. That's what I meant.
Interviewer: To her brothers and sisters?
Ken: Yes.

The difference between the reactions of Ken and Mavis is that Mavis sees the issue as revolving around the equality of the *gift* which she, as a parent, gives. By implication she sees it as irrelevant what any of her children might receive from other sources. Ken on the other hand is more concerned with equality of *outcomes* and speculates that his children would be decent enough to see the importance of this, sharing whatever any of them receives between themselves. Again, the effect of divorce and remarriage is to bring into conflict two principles – equality of the gift and equality of the outcome – which can remain harmoniously consistent with each other where parents have been married only once.

Conclusion

What has this exploration of divorce and inheritance told us about contemporary English kinship, and the ways in which it might be changing?

Most obviously it shows that the experience of divorce, remarriage and the creation of step-families makes questions of inheritance much more difficult for people to handle in practice, because it creates tensions between the various principles which most people appear to use when working out questions of inheritance in their own families. I have suggested that three key principles which people commonly use are: the claims of the surviving spouse should take priority; children can expect to inherit eventually; children should be treated equally. Whereas in families which have not experienced divorce and its consequences the application of these principles can be a relatively straightforward matter, if that is what the key actors chose, in reconstituted families attempts to apply them can cause considerable tensions because they can prove incompatible with each other. Similar tensions may arise in other circumstances where the basis of kinship is changing, for example where children are born following processes of assisted conception where the genetic ties between parents and children are not straightforward (Edwards *et al.*, 1993).

In the process of managing these tensions consequent upon divorce, we see an excellent example of the individualistic character of English kinship in action as people try to accommodate a series of marriages, and the step-relationships which they create, within a model which is going to 'work' for their *own* family. The characteristic individuality of English kinship allows this to happen.

At the same time, that individuality does imply greater diversity. In essence, individuals are left to work out for themselves how to handle these complex situations within their own families, with no explicit steer from the law and no clear cultural guidelines. So individuality means that different people, and different families, can choose to act differently from each other, for example with some families trying to treat stepchildren on completely the same terms as full-blood children, and others making a distinction between these two categories. So a further consequence of this capacity to be highly adaptable is that a range of different decisions about inheritance – and of course about other aspects of relationships in reconstituted families – is almost bound to lead to further diversity in the forms which English kinship takes.

Notes

1. Thanks are due to the Economic and Social Research Council who provided funding for two projects referred to in this chapter; Inheritance, Property and Family Relationships, 1990–93 (Grant No. G00232197) and Family Obligations 1985–89 (Grant No. G00232035).
2. In the UK, wills of people who have died are public documents once they have been through probate. We were able to draw a random sample from the probate calendars for the relevant years, since the lists of probated wills are arranged in alphabetical order. We chose, for reasons concerned with the project as a whole, to sample half from testators who had died in the south-east of England and half from the north-west region.
3. Our interview sample was not randomly selected, but was constructed in the basis of filing pre-defined target quotas. The quotas were defined theoretically, not representationally. Our main aim

was to study 'ordinary' families for whom inheritance was a live issue, which meant that the majority needed to belong to house-holds who were home-owners, and that a substantial number should be first-generation home-owners. Within these broad para-meters, we sought to include people with a wide range of ages and social backgrounds. Where appropriate, we tried to interview people who were members of the same family. Thus, of our 98 interviews, 66 have at least one relative included in our study and 46 have more than one. The maximum number of kin interviewed in a single family was eight.

8

INHERITANCE AND RELATIONSHIPS
BETWEEN FAMILY MEMBERS

Ali de Regt

Introduction

After the Second World War, the study of family relationships in the Netherlands was focused on the relations between members of the nuclear family. Since three-generation households have traditionally been the exception and even the elderly mostly live separate from their children, social scientists have paid little attention to the importance of the wider family network in people's lives. In the last few decades, however, adult children's support towards their aged parents has become a much debated and investigated topic and this has led to a reconsideration of intergenerational relationships in general. The importance of the wider kin comes to the fore – also when living arrangements are of the nuclear type.

One way in which family members are connected is by the transmission of goods and money at death. Almost everybody gets involved in inheritance matters at some moment in the course of his or her life, be it as a potential bequeather or a beneficiary. Succession is a moment of great importance for family feeling and family solidarity. Transfer of property has not only an economic but also a symbolic function: the death of a family member calls for the distribution of his or her estate as part of a rearrangement of family relations. No wonder that a lot of stories go around about inheritance leading to family quarrels and family feuds. Such stories contain a warning about what might happen between family members at moments when their relationships have to be given a new form.

In advanced industrial societies, the inheritance of wealth has lost its dominance for people's economic position. Though an inheritance may have a considerable economic value, for most young people it is education, and not the transmission of means of production or other forms of property, that has become decisive for securing a good position in life. The development of the welfare state has further diminished the economic importance of inherited wealth. Property has lost its predominance in favour of pension schemes and benefit rights in periods of financial adversity or loss of earning power.

This is not to say that inheritance has become unimportant in highly developed welfare states like the Netherlands. State welfare arrangements have not reduced the wish to hand something on to the next generation and, for many people, such arrangements have even made it easier to fulfil this wish. Therefore, recent trends to reduce welfare expenditures by stricter regulations and privatization, interfere with people's wish to distribute their property at death instead of spending it on the costs of their own care.

This chapter deals with the meaning of inheritances for family relationships. The main question is how the transmission of property influences the relationships between parents and children and between brothers and sisters. The answer to this question will be related to changes in the economic structure of society and the workings of the welfare state.

The analysis is based on two kinds of data. In the first place, the research consists of four case studies which show, each in its own way, how families can handle an inheritance, with what kind of problems they are confronted and how these have affected their relationships. Each of these four cases illustrates one specific problem that may arise. The story of Walter K centres around the resentment towards his father, who left all his possessions to his second wife without regard to the children from his first marriage. The stories of Inge R, Anne J, and Thomas G concern the sharing out of their parent's estate. Thomas G's story shows the tensions between brothers and sisters that arose when the parental goods were divided. Anne J tells a story about the conflict between her brother and their father which influenced the relationship between the brother and sisters at their mother's death. And in Inge R's story we can see how the fear of family quarrels led her and her husband to make a last will.

In the second place, much information is inferred from legal and political discussions about changes in the law of inheritance. Succession takes place within legal boundaries. People's actions in succession matters can only be understood by reference to the law and its implications. Therefore, the four case studies will be situated in the context of legal rules and their changes in this century.

The surviving spouse and the children

Until the beginning of the nineteenth century, inheritance practices in the Netherlands varied by region. In 1838, the Napoleonic Civil Code was introduced throughout the realm, which laid down the rules according to which the estate had to be divided. Since then, the law of succession has undergone several changes, but the principles have remained the same. Testators can make a last will, but have no testamentary freedom. The nearest blood relatives – their children – can not be disinherited. However, the making of a last will is not common practice: most transfers were, and still are, conducted without a last will. Therefore, in the majority of the population property is passed on according to the rules of intestate law.

In the 1838 law the surviving spouse had hardly any rights to the estate. Following the older inheritance rules in the different regions of the Republic, the law of inheritance was based on consanguinity and focused on the transmission of the estate within the family. The accent on blood relations meant that spouses, who were after all not related by blood, only could claim a right to the estate when there were no kin in the direct upward or downward line, and no further kin till the twelfth grade. When spouses had community of property, as was often the case, the surviving spouse came into possession of half of the estate after the death of the other, but had to leave the other half to the spouse's relatives by blood.

In the second half of the nineteenth century, this 'family law' was contested for the first time. Voices rose in favour of a law in which the members of the nuclear family would get more rights to the estate at the expense of more distant kin. This was related to new developments in family behaviour. The relationships between members of the nuclear family – between husbands and wives and between parents and children – were strengthened. These emotionally tighter family bonds were, among others, brought about by a free marriage choice based on affection. Such a strong emotional bond, it was thought, should also be expressed in the inheritance practice. Therefore, the nearly complete exclusion of spouses in the law of succession was seen as a flagrant injustice and contrary to the prevailing sense of justice.

Champions of a new law of inheritance were public notaries in the first place. They said they frequently came into contact with legators who made a last will in favour of the surviving spouse. Such a will gave a guarantee that the survivor could use the whole estate and was relatively safe against the claims of the children, so that he (or mostly she) would not lose out after the partner's death. Notaries argued that the public sense of justice demanded that such rules should also be applied in the majority of cases in which no last wills were made.

At the beginning of the twentieth century the general opinion was that the position of the survivor should be strengthened, but there was little agreement on the specific way in which the law should be changed. In 1923 a compromise between different options was reached; from then on the surviving spouse was a preferred legitimate heir and had the same rights as each child.[1]

Soon after the introduction of this new law, however, it became clear that the amount the surviving spouse (the wife in most cases) could claim, was not enough to allow her the same standard of living as before. Gradually a new element was introduced into the discussion: the surviving spouse had the right to be cared for. According to the Civil Code, spouses had a duty to maintain each other while alive; now it was said that partners should be allowed to extend this duty after their death and must be enabled to use the whole estate for the maintenance of the survivor.[2]

In the 1970s still another argument in favour of the surviving spouse was introduced: the survivor had a right on the whole estate because spouses had both contributed to the value of the estate; therefore it was reasonable that after the death of one of them the other could dispose of everything.

The position of the survivor in the law of succession is a highly contentious topic because each extension of the rights of the surviving spouse means an impairment of the rights of the children. Essentially, the question is about blood relations versus contractual relations.

Advocates of more rights for the survivor stress that they follow public opinion (Cozijn, 1978). According to them, the public wishes spouses to have use of the whole estate after the death of the partner because they need it and because they have contributed to its value, while children have not contributed anything and therefore have fewer 'moral rights'. Opponents to a law in which the survivor can dispose of the whole estate stress two things. In the first place, they attach great importance to blood relations and the transfer of property within the family. In the second place, they are afraid that in cases of second marriages, the children from the first marriage will be disadvantaged in favour of the second spouse, especially a new and younger wife of the deceased. They regard it a great injustice that children from a first mariage should see the second wife of their father profit from the inheritance which should be theirs. For these children it would be painful to see their 'stepmother' favoured above themselves.

In the most recent legal proposal, a compromise is worked out between the principles of consanguinity and marriage. The survivor and each of the children inherit the same portion, but the surviving spouse has the right to make use of the whole estate during the rest of her life. Children keep the right to their 'legitimate portion', but they can only claim that portion after the death of the surviving spouse.[3]

Until now all attempts to change the law of inheritance have failed. Spouses who want to favour their partner, therefore, have to make a last will. In earlier times the making of a will was limited to a relatively small proportion of owners of wealth, but this practice has grown in the last few decades. This is connected to the fact that more and more people own some property, especially houses (Thorns, 1994). Though in the Netherlands home ownership is less widespread than in, for instance, Spain, Belgium, Great Britain, Italy and France, it increased after the Second World War from less than 30 per cent in 1950 to 47 per cent in 1992. Home-owners think about the best way in which they can transfer their property after death. Most last wills concern the wish to protect a spouse against the claims of the children; that is, to guarantee that the house will not have to be sold in order to give the children their portion.

Inge R and her husband, one of the four cases on which this chapter is based, come from a working-class family in which the making of last wills was out of the question. Now they own a house of their own. The possibility that their four children might be able to sell the house after the death of one of them has led to the decision to make a will favouring the survivor. Inge presents the following argument:

> 'For then the children could say, for instance . . . yes, that would be possible, we want our portion. Now, we have four children, and say that all our property is worth 300,000 guilders. Of course I get half of it [they are married in community of property], but the other half has to be divided by five. That's 30,000 guilders each. If all four of them want to have that amount of money, where do I get all that money from? Of course I don't have that amount, so . . . '

Though Inge does not expect that her children will react in such a manner and claim their portion, she says you can never be sure. In this opinion she is encouraged by notaries, the mass media and public opinion in general, which help to spread the idea that inheritances often lead to family quarrels, even if you do not expect this, and that to make a will is very sensible. As Inge says:

> 'Everybody says you should do that. Everybody advises you to make a will. One talks about it, one writes about it in the magazines, that it is a very sensible thing to do. And then we said, yes, actually we should do that . . . . Because people have experience of children making rows about money.'

Inge told her children they had made a will and they too found it a wise decision. So the prevention of future conflicts between parents and children was acclaimed by all parties concerned.

A last will in favour of the surviving spouse, however, does not guarantee that children will not claim their portion. The blood relationship is dominant in inheritance law: children have a legal right to a part of the parental heritage, which cannot be taken away. Though children who claim their portion when parents have made a will in favour of the survivor are frowned upon by notaries and public opinion, and to substantiate their claims is legally very difficult, children may have their reasons to try it anyway, for instance in the case of a second marriage.

The opposite interests of a surviving spouse and the children comes to the fore in the case of Walter K. He and his brothers and sisters have indeed tried to contest their father's will. The father, divorced from his first wife, had stipulated that his second wife could make use of the whole estate so that the children from his first marriage would only come into the inheritance after her death. The likelihood would be that the second wife would use up the greater part of the estate for her keep, and that after her death hardly anything would be left for the children from the first marriage.

Walter tells that in the decision to contest the will different reasons played a role. Probably the most important motive was disappointment that their father favoured a 'stranger' above his 'own children'. Besides, economic motives played a part, because some of the children were in limited economic circumstances and an inheritance was more than welcome. Finally, the children had some hard feelings against the second wife, who was seen as the disturber of the parents' marriage. They found it unnecessary that the second wife should be cosseted while the children missed out. Walter summarizes the different motives as follows:

> 'But yes, that we could use the money was one thing, and that we wanted to do the widow a bad turn was another thing, and I think it was something in between.'

One of the points on which they contested the will was the main-tenance duty of the deceased towards his surviving spouse. In the 1940s the Supreme Court had decided that legators are allowed to use their estate to fulfil this duty and that children cannot resist this. But there are no rules about the amount of money which is necessary to 'maintain' a survivor. Walter K thought that his father's widow had no right to a more than medium income and that the estate was large enough to give the widow a reasonable income and the children their legitimate portion. He says:

> 'We made gigantic calculations. How much has the widow to expect according to father's former income. How much will she get from father's pension and so on. We thought that that was a nice medium income and we thought that was enough. And she would have a reasonable amount when she gave us our legitimate portion. She would not be reduced to beggary, so that would be enough.'

The courts, however, decided otherwise and were of the opinion that the widow must be enabled to live according to her former position and therefore needed the use of the whole estate. Walter does not agree with this 'class justice', but he is especially disappointed about the fact that a 'second wife' is protected at the expense of children from a first marriage:

> 'Yes, I do have the feeling that you have some rights against a second wife, who is not family, who is not a mother. I think all the children had that feeling. That it had not been necessary that father's widow was coddled and therefore nothing was left for us, his own children.'

Walter's story is a nice illustration of the feelings of injustice which can arise when marriage relationships are predominant over blood relationships, as will be the case when the position of the surviving spouse is legally strengthened and the survivor gets preference over the children. Yet, as we will see later, Walter's grudge is not so much directed towards the second wife as towards his father who made the last will.

Parents and children

In 1838, when the law of inheritance was laid down in the Civil Code, it went without saying that consanguinity would be the main criterion for succession. The lawyers dealing with the codification of the law all presumed that an owner wanted to transfer his property to those who were closest to his heart, and that these, in any case, would be relatives by blood: children or grandchildren or, if these were not alive, parents or more distant blood relations. This opinion went hand in hand with ideas about the continuation of families, family enterprises and family wealth. These ideas were dominant in a society in which inheritable wealth consisted for the main part of means of production, which allowed the next generation to carry on the family's position in society. The exclusion of the spouse was seen as an inevitable consequence of the principle of consanguinity.

In the course of the nineteenth century, and even more so in this century, ownership of means of production has become less important and income by wage-earning more important for the social position of the greater part of the population. The transfer of inherited wealth is less determining for the life chances of the next generation. Nowadays, most children are not dependent on an inheritance for their occupational position. For a good position on the labour market, 'cultural capital', particularly formal education, is much more important. Actually, children of more well-to-do families have a better start in life, but the dependence on a legacy for one's life course has diminished considerably.

These developments have contributed to an acceptance of the restriction on the children's succession rights in favour of the rights of spouses. The spouses' gain, for instance, can be seen in the relative share spouses and children have in the total amount of transfers in this century. In 1921 spouses got 13 per cent of all the wealth transferred by succession, children got 56 per cent. In 1981 spouses got 31 per cent, while the share of children was reduced to 47 per cent (Wilterdink, 1984, pp.52-3)

On one point, however, the children's legal position has remained stronger than that of the spouse: children have a guaranteed right on a legal portion and cannot be disinherited by will, as can spouses. A guaranteed portion for the children has been a much debated issue during the whole of the twentieth century. Again and again the same arguments for and against were brought forward. Opponents to such a portion argue, for instance, that it restricts the testators' freedom to dispose of their own property. Proponents of a guaranteed portion think children have inalienable rights based on blood. Besides, they argue that a guaranteed portion protects children against second or later spouses. With the increase in divorces, this argument has gained weight. In this way the danger that children from a first marriage lose their portion to a stepmother can be prevented. The example of Walter

K, however, shows that a last will can endanger the guaranteed portion. To be sure, children do have a claim on the surviving spouse, but they can only substantiate that claim when the survivor dies. When the new law comes through, this will be the normal procedure.

The preferential treatment of the spouse does not mean, however, that parents do not want to leave their property in the hands of the children. Actually, they do. Dutch research on inheritance matters, carried out in 1978, showed that the greater part of those interviewed thought children should not come into their money while one of the parents was alive, but that children should be the principal heirs after the last parent's death (Cozijn, 1978). In a study in Boston, in the United States, it was found that nearly all persons researched named their children in their last will (Rossi and Rossi, 1990). Another study in New Zealand showed children next to spouses as the main beneficiaries (Thorns, 1994). In the four cases I have studied it appeared that all four mothers who had survived their husbands found it self-evident to transfer their property to their children.

For parents it is important to leave something behind for their children, even when the latter are in a comfortable economic position and do not need the money. An inheritance has not only economic functions, but the symbolic meaning is as important. Bequeathing is a way in which the older generation can contribute to the perpetuation of the family. For instance, this was the case with Thomas's mother. Thomas commented:

> 'While she had the idea, without saying so directly, I save for you all, and when I die all of you get something . . . . She had that motive very strongly; to be able to transfer something to the children.'

In this way parents probably want to demonstrate for the last time their care and love for their children and symbolize the continuity between the generations.

According to Dutch law, people cannot disinherit their children, but most parents want to leave their possessions to their children anyway. This wish is widespread, even among parents who deny their children a moral right to their estate. Inge and her husband think they do not owe their children anything. Yet Inge says:

> 'But yes, you feel you want to give it to your children. I would not think of leaving everything to somebody else, without giving something to the children. Even if they do not need it. I would not think of it.'

Walter, who calls the system of inheritance old-fashioned and unjust, does not think it will disappear in the near future:

'It has been like that since time immemorial. It looks like a kind of natural drive in parents, to leave something to their offspring.'

In a time when inheritance determined the social position of the beneficiaries to a larger extent, the possession of an estate gave parents a certain amount of control over their children. In modern societies parents have lost this type of control because, as said before, an inheritance has become less important for their children's station in life. Moreover, the age at which children come into their parents' money has risen considerably; they benefit when their position is already settled. But still parents try, maybe unconsciously, to tie their children by their property. They can do this, for example, by promising some-body certain objects after their death. Anne tells that her mother 'always talked about who was to get what' and promised different things to her children and grandchildren. In Thomas's case, his mother's promises led to conflicts during the sharing out of the contents of the house:

'One of the complicating factors was that she had said to some of the children, you can have that and that. And she had promised the same things to different persons. So there were all kinds of claims on the same objects. That was one of the problems.'

Even Inge's mother-in-law, who never talked about her death, proved to have promised during her illness a set of vases to one of her daughters-in-law who liked them.

For children, a parental inheritance has various meanings. In the first place an inheritance has an economic value. Parents leave money, a house, valuable objects or consumer goods. In our four cases all the inheritances included money as well as goods; Thomas and Anne got a considerable sum, Inge got a small amount and Walter got nothing from the fairly large estate. The goods also had a certain economic value, though in Inge's case there was 'nothing to speak of'. Anne, Thomas and Inge stress that the money was welcome and that they were glad to get it, but that it was not really important to them.

Yet, in the stories of our respondents, greed plays a role. For Inge, the greed which she had heard about and which she feared, gave rise to avoidance strategies. For Thomas, greed was a factor in the conflicts about the share-out; and Anne acknowledges it in her own feelings after her mother's death:

'She always talked about it and on the rebound we thought we would not bother about it, but this is very strange . . . . The moment it was there, and we stood around it to share it out, I wanted to have it.'

In addition to economic meaning, legacies can have other meanings which have little to do with the economic value of the objects of the estate. For some people the goods symbolize the relationship which existed between legator and heir. Thomas explains the tensions between the siblings which arose when his mother's goods were divided as a consequence of the relationship between the mother and her children:

> 'And the tensions each child had with his or her mother come to the fore in discussions about the division of the estate.'

Anne gives a similar interpretation when she tells about the way in which her elder brother handled their father's possessions. At that moment his negative feelings against his father came to the surface and he did away with all objects as quickly as possible. Walter, who contested his father's testament, saw in its stipulations a new proof of the lack of care for his children:

> 'I felt it as an abandonment in the first place, as a confirmation of his indifference. While his own children were already disadvantaged so much by the divorce and had been badly off since that time. Living below a minimal level actually. So that had given us the feeling, he owes us something. And when that was not the case, yes, it was a disappointment, a feeling of injustice, one person, the second wife is coddled, while we, the children are kicked out of the nest. Yes, that contrast was felt by all of us, and I still feel it.'

Finally, goods can have an emotional value for the children: remembrances of the parental home, a feeling of continuity between generations, things one is attached to. Objects can symbolize a shared identity over the generations. Anne, who grew up in a home with nice old things, expresses this kind of value: 'things from her, to which I am attached'. Thomas says that the objects out of his mother's estate had little value for him: 'there were hardly any things from home'. Inge, too, stresses several times that her mother-in-law had 'nothing' which could be valued, except one picture which had been in the possession of her husband's grandfather, after whom he was named.

Children have a legal right to the estate and this right has not disappeared in the recent proposals for a new inheritance law. The fact that transfers between parents and children lead to a continuation of social class differences is hardly ever seen as unjust. The socialists' alternative of inheritance by the state, is no issue anymore.[4] Inheritance within families is seen as just and proper by the majority of the population (Vinke and Berghuis-van der Wijk, 1975). Even those persons who contest the existing law do not want more rights for the state, but more freedom for the testatator to do whatever he wants without being forced to leave a guaranteed portion to the children. Such freedom, however, would make hardly any difference to inheritance practice and therefore for the distribution of wealth in the population.

Brothers and sisters

Traditionally the Dutch law of inheritance contains the principle of equal rights for all the children. Sons have no precedence over daughters, nor have elder children over younger.

In pre-industrial times other types of inheritance could be found in different parts of Europe. In some regions the law favoured the eldest son, in others the youngest, in some parts daughters were excluded (Goody 1976; Medick and Sabean, 1984). The kind of system followed had important consequences for the relationships between brothers and sisters: co-operation or competition, loyalty or conflict were intrinsic to certain types of division. The system of equal inheritance could give rise to competition between siblings, because an estate in the form of a farm or some other enterprise could not be divided without fragmentation (Segalen, 1984; Collomp, 1984). In Dutch agricultural regions this problem has often been solved by a testamentary practice in which the enterprise is given to the succeeding heir, while the other heirs are compensated in money. Now that most of the estates only consist of money and other moveables, or at the most a house in which the heirs do not themselves live, the division between siblings has become much easier.

Yet, the share-out can lead to all kinds of conflicts between the children. These conflicts concern mostly the division of the furniture and other moveables, which often have both an economic and an emotional value. When siblings are conscious about the fact that the division may lead to conflicts, they can try to avoid quarrels by following a pre-arranged and therefore 'just' procedure. With our respondents this was the case.

Inge and her husband had been on bad terms with his youngest brother and sister-in-law for years, but during their mother's illness the relationship was mended. After the mother's death the three brothers and their wives understood that here was a new occasion for conflict. That is why they explicitly agreed on a harmonious division. 'The three of us had made up our minds not to fight, and we succeeded'. Brothers and sisters-in-law came together, divided the most expensive pieces of furniture, shared the three jewels among the sisters-in-law and divided the rest into three. There were no disagreements, but actually, in Inge's words, 'there was nothing to quarrel about'.

Anne's mother left a lot of valuable pieces, and experiences with the division of their father's things had shown how unsatisfactory such a division could be. At the time, the eldest son, out of spite against his father, had done away with objects which Anne and her sister had valued. Anne's mother had decided in her last will not to let her eldest son execute the will, but her youngest daughter. This was a very painful decision, which was, however, as Anne told, 'our rescue'. They devised a very strict sharing system: the value of all the goods present was estimated in advance by a professional; on the day of the share-out each of the three children (without in-laws) had turns in choosing an object. Afterwards the total worth of the choice of each of the children was calculated and evened out with the inheritance in money. Nobody could feel wronged afterwards, everybody had had a fair choice. After all those years, Anne is still glad that they have avoided resentment and spite by means of this procedure, and that the relationship between the siblings has not suffered because of inheritance matters.

In Thomas's case, Thomas and a sister-in-law made an inventory of all his mother's possessions. All children could indicate what they wanted to have; when more than one person wanted the same object, they drew lots. In spite of this approved system, the division gave rise to conflicts and irritations which have their influence till this day. Tensions rose already after the somewhat hasty sharing out of their mother's jewels; some sisters felt themselves disadvantaged. The day on which the contents of the house was to be divided, saw more quarrels:

'They fought about whom would get a certain item, a table, the bed-linen, a radio or an iron. About everything she had, actually.'

Thomas explains that these conflicts arose not only from greed, but also from what is called 'sibling rivalry': competition between brothers and sisters about the mother's love was now fought out over the mother's estate.

'I think it was about the question whom did she love most. And tensions, and also sorrow from the past came back in the division.'

Brothers and sisters inherit, but indirectly in-laws are drawn in too. Sisters- and brothers-in-law can have a voice in the division, as in Inge's case, where the daughters-in-law had a big say in the sharing out of the moveables. In Anne's case, on the contrary, the in-laws were expressly left out of the procedure. In Thomas's family, the fact that a sister-in-law, who was in charge of the mother's administration, had an important share in the procedure led to a protest by some of the children:

> 'And from the beginning that made difficulties with some of them, especially with my sisters. They thought that only relatives by blood should concern themselves with the estate and no in-laws.'

In-laws, in popular speech 'the cold side', are often seen as the instigators of quarrels between siblings. Because they do not feel loyalty and solidarity with the parental family they are supposed to act solely for monetary gain and are often said to have a negative influence on their partner. My research was not extensive enough to corroborate this point, but in two of the four cases the distinction between blood relations and in-laws was explicitly made.

Conflicts between siblings about the division of the estate are in most cases about an 'honest' share for each. An honest share is mostly equated with an equal share. Parents, however, might have various reasons to favour some children above others. For instance, some are more in need of money, some are more dear or have done more for the parents. Yet parents do this much less than could be expected. An unequal treatment of children goes against a deeply rooted ideology that all children should be loved in the same way and that all children should be treated equally. That is what children expect too. Preferment of one child above the other is contrary to the equal love and attention which children demand from their parents.

To bequeath or to grant: the workings of the welfare state

Property owners do not have to wait until after their death for their property to be transferred; they can give away part of it during their life time. The growing number of registered donations, compared to registered inheritances, might indicate that transfer during life is on the increase (Wilterdink, 1984, p.250). On this point too, children are the most frequent beneficiaries. One of the reasons to prefer a gift over an inheritance is the avoidance of death duty. Recipients of capital gifts actually have to pay a duty on gifts, but parents can give their children a considerable amount free of tax. Another reason not to wait to transfer capital till death, is to let children profit from their parents' money when they are relatively young and have more use for it than at a later stage of their lives. Because of the rise in life expectancy, inheritances often come free when the beneficiaries are already in their fifties or sixties. Therefore parents find a gift more satisfactory than a bequest after death.

Anne and her husband, for instance, have decided to give their two young adult children, who are short of cash, a monthly allowance. Anne says:

> 'We are the parents of luxury kids. You know what it means to them and you think, now they are young, now they really need it, between quotation marks that is to say, and why shouldn't we help, if possible. Even a few hundred guilders a month is a support, then they can say, now we can manage.'

Her children have accepted this money gratefully, though they tell their parents not to cut back on their own expenses. Yet Anne is surprised about the fact that her son and his friends seem to find a parental gift normal – 'as a kind of advance on the inheritance'. Inge, too, intends to give her children a certain amount now and then, not because they need the money, but because this is more pleasant than a legacy in the far future. For her such a gift symbolizes the good relations they have.

A final reason to prefer a gift over a bequest has to do with the workings of the welfare state. In the Netherlands, the social security system grew rapidly after the Second World War. Social insurances in cases of illness, invalidity and unemployment, and state and private pension schemes for the retired, made the possession of saved or inherited private wealth less urgent. The introduction of these various welfare arrangements lessened the material dependence between family members and questioned the whole idea of maintenance duties towards kin. Spouses and children are not left without means of living after the death of a husband or parent, and the idea of maintenance as a motivation for mandatory inheritance could be called outdated. It might be argued that in welfare states inheritance has lost its importance for all parties concerned.

However, this is not as bequeathers see it. They see quite another problem, namely how to save their property for the next generation and defend it against the claims of the state. Until far into this century property was a means to take care of oneself, in particular after retirement. But after the Second World War there is less need to save for old age. As public and private pension schemes provide an income, and health and welfare arrangement are paid by insurances or the state, savings can be used to hand on to the next generation. However, elderly people who have a reasonable income or a certain amount of property do have to pay the costs of an old people's or nursing home themselves, while people without income can live there without paying. This can lead to strong feelings of injustice: people resent having to use up their savings, while others live for free. They want to pass on their property to their children, not use it up for their own keep.

In the last few decades professionals, like notaries, tax advisers and bankers, have thought of different ways to give away a large part of one's property to the next generation, so as to be able to live for free in an old people's home. Inge is very often confronted with this topic among friends and acquaintances:

> 'People sit to think ... there are all kinds of tricks to sell your house to your children .... All those people in my age group, they have a house of their own and they think, I want to give it to my children and I do not want to wait till I have to sell my house to pay for an old people's home. I don't want to eat up my house. To "eat up your house", that's a popular expression nowadays. That's a great trouble, that's even more trouble than having no money at all (*laughs*). This is very common.'

Thomas's father-in-law is confronted with the workings of the welfare state in another way. He expects to leave his children a fair amount of money after his death. But he is troubled by the fact that one of his daughters, who lives on social assistance, will lose her benefit rights when she gets her share of the estate. Thomas comments:

> 'He said I feel uncomfortable about it, that I have to give that money to the state and that she does not profit from it.'

The wish to transfer one's property to one's children and not let it fall to the state, together with the feelings of injustice to have to pay for something others get free, stimulate parents to transfer their property to the next generation during their life time. The development of the welfare state has not led to a diminishing concern with transfer of property, but to attempts to defend one's property against state claims. In this way welfare arrangements had an unforeseen part in the shift from inheritance to gift-giving.

Conclusion

Traditionally, the law of inheritance and inheritance practices in the Netherlands focused on blood relationships. Inheritances contributed to a continuation of the family by transferring property within the circle of kin related by blood. Since the last decades of the nineteenth century the emotional bond between marriage partners got more emphasis; this was, among other things, revealed in the wish to appoint the surviving spouse as the main heir, even if this limited the rights of the children.

Reinforcement of the conjugal tie paradoxically has gone hand in hand with a rise in the number of divorces, which might suggest a weakening of the conjugal relationship. However, this is not a real contradiction; both developments can be explained by the way in which the marriage relationship is envisaged these days. Marriage is seen as worthwile only when based on strong mutual affections and not on economic necessities, and the disappearance of love is a ground for divorce. Marriage partners who stay together, therefore, can be supposed to have positive emotional feelings towards each other and that means they want to take care of each other, even after their death. This is also true for second and following marriages. Each subsequent marriage is made out of love and the wish to leave one's estate to one's spouse applies to each new partner.

The wish to favour the spouse restricts the inheritance rights of the children. This seems to contradict the strengthening of the position of children within the family, which is noted by all family historians. This seeming contradiction can be solved by looking at the changing economic structure of society. Nowadays children are hardly dependent on an inheritance for their social position. Parents express their affection by giving the children an extensive education to give them a good start in life and provide their teenage and young adult children with money to live on. Later on they give money and goods to their adult children. These material transfers are more important for their children's life chances than an inheritance in a much later stage of life.

A change in economic structure and the workings of the welfare state have diminished the role of inheritance for the material perpetuation of families. But this does not mean that inheritance has lost its functions in present-day society. Some categories of the population remain dependent on the transfer of means of production, like farmers and self-employed persons. This category is small, but not insignificant socially. In the second place, the transfer of great fortunes means a continuation of class inequalities.

The importance of inheritance, however, is not restricted to the transfer of capital, class position or social status, but inheritance practices have also symbolic functions for family members. By giving and receiving inheritances, partners emphasize their mutual love, parents the care for their children. Conflicts about inheritances within families involve cash and goods, but these conflicts always turn around something else too. Inheritance matters are about feelings of love, appreciation and redress and about an honest treatment by which everybody gets what they think they have a right to. Inheritances play an important role in the continuation of family feeling and family identity, even in those cases in which material transfers have only a small economic value.

Notes

1. In ordinary language spouses get 'half and a child's share'. This refers to cases in which partners are married in community of property, so each owns half of the estate. For the discussions about the change of the law, see the debates in the Dutch parliament in the years 1919–1921.
2. In the 1940s the Supreme Court decided that testators had the right to use their estate to provide maintenance to the surviving spouse.
3. From the 1950s onward, legal proposals have been formulated and discussed with a view to changing the law of inheritance. Each proposal has been contested and until 1994 no agreement had been reached. Notaries have had a considerable say in resisting all these proposals; they advocate the strongest position for the survivor. See parliamentary proceedings from 1950–1990.
4. At the end of the nineteenth century and the beginning of the twentieth century, the socialists advocated abolition of inheritance within families. In the 1950s, some socialists were still in favour of inheritance by the state. Nowadays hardly anybody takes that position.

9

HOME-SHARING AND THE TRANSMISSION OF INHERITANCE IN FRANCE

Claudine Attias-Donfut

The profound changes which have redefined the modern family relate to changes in gender relations as much as to those between the generations. The trend of greater individual autonomy within the family, the decline of hierarchical structures in spouse and parent/child relationships, together with the development of a wage economy and social security system, have resulted in a growing independence between one generation and another. Furthermore, the increase in life expectancy has also revolutionalized the structure of the family as well as producing entirely new problems. The significant rise over the last 30 years in the age at which an individual still has parents or grandparents alive is now well established. The filial bond is now in place for the greater part of an increased life span, making possible the interchange and sharing of experiences between generations. These changes must be taken into account in order to understand and interpret the events which characterize the family life cycle.

The length of time children are at school, the stage at which they are preparing to leave home and the reunification of some children with their elderly parents through cohabitation all interconnect as a series of phases in a continuum of generational relationship. To share one's home with parents or children certainly implies the recognition of a close bond, but also one of interdependence, of give-and-take, with each generation deriving some form of benefit whilst providing help and support as well. In this system of interchange, whether immediate of deferred, the use made of the home and its eventual transfer are crucial factors.

These questions are addressed in this chapter using data from research on 'The Three Generations'.[1] This survey was anchored to a particular cohort representing a 'pivot' generation born between 1939 and 1943. This resulted in a limited age-spread in the case of the parents' generation – between 70 and 90 years, average age 77 – and a narrower one in the case of the grown-up children – most of them being between 19 and 30 years, average age 27.

The three family generations who are thus subjects of the survey provide the advantage of having led, or are leading, lives that cover distinct and recognizable periods of history, thus circumventing one of the major problems in this type of empirical observation which lies in the fact that the notion of generation is susceptible to wide and varied definition (Attias-Donfut, 1988). This method has enabled us to follow the process of social change across the interaction between generations, as well as to examine the part played by relationships within the family in transmitting or absorbing such change. The experience of living in the same home is in this respect revealing and represents a significant aspect of family life and the changes it is undergoing.

Contradictory developments in the form of home-sharing

About one-fifth of persons over the age of 60 are today estimated to be living with one of their children (Audirac, 1985; Baraille, 1993). This practice, though still relatively common, has decreased considerably over the last 30 years, and by more than 50 per cent in the case of widows aged over 85 (a category where it was most prevalent), dropping from 57 per cent in 1962 to 29.6 per cent in 1990. Over the same period, the proportion of elderly people living alone rose considerably, particularly among women (from 29.7 to 50.1 per cent for widows over 85), while the figure for people living in retirement homes showed little change – 2 per cent under age 75, 5 to 7 per cent for men and women between 75 and 85, 12 per cent for men over 85 and 20–22 per cent for women (Baraille, 1993).

On the other hand, the decline in generational home-sharing has been accompanied by a growing tendency for elderly people to have separate accommodation, suggesting both greater independence between one generation and another and the predominance of a model of 'intimacy from a distance', to use the term proposed by Rosenmayr (1963). Improvements in pensions and in living conditions have given impetus to this tendency.

On the other hand, with the younger generation at the start of adulthood, the last ten years have seen a contrary tendency develop – that of staying on longer at home. In 1950, 56.2 per cent of those between the ages of 20 and 24 were still living with their parents as against 49.3 per cent in 1982 (Desplanques, 1993), and some who had previously left home had returned for indefinite periods. The transitional period between the end of adolescence and taking up a job, finding a home and getting married and settling down, has become longer and now takes place in successive stages (Galland, 1991).

In the tri-generational survey alluded to above, the overall findings per generation show the same trends as identified by official statistics despite the specificity of the sample – three family generations and specific age groups. Each of the three generations followed a different route with its own models for filial and parental relationships.

In the elderly generation, the length of schooling was short: 72.5 per cent of men and 83.5 per cent of women completed it at the age of 14 or under. The age of leaving home was 22.7 on average for men, 21.5 for women. Almost 11 per cent of the older couples have always lived with either their parents or in-laws, which for the previous generation implies a far higher rate of permanent cohabitation, augmented of course by the number of children there may have been. The survey does not provide the non-permanent rate of cohabitation but, as shown earlier, home-sharing between different generations was very frequent 30 or 40 years ago during the period in question. Furthermore, 52.7 per cent of this age group state that they looked after elderly parents, 27 per cent of them for more than ten years – evidence of a considerable degree of proximity between these two generations.

The situation changes somewhat with the relationship between this same generation and their children. These children left home sooner, the males at age 21.8 on average, the females – earlier as before – at 20.8; the time being the turn of the 1950s and start of the 1960s. They also enjoyed longer schooling than their parents: 39 per cent of the men and 36 per cent of the women continued studying to 18 or beyond as against 15.2 per cent and 5.5 per cent in the case of their own parents – the older generation – who are still living. This proportion is lower still for the spouses (a majority of them deceased) of the elderly women questioned (8 per cent) because of the differential in mortality between one social group and another, particularly among men.

The age of leaving school in the case of men in the 'pivotal' generation does not appear to have been instrumental in when they left home; in fact there is a negative correlation between the two ages: males who

Table 9.1   Comparing generational differences

Feel a greater difference between	elder (%)	Pivotal (%)
Their generation and that of their parents	38.9	58.7
Their generation and that of their children	55.1	38.8
Don't know	6.0	2.5
Total	100.0	100.0

went on with their studies beyond age 18 left home sooner than those who did not. Females, who generally tend in each generation to leave home earlier, show a tendency to hang on longer at home if they prolonged their studies: among those who left home at 21 and under, 17.5 per cent continued studying to the age of 19 and beyond whereas the figure was 29 per cent for those who remained at home till the age of 22 and beyond. More males who left home at 21 or under continued with their studies beyond 19 (28 per cent) than did those who left home after 22 (23 per cent).

A split is apparent between the older and the 'pivotal' generations, which is a direct result of the disruption in the 1960s, which even now, 30 years on, markedly affects their relations. It is something they themselves all draw attention to when comparing their generation with the other two (see Table 9.1). The older generation feels closer to their parents than to their children who, themselves, feel less close to their own parents than to their children. This discrepancy would seem not to have occurred before, nor since. It remains as an isolated fracture.

The children of the 'pivotal' generation have not yet completed their transition to adulthood and cannot yet be compared with the two previous generations, but they show a tendency to postpone leaving home at least as late as their grandparents did. Sixty-five per cent of the total of this younger generation have already left. Among those over the age of 22, 19.6 per cent[2] are still living with their parents – i.e. 25 per cent of males and 13.75 per cent of females aged over 22 live at home. In one out of five families a child has left and then returned; in this generation too, sons tend to leave later than daughters, and to return a little more frequently.

Both parents and children corroborate in giving two main, equally important, reasons for staying on at home – the economic benefit it brings and an act of choice in the absence of any strong reason to go; and there is a third reason – reluctance on the part of young people to live alone. But these young people see their situation as provisional, almost half of them contemplating leaving in the course of the year, the

Table 9.2 Departure rate of under-twenties depending on sibling ranking and parental discord

Parental discord	Ranking (%)		
	1	2	3
Yes	26.5*	23.8	20.8
No	23.0	17.4	13.0

* i.e. in families where there is parental discord 26.5 per cent of the firstborn leave home before age 20

rest at some indefinite time in the future. Only half of those who still live at home express a desire to live on their own. Certainly unemployment or job and financial insecurity count for more with those still at home than with their peers who have left home but there are relational factors too that delay departure, in particular the family climate in which they grew up.

Those who have had a 'broad-minded' upbringing will stay on longer at home than those whose upbringing has been strict or authoritarian; and those who as children experienced strife between their parents, more frequently the case in larger families, are likely to leave home sooner (see Table 9.2). Leaving home at an earlier age where such dissension exists continues with the third child, and this suggests its effects have little to do with the size of the family as such. Moreover, place in the family has its importance too; the older children leave more often earlier and the age of leaving tends to rise down the sibling line.

What about home-sharing at the other extreme, when parents become old and frequently frail and dependent? The sociological profile of the elderly who cohabit with their children is well-documented on the basis of census results. They include a high proportion of people in farming and working people generally, a strong rural element and marked regional disparities, cohabitation being more prevalent in regions which traditionally contained stem and community families (the south-west and north-east and the Mediterranean region) (Audirac, 1985; Le Bras and Todd, 1981). Cohabitation is a little more common with sons than with daughters and generally concerns couples living with their children before they turned 80; beyond this age, it is mainly one or other parent, most often a widow.

In the tri-generational survey, the same characteristics reappear, clearly indicating the determining role played by social category. But the basis for observation still remains the one generation, that of the elderly. The group represented by children living at home needs to be analysed as much as does that of their parents, as does the question of intergenerational social mobility too. Moreover, the perspective here adopted here also takes into account the length of time cohabitation lasts. The findings given below confirm the fundamental importance of these two dimensions – social mobility and length of cohabitation – and enable the problem of home-sharing to be seen as two contrasting realities.

Two contrasting situations: uninterrupted home-sharing and 'recohabitation' – a return to home-sharing

Two contrasting patterns stand out from the welter of forms of home-sharing: one where parents and children have always lived together, the other where parents in their old age revert to a pattern which was discontinued as children reaching adulthood sought a 'normal' independence. In the older generation these two situations occur in roughly comparable proportions, with 54.4 per cent having always lived with a child with whom they are sharing a home, and the remainder having gone to live with a child (or children) following a prolonged period of independence. Far less often is it the case of a son or daughter returning to live with ageing parents. In a very small number of cases there is 'alternate home-sharing', with a parent dividing his or her time between one or another child's home.

The extent of uninterrupted home-sharing observed is surprising. It is not, however, possible to compare the result with overall figures for households since these do not show the length of cohabitation. But it may be assumed that unbroken home-sharing is still more common in the population as a whole than in our sample which is limited to multigenerational families. As the evidence shows, single children especially, for the most part sons with no children of their own, remain with their parents for life. The sample then by its nature excludes one category of old people whose situation this represents – they have children but no grandchildren.

For a clearer definition of these situations, a comparison needs to be drawn between the facts relating to the two generations – the older one and their children – to whom home-sharing applies (see Tables 9.3 and 9.4).

Observation of the older generation reveals that if widowed mothers

Table 9.3 Characteristics of parents according to type of home-sharing with offspring

	NON-DECOHABITATION (n=98) i.e. permanent	RECOHABITATION (n=82) i.e. return to home-sharing
Both parents	24.5%	6.1%
Mother alone	68.4%	76.8%
Father alone	7.1%	17.1%
Number of children	4.3 children	3.7 children
one child	4.1%	15.9%
2 or 3 children	42.8%	37.8%
Mean age	79.2 years	80.2 years
Under 75	28.5%	19.4%
75–79	19.4%	25.6%
80–84	31.6%	29.3%
85 and over	20.4%	25.6%
State of health		
Good or very good	31.3%	36.6%
Average	40.6%	30.5%
Poor or indifferent	28.1%	32.9%
Daily help needed with		
Washing, handling	24.5%	36.6%
Shopping, meals, housework, transport	23.5%	30.5%
No help needed	52.0%	32.9%
Man's job		
Farming	45.8%	22.5%
Trade and crafts	8.3%	6.3%
Management	–	2.5%
Supervisory	8.3%	6.3%
White collar	8.3%	12.5%
Blue collar	29.2%	50.0%
Locality		
Urban, suburban	36.7%	59.8%
Rural	35.7%	25.6%
Isolated	27.6%	14.6%
Milieu		
Wealthy	27.6%	36.6%
Average	49.0%	47.6%
Poor	20.4%	7.3%

Source: CNAV 92 (parents)

Table 9.4 Characteristics of offspring according to type of home-sharing with parents

	NON-DECOHABITATION (n=98) i.e. permanent	RECOHABITATION (n=82) i.e. return to home-sharing
Sons	64.3%	25.6%
Daughters	35.7%	74.4%
Unmarried	70.4%	6.1%
Married	25.5%	62.2%
Divorced	1.0%	23.2%
Widowed	2.0%	8.5%
Working	67.4%	56.1%
Job-searching	7.1%	4.9%
Retired (or early retirement)	9.2%	9.8%
Otherwise not working	16.3%	29.3%
Farming	29.9%	11.0%
Trade and crafts	5.2%	7.3%
Management	–	3.7%
Supervisory	5.2%	6.1%
White collar	17.5%	30.5%
Blue collar	30.9%	20.7%
Unemployed	5.2%	15.8%
Only child	27.6%	37.8%
First-born	24.5%	26.1%
Last-born	40.4%	33.3%
Mean age	46.9 years	50.3 years
Under 35	14.3%	1.2%
35–44	17.4%	14.6%
45–49	16.3%	22.0%
50–54	29.6%	48.8%
55 and over	21.4%	13.4%
Mean number of children	0.7 children	2.3 children
No children	66.3%	6.1%
1 or 2 children	24.5%	57.3%
Educational level		
Primary	57.1%	50.0%
Vocational	30.6%	35.4%
Baccalauréat	9.2%	3.7%
Higher	2.0%	6.1%
Upwardly mobile	45.7%	71.6%

Source: CNAV 92 (parents)

are in the majority in both cases, there are many more couples in uninterrupted home-sharing (24.5 per cent as compared with 6.1 per cent). Those who worked on the land most commonly share a home permanently with one of their children: 45.8 per cent being in this category as compared with 22.5 per cent in the other; whereas the situation is reversed with industrial workers, 50 per cent of whom 'recohabit' after living on their own as against 29.2 per cent.

But the particularity of each situation is shown most clearly with the children's generation, the most striking difference residing in the pattern of co-residence by sons on the one hand and daughters on the other: sons continue to live with their parents in two cases out of three, while daughters 'recohabit' in three cases out of four. This pattern of distribution accounts for the fact that overall figures show as many sons as daughters 'cohabiting' with parents – slightly more in fact, and this is in line with our assumption that, overall, uninterrupted home-sharing, involving mainly sons as it does, is rather more common than a return to home-sharing.

Children who never leave home are for the most part those who remain single (70.4 per cent), and they number more sons than daughters. 'Recohabitation' is not a formula common to the child who remains single (6.1 per cent); it is practised mainly by those who are married (62.2 per cent) and also, significantly, by those who are divorced (23.2 per cent) or widowed (8.5 per cent).

Home-sharing fairly frequently involves three generations but in one out of two cases following a prolonged period of independent living – only in one out of five cases has it been uninterrupted.

In the case of the children cohabiting, social groups vary. Those who have always lived with parents are in the main blue collar workers in industry (30.9 per cent) or on the land (29.9 per cent), and to a lesser extent white collar workers (17.5 per cent). There are few in independent trades and virtually none at management level. Those who 'recohabit' tend to be more often white collar workers (30.5 per cent) and less often blue collar workers in industry (20.7 per cent; while the cohort numbers 24 per cent in this category); and a few (3.7 per cent) at management level.

Schooling is on average better in the case of those who 'recohabit'. Intergenerational social mobility, measured by a subjective indicator, is far more evident where a return to home-sharing follows prolonged independence than where it has been uninterrupted. This indicator tallies with comparisons between social and professional groups: 'recohabitation' is in evidence where the younger generation have been greater achievers than their parents. This – but only with this type of home-sharing – confirms our hypothesis of the spin-off resulting from social mobility (Attias-Donfut, 1993), shown here insofar as the cohabitation of different generations is a factor in raising the parental standard of living. Geneviève Canceill has already shown, across her analysis of revenue provided by women so cohabiting, the benefit that accrues essentially to women on their own. Their standard of living is raised by 17 per cent compared with their situation if they lived alone. And this is not so, either with elderly couples or with men on their own cohabiting with their children (Canceill, 1989). Uninterrupted home-sharing is further characterized by social immobility between generations.

The significance of social mobility in the distinction between these two forms of cohabitation raises the question of the child 'chosen' for cohabitation in preference to siblings. There, too, the situations are very different in spite of having some aspects in common. Those in this generation who do not cohabit number more couples, fewer unemployed or non-working and far fewer employed in agriculture than the children who participate in one or other form of cohabitation.

The difference lies mainly in the social positioning of the child 'chosen' in relation to siblings. An uninterrupted sojourn with parents clearly tends to indicate being disadvantaged, socially and professionally, in regard to schooling as well as by the subjective indicator of social mobility. But in the instance of 'recohabiting', the position with regard to siblings is one of advantageousness, particularly if the subjective indicator of social mobility is to be believed, but without the distinctions being very pronounced.

There remains a constant factor in these two forms of cohabitation insofar as the last born of the siblings more often than not lives with the parents either uninterruptedly or after a period of independence.

The determinants of these two forms of home-sharing are clearly quite distinct and relate to two important factors – the degree of health and autonomy enjoyed by the elderly parents and considerations of inheritance.

Cohabitation between the elderly and their now adult children is often thought of as a form of substitution by the children for the partial loss of autonomy suffered by their parents. Assessment of the need for assistance in regard to daily living effectively shows there to be a higher proportion of 'dependants' among those cohabiting than in this particular generation taken as a whole, but this is much more the case with latter-day than with uninterrupted home-sharing; the need for help in regard to everyday living counting respectively for 64.7 and 49.5 per cent. The question of the older generation's aptitude for independence has of course major bearing on a return to home-sharing, though naturally there are other considerations such as widowhood or, less frequently, marriage difficulties.

Uninterrupted home-sharing, which is more common in rural and independent occupations, is far more a feature of rural than of urban communities. More often it implies the handing down of a trade and of a lifestyle, also of an inheritance bequeathed as a form of privilege to the child who remains in the family home. This is an important feature and will be returned to later.

Home-sharing thus would appear to concentrate diverse and complex forms of exchange between the generations who live together and in whom are formed symbolic equivalences between possessions, culture, education and feeling. When the trajectories of successive generations are reconstituted, from their spatial separation to their eventual reunion, the long duration of reciprocity comes to light in a remarkable way.

Separation in the course of the children's youth, reunion when the parents are old

The generation of today's 50-year-olds left the parental home relatively early, on average, compared with the preceding and the following generations, and generally speaking is less inclined than its predecessors to live with ageing parents. Is there a connection between these two key events in the family life cycle? Analysis does point to a significant link here, in that children who leave the parental home later show a significantly higher frequency of 'recohabiting' than do those leaving earlier. A majority (54 per cent) of those, for instance, who are now home-sharing with their parents left home between the ages of 22 and 34, whereas, at the time, most of their generation were under the age of 22 when they left. Is it possible to deduce from this that a particular quality of parental relationship might be at the origin both of the prolonged time at home in their youth and the resumption of this shared life in their parents' old age? If this were to be true, it would mean the further verification of a special kind of relationship between parents and non-cohabiting children who left home later. To put this hypothesis to the test, relations between the 'pivotal' generation and their parents, differentiated in line with the age at which departure from home occurred before or after age 22, have been measured using an index of relational intensity that combines frequency of contact with leisure and holiday time spent together. Comparison between the results obtained by 'pivotal' individuals who left before age 22 and those who left after indicate a tendency for the latter to be significantly closer to their parents. This observation supports the hypothesis of there being a favoured relationship between the younger generation who postpone leaving home and their parents, and one such as to favour the possibility of their living together again later on. The two periods of life spent in common respond to one another, and correspond to forms of exchange, immediate and deferred, which in turn establish a degree of reciprocity between generations.

By staying on at home, young people have the benefit of receiving support during their studies while preparing to earn their own living and seeking to improve their prospects. This is particularly so with girls of the 'pivotal' generation who happen also to be the ones who return to home-sharing most readily. Having contracted a debt towards their parents, they are more likely than others to be ready to provide support for them in old age, cohabitation here representing both affection and practical support to the extent that they are dependent or needy.

Such a model of mutual help as life takes its course certainly needs to reckon with the special emotive ties that may incline one child rather than another towards this kind of supportive relationship with parents. Research conducted by Tamara Hareven and Kathleen Adams among former textile workers who had emigrated to the United States at the turn of the century and among their children has shown that the help given to very elderly parents largely depends on the relationship that has been established through their lives from childhood on. The child who is to become 'parent-minder' is frequently selected in advance by parents themselves, who want to be sure of companionship when they are old. The child who is chosen, often a girl and the last-born, generally dedicates herself to this role through life (Hareven and Adams, 1994).

The preference shown for the last-born as it appears statistically in both types of cohabitation seems to have less to do with cultural traditions, which are fairly diverse in this context and point normally to the first-born, than to psychological mechanisms. Could there be a tendency among parents to maintain the last-born child in a state of dependence through fear of the nest becoming empty? In which case the elder ones would find it easier to acquire their independence, since the younger are there to take over when the parents need them.

And what happens when a life lived in common continues unbroken? Here the customary give-and-take leads on more obviously to the question of the succession.

Transmission of inheritance wealth

The transmission of inheritance wealth has undergone significant development in more recent times. Its post-war growth is reflected in increased resources under the dual influence of government assistance and incentives and of inflation. Pensions have become generalized and more generous, property and savings have accumulated in value. So legacies and gifts have grown, to the extent that now in France nearly two out of three households are or will be beneficiaries. Arrondel and Laferrère (1992) have shown that parity of inheritance has become the norm and that in the vast majority of instances division between siblings does not appear to be to the advantage or detriment of one or another, a function neither of their respective attributes nor especially of their achievements. Yet this norm of equal apportionment should be qualified, because, as the authors show, it is flexible to the extent that more often than not it is applied by the making of gifts which renders the possibility of what each child will get somewhat arbitrary. Gifts are more common among those in farming and the self-employed than among wage-earners. According to tax sources, they count for about a third of legacies (Laferrère, 1991), which is probably an underestimate since they are frequently undeclared.

The 'pivotal' generation, with many of their parents still living – in 34 per cent of cases both parents, and in the case of those home-sharing with children 21 per cent – so far has not inherited greatly. And in most cases the death of one spouse has merely meant that the surviving one has retained possession (or at least enjoyment) of the assets or that there was nothing to pass on (26.8 per cent of cases). Frequently an earlier gift between spouses provides security to the surviving spouse (this practice is attested by 38 per cent of widows or widowers and 56 per cent of elderly couples). In all, in only 16 per cent of cases was the death of a spouse followed by an actual succession. Transmission by way of gift is thus much more frequent in these families, practised by 21 per cent of all parents, chiefly on behalf of the children (95 per cent) but of grandchildren too sometimes (8.3 per cent).

Is there a connection between the act of giving and home-sharing? It all depends on what form home-sharing takes. With 'recohabitation', gifts are much more rare (16 per cent), more common in the case of uninterrupted home-sharing (27 per cent). The type of goods transferred is different too, lifetime home-sharing being characterized more by transmission that has to do with land and assets that have a professional use. This also holds *mutatis mutandis* among those who are self-employed. The most frequent motives for such gifts are the wish to 'avoid the share-out' (45 per cent of those not cohabiting, 61.5 per cent of those who 'recohabit' and 53.8 per cent of permanent cohabitors) and to avoid tax (respectively 16.6 per cent, 38.5 per cent and 15.4 per cent). A smooth transition for the business is a reason mainly given by those who have lived together permanently (27 per cent), as is the intention to retire (11.5 per cent). Other motives that crop up among all those making gifts – a legacy (6.4 per cent), coming into money (5.2 per cent), a child's marriage or similar celebration (4.4 per cent) or providing help where needed (13.6 per cent) – are of no greater frequency in families that cohabit than in others.

Transmission may be linked to the form cohabitation takes but it has still more to do with being given a home either by parents or by children and paradoxically this does not tie up with one type of cohabitation rather than another. When asked: 'Have you taken your child into your home?' or 'Has he(she) given you a home?', more than 60 per cent of parents say they are looked after by their children, who in 54 per cent of cases have never in fact lived away from home. This apparent contradiction is explained simply enough by the fact that 43 per cent of the younger generation having always lived at home. They have in fact received the same home where they now look after their parents as a gift from them. With those who 'recohabit' the figure is 20 per cent.

Transfers of property in fact hide the significant part played by the older generation in the forms of cohabitation. With the transfer of inheritance that follows on from a gift or with the death of one of the parents, the children become owners or co-owners of the property of the parents with the surviving parent. It is not uncommon to find that the child who has always lived at home takes possession of the family house, with either the parent having or not having enjoyment of its use. This being so, the notion of who is providing a home for whom becomes inverted following such a transfer of inheritance, without there being any noticeable change in the conditions of existence.

The 'cohabiting' child thus seems to be advantaged in the matter of succession over his or her siblings. Out of all parents with more than one child who have made gifts, only 11 per cent declared they had divided these unequally, but the figure rises to 19 per cent with those who have always lived with one child. Unequal division is further more common among the self-employed, tradespeople mainly, and relatively less common in farming. With those employed in farming, varying regional traditions need to be taken into account and the basis of the sample was too restricted for this to be done. Druhle and Clément in their study of elderly people in the rural south-west mention the three chief methods of transmission practised in farming in France as defined by Pierre Lamaison (1988): effective division (mainly in the north and west); property not divided but held jointly (more common in the Aube and the Côte-d'Or); and unequal division on the basis of a quarter of the value of the assets going to the child taking over the enterprise (prevalent in much of the Midi) (Druhle and Clément, 1992, p.95). The diversity in transfer customs in the world of farming in France, and declining traditions in France, may explain the fact that the sample only contains instances of unequal settlement in other social categories.

It remains the case that parents who cohabit with their children have to a considerable extent pre-empted inheritance in making gifts which allow them to amend the principle that the estate should be divided equally; and this seems to be confirmed by the dearth of assets to be passed on at the death of the spouse, as declared by more than 45 per cent of widowers who have been given a home by a child and fewer than 20 per cent of those with whom a child is living. Where in cases of 'recohabitation' a settlement is made by parents in favour of a child (or children), as often as not it occurs at the time that their lives begin to be shared again. The practice which suggests a correlation between such a settlement and cohabitation remains, it has to be stressed, exceptional where there is 'recohabitation'. In any case, it would appear that the value of property passed across is often limited, reflecting the means of the elderly who live with their children and, in fact, the vast majority of inheritances in France whose disparity has been time and again pointed out. Fewer than 10 per cent of successions account for half the inheritance transferred.

Households consisting of elderly people and their children, as has been said earlier, are far more frequent in regions where in the past extended domestic groups were common and there was a continuity in sharing. It might be thought that the model would persist there, but this is hardly confirmed by the findings in the survey, though its relatively narrow base must be allowed for. Nevertheless, in line with official figures, these findings show cohabitation to be more developed in the south-west and north-east than elsewhere in France.

Even though households characterized by uninterrupted sharing may recall extended family patterns, there is clear divergence. Martine Segalen has warned against such 'comparisons out of context' and sees the continuance of complex households as a 'sign of dysfunction', of 'social and economic crisis', enforced home-sharing due to poverty (Segalen, 1993, p.37). In general, the picture offered by such types of

Table 9.5 Geographical distribution of types of home-sharing

	Number	Overall rate of home-sharing (%)	Permanent home-sharing (%)	Return to home-sharing (%)	Total (%)
South-west	(192)	26.6	52.9	47.1	100
North-east	(159)	23.9	56.3	43.8	100
Other	(866)	12.4	54.6	45.4	100
Total	(1217)	16.1	54.4	45.6	100

sharing seems to confirm this.

The links between family traditions, types of transmission and types of cohabitation are in fact extremely complex. Drulhe and Clément have shown that in the rural south-west although unequal division at the time of succession is still an important feature in uninterrupted home-sharing between generations, it is often counterbalanced by other economic and social factors – the value of property handed down, and the nature of the relationship with children or with their spouses. More importantly, young women tend to reject a cohabitation model that imposes a heavy burden or submissiveness on them. Such an attitude, which strikes as it does at the foundations of the model and which has been observed within the region by the authors, is very probably generalized since women, whether daughters or daughters-in-law, are to a greater extent absent from households practising this type of cohabitation, where normally only an unmarried son remains (cf. Annex II). The same study shows that in the country there is no easy correlation between size of inheritance and type of home-sharing. When families prosper, they adopt a different lifestyle, live closer to one another and envisage a return to sharing should the parents become dependent. When the property is unprofitable, the likely heir has little incentive to acquire possession. A mediocre inheritance 'can only be given as a condition of cohabitation in cases where the likely heir can see no other source of means' (Druhle and Clément, 1992, p.106). In cases of necessity, where the precariousness of living dictates cohabitation – and this is often the case when it is uninterrupted, home-sharing is fraught with tension and conflict and bitterness, and this is clearly borne out by the evidence of this study.

Other studies have produced evidence of the cross-effect of the overall economic context and relationships in the choice of this or that mode of life in rural society. Glen Elder has made a study of such transmission across three generations that cover a large part of the present century and its major economic crises. He has shown that the son's taking over of the father's enterprise (which does not necessarily imply cohabitation) depends both on the nature of their relationship and on the economic context, the one being all the more decisive when the other is unfavourable (Elder *et al.*, 1994).

Conclusion

The major transformation brought about in the 1960s did away with the traditional – now obsolete – model of intergenerational relations: the split between the younger generation and their parents became an accepted fact and led on to the creation of a new type of relationship with the emerging generation. By loosening the constraints it required of its members, the family has provided space for these several members to renegotiate and more freely define their respective positions and commitments (Finch, 1989), while normative or formal models have become rarer or less meaningful in new family structures. Hierarchical relations have made way for a recognition of greater autonomy within and between generations and an emotive interdependence which fulfils a bonding function (Hagestad, 1995). Family patterns and the experience of home-sharing in the lives of successive generations at the present time bear the mark of this change. The family must withstand and assimilate the mass of economic, social and emotive cross-currents that assail it and find expression in different forms of cohabitation which, despite a general preference for living independently but close, remains widespread. Hence cohabitation figures as a 'compromise' in which interdependence is the controlling factor; but it is revelatory too of the continuity of relations and the powerful and lifelong cohesion that develops between generations. Certainly it only represents one aspect of family life: if it brings out the strength and permanence of ties, it draws a veil over the failures and the links that sever as well as strengthen and that also follow from an easing of constraints.

Nevertheless the foregoing enquiry gives ground for thinking that the various forms of interrelationship that have come to light are likely to endure. Indeed, on the basis of the trends displayed by the three generations under observation, one might venture a few comments.

The more apparent proximity of the 'pivotal' generation to their children (as compared with that to their parents) may well bring about a reversal in what seems to be the current attitude to the situation of the older members of the family, ties here being reinforced. In the years ahead, when those who are now aged 50 or so come to face the trials of old age, their children will be middle-aged, perhaps thinking of retirement (if the present tendency towards premature retirement subsists). Then it is highly possible, given all that they have received from their parents and their own greater availability, that they will be likely to be there as a source of support if and when needed, to 'recohabit' with them too.

And if one considers the same two generations in the light of the observation which shows that those who leave home late are more likely to return to home-sharing with their parents, when widowed or handicapped, one is entitled to conclude that the longer time spent by young people at home nowadays may lead to an increase in cohabiting in the future. The mechanism of indebtedness has taken on added significance in that the considerable help many young people receive from their parents will probably continue for longer in life, given both the problems of the labour market and the relatively privileged situation – in terms of income and assets – enjoyed by the older generation. And that same generation may well find their life expectancy extended and thus their self-dependence, so postponing the moment when 'recohabitation' becomes a pressing need.

The continuity of a life lived in common, whether due to economic uncertainty or to the demands of a family enterprise which is exploited and handed down as a collaborative effort, is conditioned by the overall economic context and by the way the children resolve the problem of how and where they live, all of which cannot be foreseen. It may be that an increase in poverty will bring about new forms of uninterrupted home-sharing in urban as well as in rural areas. Besides, the outlook for cohabiting children, particularly single ones, after the death of their parents, could present a problem which it may not be possible for depleted family structures to tackle and may require governmental action.

Such thoughts on possible changes in the modes of cross-generational home-sharing should, however, be qualified by the prospect of new technologies applied to housing and of architectural conceptions in the future that may be able to resolve problems of the need to be both close and cosy, and yet to be independent.

Notes

1. The survey, undertaken in 1992–3 by the CNAV in conjunction with INSEE, was conducted by C. Attias-Donfut together with S. Renaut and A. Rozenkier. A random sample of 1,958 respondents, aged between 49 and 53 years, and with at least one parent still living and one grown-up child, were interviewed at home by questionnaire. This initial survey led to the identification and further interviewing of parents (1217) and children (of whom 1493 responded). The total sample comprises 4668, including close on 1000 triads. Initial results were presented in C. Attias-Donfut (1995b).
2. The rate is lower than government figures show on account of the choice made in the sample to give precedence to families where one child at least had left home.

10

FASHIONING A NEW FAMILY TIE: STEP-PARENTS AND STEP-GRANDPARENTS

Didier Le Gall and Claude Martin

The increase in divorce to a point where at the end of the 1980s there were about 30 divorces per 100 marriages is probably, along with the increase in births outside marriage, one of the more obvious signs of the profound changes that have occurred in the institution of the family in France. Fertile couples who break up is the major cause of single parenthood (the term first appears in France in the mid-1970s), where one or other parent – most often the mother – brings up a child or children alone (Le Gall and Martin, 1987). And indeed in roughly two-thirds of cases this is brought about by break-up in the marriage or partnership, whereas in the past it was generally the consequence of being widowed. In 1991 INSEE records 1,229,000 single-parent families, counting for 13.5 per cent of families with offspring under 25. This figure has grown significantly since the start of the 1970s and now represents a good 15 per cent of families with children.[1]

If, over the last 20 years, this situation has become relatively widespread so to some extent lessening the stigma that attached to lone mothers before the end of the 1960s, it continues to pose a number of problems – in particular, financial – to government insofar as mothers so placed are economically vulnerable. In France a quarter of these households live below the threshold of poverty (Lefaucheur and Martin, 1993; Martin, 1997).[2]

Such separation, which was virtually always thought of as incurring a 'social risk', such as the lack of resources and the children being prone to behavioural problems, is now seen as a potential threat to the family tie itself. Will the parents continue to maintain the contact needed to ensure the children's subsistance and schooling? Will the family do all it can to support parents who are separated? How and when can the state take upon itself personal commitments?

Divorce now is compounded by the constant rise in dissension between couples who cohabit and whose partnerships demographers point to as being even more at risk than married ones. Hence separation and divorce result more and more frequently in so-called reconstituted families.[3] What is the exact nature of this family tie? To what extent can step-parents take over the role of the parents who have abdicated? What function have they otherwise? Can they or should they become involved in schooling, in the process of socialization and in providing material support? What kind of tie develops between them and their stepchildren? Or between the children and their step-grandparents?

Such families may in common with single-parent families be branded with the vestiges of 'second marriage hatred' (Lefaucheur, 1993), but one is nonetheless struck by their image, as conveyed in particular by the media where they are presented in a far more sympathetic and reassuring light compared with one-parent families: reconstituted families are a new type of large family, genuine small tribes in which adults and children invent a new form of family democracy, establish new norms and a new type of family relationship founded not on ties of blood but on the fact of living together. How is this supposedly innovative pattern of behaviour, which is more or less totally disregarded in law, likely to develop (Meulders-Klein and Théry, 1993)?

Since 1987 – and still more markedly since 1993 – French civil law has been moving towards a new prescriptive model of parental ties being indissoluble. 'Once a parent always a parent' is the notion that best sums up this model (Théry, 1993). But what does this imply in practice? How far are family bonds weakened by dissension? Are they reconstituted subsequently? What follows is an attempt to provide an interim reply to questions such as these on the basis of a number of surveys carried out in France early in the 1990s.

Firstly, we shall consider in what ways and to what extent the process of reconstitution reshapes the bond of family; and then turn to the impact of partnership break-up on relationships within the inner family. This will involve rehearsing a series of factors which affect the course of events following a break-up. Further, we shall try to discover what forms of action are adopted by near relations when break-up occurs and how their impact affects the social aptitudes of those it most directly concerns.

The step-parent in the context of everyday

Despite the investment it is only now beginning to represent in France, family reconstitution still eludes our everyday mental categories (Théry, 1991). The mere fact of separation presents one with a bifocal family situation which becomes somewhat complex when one ex-partner (or both) form a new couple (remarried or living together); in which case, there is the addition of one new participant (or two) whose precise role and status it is not easy to determine, our form of society being focused entirely on the first family. What reorganization of family ties does such reconstitution induce, and what sort of ties develop between the members of these complex families? These are the questions we propose to tackle.

With these new unions a child from the first marriage comes to have one step-parent, if not two; but the two need to be distinguished in terms of the 'place' they occupy for the child of the first marriage. Use of the same term suggests an identical situation, this is not, however, quite true. With the partner of the parent having custody[4] there are daily encounters; with that of the parent not having custody they are intermittent. Hence depending on there being a 'step-parent in the context of everyday' or an 'intermittent step-parent' (Le Gall, 1996), the terms of the relationship vary considerably. For the reason that divorce settlements tend more often to leave children in their mother's care, there is the likelihood of a stepfather 'for everyday' at the children's main home and a stepmother 'on an intermittent basis' when they visit their other home. But since fathers not having custody tend to set up with a new partner more often than do mothers having custody, children of the first marriage more often have a stepmother 'on an intermittent basis' than a stepfather 'for everyday'.

Being unable to perceive this social relationship in all its complexity yet nonetheless concerned to investigate this 'new family figure', we shall here give special emphasis to step-parenthood in the context of everyday. And in the interests of simplicity, we shall limit the field to 'everyday' stepfathers, who are statistically in the majority. How then, knowing that stepfathers are without the benefit of either legal status or of any other form of institutional support (Cherlin, 1978), is their social role mapped out?

If a stepfather's situation is doubtless different from a father's, it is nevertheless possible to speak of it as a social construction. But the process is only really set in motion when a mother having custody envisages setting up with a partner, with or without a child (and he, the partner, having or not having custody). Therefore the stepfather's role can be apprehended in terms of the regulation that follows from the divorce and informs the whole process of family reconstitution and which, in our opinion, differentiates reconstituted families more significantly than their own structural diversity (Le Gall and Martin, 1991; Le Gall, 1993). On the basis of the regulation in the wake of divorce which serves to fashion the way in which step-parenthood is established, we propose to distinguish different models of step-parenthood and to compare them with other patterns of relationship (parenthood and friendship).

Family reconstitution and types of regulation

We have lately made a study devoted to the process of family reconstruction, that is to say how the transformation from break-up to the reconstitution of family is realized (Le Gall and Martin, 1993). To this end we carried out two series of interviews, at an eighteen months interval, of the parent with custody, the new partner, the former partner and, where possible, the children of the first marriage, all from different social backgrounds. Thus we were provided with a multiple cross-reflecting discourse, the participants in each constituent family giving, from their own stance and with their own trajectory in mind, their point of view and their perception of the way in which the family had achieved a form of reconstitution.

Analysis of the material suggests there being a marked cleavage resulting from three closely-linked factors – social background, representation of the family and the way the divorce settlement affected the arrangement of relationships. In line with the distinction proposed by Théry (1993), as it is apparent in the post-divorce situation, between the need for replacement and the need for continuity, we sought to establish two opposing points in a continuum of attitudes on the part of those we were interviewing. In regard to replacement, the participants gave special value to the reconstitution of a family as a means of restabilization, one family 'erasing' the other. In regard to continuity, primacy was accorded to the parental bond over the conjugal bond via a reorganization of family in new and complex forms. Two ideal models can be contrasted.

Among the more disadvantaged, the following tendencies can be observed: divorce motivated by conflict, with culpability – adultery, alcoholism, violence or desertion – informing the proceedings; a sequel to divorce during which parental relationships remain characterized by conflict or else fade gradually and result in an almost complete end to relations between parent with and parent without custody, then between children and parent not having custody; pressure for replacement clearly dominant, accounting for the fact that parents accorded custody are often motivated to 'have another try' almost immediately. Clearly what is involved here is the concern to avoid isolation, the compulsion to give renewed economic stability to the home and the desire to adhere to what is seen as 'normality'; a determination to translate new encounters into remarriage, if they seem to offer a chance, in the knowledge that there too the economic argument plays a role, either in slowing down the process (on no account losing out on a single parent's allowance, for instance) or in speeding it up. This observed pattern may need some modification but in general terms it represents the stance here adopted towards marriage. It also represents a relatively traditional concept of family, with a fairly marked division in sexual roles, where remarrying provides a guarantee of the officiality and the legitimacy of the union and where family cannot be conceived of without children, whether they are one's own or cared for by one.

The attitude towards remarrying is also transparent. Partners are irresistibly drawn to marriage as an institution, earlier failure being construed as the consequence of an ill-chosen match. If it has not 'worked out', it is because one simply chose the wrong partner. However, remarrying can be contemplated on the grounds of its being the 'normal form' of family life. Hence, the new partner is often depicted as being the converse of the previous one. Besides, the couple think of themselves as forming a family and the presence of children immediately gives substance to this. Couple and family are all one. A reconstituted family is primarily one that needs to approximate to the norm of the traditional nuclear family. The press for a new partnership accentuates the rationale of replacement already adopted and going to law – that is, hetero-regulation – is the only legitimate course left open.

Among the more fortunate and better educated, the overall pattern is entirely different. There, too, enduring features are discernible: breakups apparently involve less violence; for example, they are the product of incompatibility, of overmuch latitude on one side or the other. Partners try to work out together, if possible in an amicable way, the terms of their separation without immediately resorting to law. For the most part they are able themselves to devise a mechanism for negotiation and the law comes in at a later stage, often merely to endorse agreements reached. Divorce is better handled, more often than not by mutual consent. Parents not having custody as a rule assume parental responsibility and see to it that their role is not negated by the parent with custody forming a new partnership. The children move about fairly easily between families. Clearly the will is there to maintain a basis of communication in spite of glitches. Marrying again is seen not as an absolute necessity – sometimes merely as a convenience. Living as a couple and living as a family are not assimilated, and the future can be contemplated otherwise than in a traditional form.

Within this social background, new partnerships form and are gradually adapted to a new family situation, but without imposing a mould. The split is not irreversible. It is more a case of a long, negotiated, process involving both situation and relationships. What's past is past and one cannot but accept the legacy of the past in agreeing to reasonable adjustments, while avoiding the risk of a second failed partnership. Those who have custody are not of the view that the cause of breakdown is entirely due to the other partner. The general feeling is that living as a couple is both complex and difficult and that a rift is always possible.

Each partner in the initial relationship maintains a role that divorce may amend but cannot suppress. In short, the family models are entirely unalike. It is no longer a case of a step-family trying to adopt the shape of a traditional 'nuclear family', but a model where man and woman endeavour to try out a more equitable distribution of their respective roles and where each secures the possibility – in particular, economic – of promoting his or her own options before those of the family unit. The legal vacuum is less keenly felt, hence what is asked of the law has less significance. Participants go to law in order to have their negotiated arrangements ratified or a point of conflict settled. Such attitudes mesh perfectly with the present movement away from institutionalization where de facto situations are recognized for what they are, participants defining the terms of their relationship in accord as they go along and prepared to have recourse to solutions of which the law knows nothing. The rationale here is one of continuity and self-regulation.

Such are the two major tendencies that emerge from an analysis of the material we have. They reinforce the notion that reconstituted families are above all differentiated by the type of regulation they adopt. Replacement and hetero-regulation (recourse to law) as against continuity and self-regulation. Certainly there are variations within these two extremes and this outline interpretation has to be understood dynamically: the odd disagreement, for instance, may produce a shift in relationships which had been established more with a view to continuity.

At all events, the more family representations – in the main determined by cultural factors and overall by social background – present the dominant model as ultimate reference, the less likely are continuity and self-regulation to stand out, and conversely. To put it another way, the less the traditional image of family asserts itself as a constraining norm, the more will the participants be disposed to adapt to the situation by developing innovative models of behaviour so as to reconcile 'legacy' and plans for the future. In one case, family reconstitution functions through break-up, in the other it comes about by way of a degree of continuity. Thus it seems somewhat rash to suggest that reconstituted families compose a type of family on the basis of their incomplete institutionalization. The lack of established support truly seems to be experienced in different ways at the two extremes of the social scale.

Types of step-parental role in an everyday context

The step-parental role cannot be adopted in an identical way in accordance with the form of regulation that operates in the process of family reconstitution, bearing in mind that other variables come into play, variables which are harder to diagnose since they are more indefinite or peculiar to the new family situation. One thinks of passing time, the attitude of the parent without custody (sometimes that of the parent with custody too), the age of the stepchildren at first encounter, nature of relationship between stepchildren from both sides (where applicable), determining factor of age differences, and so on. In the near impossibility of containing all such factors it would seem more appropriate to cite step-parental models that suggest themselves as being conspicuous.

Two significant and relatively contrary models may be distinguished. The first, rejecting the specificity of the new family situation, is based on the parental role; the second, recognizing such specificity, invents itself, so to speak, without borrowing from pre-existing roles.

The role of replacement or the attraction of the 'space left vacant'. Among the more deprived, where a rationale of replacement holds, the conflictual nature of the break-up often makes it impossible for even purely functional relations to be established between ex-partners. With the consummation of the break-up, the parental couple 'disappears' along with the conjugal couple. At best, the father not having custody settles alimony payments more or less with regularity and perhaps maintains contact with his children. At all events, though it cannot be said that the place is 'vacant', the stepfather enjoys a degree of room for manoeuvre which predisposes him to take on a replacement role. Given the cogency of the dominant model, the division of roles in the reconstituted family is therefore organized in a traditional form: a 'family' is reconstituted. This type of arrangement further brooks little discussion inasmuch as the stepfather provides for the family and the children are likely to be still young.

Hence the domain is more or less that of parent and the replacement role is adopted and legitimized the more easily because the mother awarded custody and her children are in league against the defaulting father. This being so, any finesse in working towards or negotiating an undefined role that meets the particular situation is out of the question. In a culturally deprived environment the stepfather as often as not moves into the place left vacant. Having broken with the previous parental system, the 'new family' adopts the image of 'original family'.

A role to be constructed or the search for a new behavioural model. Where there has been the benefit of more education, the new family set-up frequently reproduces the rationale of continuity prevailing. The 'non-custodial' father, far from being a 'non-parent', assumes his role fully. It is not then a matter of substituting one family for another. The family continues to exist in spite of separation and the stepfather becomes gradually integrated and makes his own mark. It is a matter of time, but frequently he comes gradually to realize, as do the others, that he has a crucial part to play in the relations between the mother with custody, the father without, and children. In this view, clearly it makes no sense to mirror and reproduce a pre-existing role – one must construct a new one. There is no place for the taking, only that of the mother's new partner, with the proviso that the children do not raise objections. The least indiscretion may lead to heated argument. The protection of the children is paramount.

Hence it is out of the question to adopt a role that has close similarities with the father's; an altogether new role must be found, one that is in keeping with the situation and its antecedence. And the stepfather finds he must innovate, but in a way that will suggest itself the more easily in that characteristic conditions are forthcoming – the children are still relatively young, the mother having custody helps her new partner to assume his place, the father not awarded custody does not systematically obstruct but rather bends all his efforts to dialogue.

To sum up, at the risk of some oversimplification, the absence of a model ready to hand means that at each extreme of the social scale there is an opposing model for the role of stepfather. On the one hand, denial of the specificity of the new family situation produces a step-father with a role not dissimilar to the one incarnated by the ex-partner; on the other, recognition of such specificity leads to a search for new models of behaviour. Nevertheless, it should be noted that, whatever the stepfatherly model, the arrival of a new child appears to facilitate the integration of stepfathers in the context of everyday. It is as if parenthood (being parents 'together') led directly to promoting step-parenthood.

Step-parenthood between godfather and friend?

With reconstituted families, a new figure emerges in the family – the step-parent, who will either take on a replacement role or make up a role to suit the occasion. Contrary to the circumstance of widowhood, step-parental families constituted following separation do create a new set-up. There is no 'place for the taking', rather a 'place for the making'. This requires us to re-examine the nature of parenthood and family life in the light of this additional social role.

Unlike other social bonds, those between parents and children appear as 'given'. They are intense and continuous, however they are reconstituted with advancing years, more particularly when children themselves become parents. They have an unconditional element, they seem irrevocable; and in this they differ from bonds of neighbourliness. Even so, proximity often results in bonds of lasting friendship. But friendship itself, which grows out of trust, involvement and sharing and which sanctions confidentiality, differs from parental relationship by dint of its elective character, even if, as Aubert notes: 'Ideally friendship equates with parental relationship (one that by nature cannot be undone)' (1992, p.231).

How can the bonds of step-parenthood be 'juxtaposed' with those of parenthood and come gradually to take on an aura of family bond? Is it not likely as the ties of step-parenthood develop that they will cause a change in the way we represent parental ties and so, as an indirect consequence, our notion of family? In a certain number of cases – and especially where a stepfather has been with his partner's children from the time they were very young, without trying to replace the biological father – it might be said that step-parenthood in its adjacence to parenthood takes on the aspect of a friendly godfather precisely because it assumes a particular form of election (absence of choice coupled with adult/child or adult/adolescent relationship) which needs to be compatible with an educational – socializing, protecting – mission, yet without competing with or supplanting the functions that here devolve on parenthood (Le Gall, 1993). Perhaps one might then go on to relate the role to other forms of multiparenting, whether as described in other societies (Lallemand, 1993) or in social forms that have acquired new value with the development of biomedicine and adoption.

Development of family and intergenerational bonds following break-up

Family separations, which are often reduced to their conjugal aspect, can shatter the wider reaches of family and intergenerational ties. So it requires more than to trace relations between the couple who have separated, it is pertinent to consider the knock-on effect among kin. Conceivably, when one partner disappears, a large part of the sociability network could follow (grandparents, siblings, friends, the wider area of kin) along with all the services and support they provide.[5]

One should, however, first make it clear that, concerning all social categories as it does, family separation produces widely contrasting effects in relational as well as in economic terms. It is no less mistaken to equate lone parentship with poverty than to deny impoverishment as the outcome of break-up. The economic insecurity of many households which provided material for the survey is undeniable.[6] The effect of separation may not be to make every lone-parent in the family more economically vulnerable, but it certainly makes the situation more difficult for those who were already vulnerable. This is particularly the case with mothers who had not gone out to work. But for women with jobs and qualifications the economic impact is slight. Track differences hence are considerable in terms of two primary factors – social background and level of employment.

Separation or divorce does not necessarily imply an irrevocable end to the relation between father and mother. In two-thirds of cases the survey shows that they maintain ties following their break-up, most of the time these ties being restricted to decisions concerning the children. Even so, that split parenthood reinforces inequalities, since the very ones that most need the active support of their ex-partner are the most deprived. Hence, for instance, if overall six out of ten parents having custody are in receipt of alimony, the proportion varies sharply

according to social background: those who have studied to baccalauréat level or beyond obtain alimony in twice as many cases (70 per cent)
as those with no such qualifications (35 per cent).

The break-up has reverberations also on relations between children
and the parent without custody (in most cases the father). Fewer than
30 per cent of these exercise their visiting rights regularly, and one out
of three even breaks off all contact with the children, with one out of
four (27 per cent) meeting them only occasionally (less than once a
month, though here there may be questions of distance involved). This
tends to confirm the notion of there being a significant lack of commitment on the part of fathers following break-up. But then this too varies
with social background. The proportion of those who never see their
children reaches nearly 50 per cent among those with a poor education
but is no more than 13 per cent among those who have reached
baccalauréat level. However, in approximately a quarter of cases, and
whatever the educational attainment, the parent without custody
shares every second weekend and half the holidays with the children
(as generally stipulated by legally established right of access).

Following separation or divorce, the parents awarded custody are
most often the ones left without a partner (Claude Martin, 1994).
Partnership mobility is slight – 10 per cent family reconstitution (cohabitation or remarriage) for the first survey, 15 per cent for the second. If
a slight timelag is needed between break-up and a new partnership, too
long a gap compromises the possibility of forming a new relationship.
In this respect, the first few years are crucial (Festy, 1991). Among
parents who have custody, it would appear that fathers are rather more
likely to form new partnerships than mothers. Living without a partner
has, of course, much to do with age. The second survey revealed that
nearly half the parents awarded custody who were under 30 had
reconstituted a family as against only 5 per cent of those over 45. Social
background also has its part to play in that the likelihood of remaining
single increases in inverse ratio to educational achievement. Being
possessed of youth and qualifications are plus factors when it comes to
meeting people, and that also applies when one is already a parent.[7]

It is clear when one puts these elements together that vulnerability in
terms of relationships compounds economic insecurity. Thus, those
who are most likely to break off entirely from their ex-partner after a
marriage bust-up are also the least likely to be able to reconstitute a
family, so sometimes facing emotional and sexual isolation. Even so, the
'lone parent' as portrayed by social services occurs in no more than a
minority of cases studied.

*Family and intergenerational ties as a support network –
differing degrees*

Economic conditions and partnership tracks become more unequal
when one looks at material and moral support on the part of close
relatives after break-up has occurred. If the larger family almost invariably ensures some kind of minimal 'close watch', in the sense of being
the vehicle for the interchange of services, these seem to get few and far
between with less fortunate families. Networks of sociability and support depend very much on the social group one is part of. In
wage-earning classes, networks are centred chiefly on family and are
maintained by constant visiting. Among middle classes and the more
highly qualified, the circle of friends becomes more important, though
that is not to say that the family does not play a support role.

Surveys conducted in the 1970s by Catherine Gokalp (1978) and by
Louis Roussel and Odile Bourguignon (1976) on the 'network of family'
brought out the extent to which adults remained close to their older
relatives, whether in terms of where they chose to live or how often
they saw each other. Our findings point the same way. Gokalp reckoned that about 56 per cent of those who no longer lived at home lived
close by or not more than 12 miles or so away, fewer than 30 per cent
living further than 65 miles away. And our survey shows 55 per cent of
parents having custody as living within 15 miles of their parents and
only 20 per cent more than 65 miles away. Such closeness again
depends a lot on social background.[8] Contact with parents is very
frequent: more than 60 per cent of those who provided data saw their
parents at least once a fortnight, this being very much a function of their
living close by. But daily physical contact is more common among those
whose educational achievement is low.[9] On the other hand, marriage
break-up distances one set of near relatives. Those of the parent without
custody (generally the grandparents on the father's side) are far less
often with their grandchildren than are those of the parent with custody
(generally the maternal grandparents).

Even though three-quarters of the parents with custody who came
into our survey no longer have grandparents alive – so there is an
inevitable shrinkage in base numbers – a fairly clear pattern is discernible: contact with these great-grandparents diminishes in proportion to
the level of educational attainment;[10] and this general tendency is true
also for siblings. More than half the number of parents with custody, but
without qualifications, meet one or other of their brothers and sisters at
least once a fortnight, as against 29 per cent of those with a baccalauréat

at least. Lower down in the social scale, either contacts are very frequent or else relations have been broken off for one reason or another, seldom, however, because the distance between homes is too great.

Family support, provided or called on, may vary with the degree of disapproval shown when the break-up occurred. In the main, survey findings bear out that relatives are understanding and helpful (45 per cent of cases). A little over a quarter tended to show a certain detachment, or concern not to interfere in the private affairs of their children. Those who recognize the new situation without becoming in any way involved count for 17 per cent; and those who denounce and refuse to accept the break-up, 12 per cent. Again these attitudes alter according to social background. For instance, disapproval – though registered by only a minority – tends to be rather more frequent in regard to the better-qualified parents with custody. Does this imply that family separation is less readily accepted by the better educated who are generally thought of as being more progressive and broad-minded? On the contrary, the more highly educated parents having custody are generally more successful in getting parental support after marriage break-up; unconcern is a more common attitude among the less well educated. The attitude adopted by siblings differs little from that of parents. Brothers and sisters are generally helpful, materially as well as morally (in 40 per cent of cases), whatever the background concerned. Thereafter come cases of relative or tactful unconcern (35 per cent).[11]

For the purpose of eliciting help, an approach is generally made to parents (six instances out of ten), less often to siblings (three out of ten). Further, any material help from parents is more or less on a permanent basis; with siblings it is likely to be sporadic. But 'rallying round' of this sort following separation varies very much with social background, almost certainly because it is a question of material resources available: 45 per cent of low-achieving parents with custody reckon to have received no help from parents; the figure falls to 16 per cent for those with baccalauréat at least.[12] Help of this sort relates mainly to children (this is specified by 30 per cent of parents with custody). Then there is help with daily living and financial help (17 per cent in each case) – financial help is necessarily more likely to be forthcoming where attainment is greater. Help with lodging (5 per cent) or employment (1 per cent) is much rarer.

Parents who have custody but no partner are proportionately the most numerous among those left with little support from their parents. They do on the other hand receive money from them, which decreases as and when a new relationship forms: if 20 per cent in this category have been so helped, the figure drops to 16 per cent with those in a new relationship but yet without a common home, to 9 per cent with those who live together, and to 6 per cent in the case of remarriage. Monetary support is phased out, so to speak, with the arrival of a new partner. Or rather it changes character inasmuch as there is an increase in help on a day-to-day basis as a relationship becomes formalized, building up from 14 per cent with lone parents, to 19 per cent in the case of a non-cohabiting partnership, 21 per cent when cohabiting, 22 per cent when remarried.

What conclusions are to be drawn? First, that the obligation felt to provide support is generalized and functions as a form of insurance against adverse living conditions. But it might be thought also that readiness to provide is a function of resources. This may hold good for material or financial help, not for the bare necessities (Pitrou, 1992) – a helping hand here and there with day-to-day living or with the children. But even in this case, support is stronger among middle and upper classes. What seems to matter more than means are the differences in value attaching to help provided: poorly off households often take for granted such gestures of support. Another explanation has been proposed by us (Claude Martin, 1993; 1997): 'help grows in inverse proportion to its need'. Indeed need may induce a sense of dependency. Help tends to be less readily accorded by the immediate circle the more it is needed, which points to the way in which each individual involved sees independence or, to turn it round, is aware of the risk that the beneficiary may become dependent. When the provision of support seems to be one and the same with inculcating dependence, it tends to put off both the giver and receiver, one because of the risk of there being no return whatever, the other because of the social disqualification it might incur. Petitat writes: 'a gift that cannot be returned only reinforces the receiver's inability to cope or to embrace an exchange relationship as an equal' (Petitat, 1991, p.55).

The family network – sociability or confinement?

Yet the absence of a network and social back-up is not necessarily regarded as a sign of isolation. Among working people support may be less common but, as has been seen, close contact is maintained with kin. What then can be said about feelings of isolation and the notions that parents with custody have of their sociability? Does contact with kin make up for the absence of support? Are there social differences here too?

A third of those interviewed consider themselves isolated and a quarter that their largely family web of relationships is a restricted one. Other parents who have custody consider that they form part of a wider diversified network (20 per cent) or independent and fragmented ones (21 per cent). But this self-assessment differs greatly according to sex, age, educational attainment, occupation and, naturally, family situation. The feeling of isolation is slightly more marked with women than with men, also a lot more frequent with those over 45 (43 per cent of whom register this as against 17 per cent under 35). It is more often than not the case that younger people have a restricted, largely family, circle of relationships; certainly, the younger they are the more likely it is that parents having custody keep close contact with their own families. Further, being under 35 makes for a a wider network: roughly one-third consider that in addition to family their circle brings in friends, colleagues and neighbours; for those over 45 the figure drops to 11 per cent. Circles that are independent one of another are more common with parents over 45 (25 per cent of them note this as against 17 per cent of those under 35).

Sociability also appears to reflect educational attainment. Most of those with fewer qualifications consider themselves in the main isolated, which may appear paradoxical in that their level of contact with close kin (parents, grandparents and siblings) is higher. However, this does not necessarily make them feel less isolated, indeed it may be a factor in their feeling more hemmed in, hence more isolated. Those of average attainment have a largely family-centred network of relations; those whose qualifications are higher regard themselves as relating to different circles, each independent of the other. Having an occupation is an important source of sociability; those not in active employment rate themselves twice as isolated (57 per cent) as those who are (25 per cent).

But, as one might expect, these opinions change with family situation. The feeling of isolation subsides with the degree of involvement in a new partnership. If around 40 per cent of single parents consider themselves isolated, the figure drops to 20 per cent where there is a non-cohabiting partner and 16 per cent when they have reconstituted a family, whether remarried or not. On the other hand, to consider oneself as having a wide, diversified, even fragmented, circle of sociability is more the case with parents in a non-cohabiting partnership (58 per cent), even a reconstituted family (52 per cent), less commonly so with

single parents (37 per cent). Lastly, a family-centred network of relations means different things depending on the conjugal situation. With
single parents, it can mean both contact with kin and of course between
the parent with custody and her or his children. Twenty-four per cent of
single parents see their circle as restricted to family. Whereas with
cohabitation or remarriage, family-centredness is most likely to comprise the reconstituted family and each partner's kin – 32 per cent of
those in this situation report accordingly; as one would expect, the non-
cohabiting are less frequently (22 per cent) of this opinion.

The appreciation parents with custody make of their sociability or
isolation varies too with social background. A sense of isolation, and
perhaps even constraint, in family-centred relations occurs more often
among working people. After all they are more inclined not to find a
partner, to limit their contacts to family and to be out of employment,
and one knows that employment is a significant source of sociability.
But there is compensation if one is younger. Over 45, restrictiveness,
and the sense of being enclosed, increases.

These findings show how complex is the impact of break-up upon
family ties – at once differentiated by social environment and at times
clearly suggestive of the inadequacy of family contact to meet the
expectations of sociability – that is, new encounters – following separation.

Conclusion

Break-up puts the ties of family to the test and frequently undermines
pre-existing relationships. Yet the children of the partnership generally
maintain contact with their grandparents, even though, given the fact
that most children live with their mothers, links with the father's side
may be fewer, sometimes disappear even.

On the other hand, when and if the mother forms a new partnership,
the 'family' multiplies. The children come to have a stepfather, possibly
half-brothers and half-sisters and, it is sometimes forgotten, step-
grandparents. Little work has been done on this particular relationship
but the evidence available suggests that it is on the whole a warm one,
particularly when the new partnership produces children. Certainly
admission to the status of 'family' is a matter of choice, but if the direct
line of descent theoretically has the prerogative, the notion that there
should be equal treatment for all tends to prevail: 'Of course, they're not
their children, but for Gérard's parents they're as good as'.

Similarly, when a father who has not been given custody finds a new partner, the prospect of a new family on that side presents itself. But the situation is objectively different, particularly when right of access is restricted to the minimum. Hence a step-parental relationship of a sporadic kind, for want of proper continuity, is both trickier and more basic. Sexual roles being what they are, the stepmother generally sees to arrangements at home when her stepchildren come; however, when they only come now and then they are unlikely easily to accept her influence and authority and the relationship may remain distant. When things go well, a stepmother may compare the relationship she has with her stepchildren to that prevailing between aunts and nephews or nieces (Le Gall, 1996).

But in spite of more restricted contact, our findings seem to show that stepmothers, rather more than stepfathers, are inclined to accept stepchildren as full members of their own family and even regularly assign them to the care of their own parents, who then are likely to find themselves looking after the children of their daughter's partner more frequently for an evening, a weekend or a few days in the holiday, and particularly so when the new partnership produces a new child.

At all events, it seems reasonable to suppose that the mother-daughter relationship, not to speak of the role of mother, is of its nature well-placed to comprehend and adapt to new situations. Committed as it is to the institution of marriage and intergenerational relations, such a relationship and such a role is more likely than another to acknowledge and make the best of patterns of behaviour which are unusual and which in the long run even the most traditionally minded may well come to accept.

Notes

1. In 1968, numbering some 720,000 households, they represented 9.5 per cent of families as defined by INSEE; in 1989 they numbered 1,100,000, 12.6 per cent. In 1985, INED reckoned that 1,120,000 minors lived in single parent families. Five years later there were 1.4 million (Desplanques, 1993).
2. The situation of single mothers is more drastic in Britain and the United States where many of them live precariously, if not in poverty (see in particular Millar, 1992; McLanahan and Sandefur, 1994).
3. Guy Desplanques (1993) puts the figure for minors living in recon-

stituted families in 1990 at 750,000, that is 5.5 per cent of the total.

4. We use the expression 'parent having custody' (*parent gardien*) which the 1993 Act, with its emphasis on joint parental authority following separation, has made redundant. Yet it still has relevance since the home of one of the parents still constitutes the 'main residence of the children'. Also, rather than use the expression 'parent with whom the child or children mainly reside', we have chosen to maintain the expression 'parents with or without custody' which well conveys the disparity of situation on a day-to-day basis.

5. Across a study of the trajectories and sociability networks of 336 parents with custody and either separated or divorced, based on two postal surveys carried out at a three-year interval (1987 and 1990), we analysed the different sets of relationships maintained or created following break-up, so taking the measure of relational vulnerability (Martin, 1997).

6. Roughly one quarter of the sample were below the 'very low income' threshold as defined by INSEE; that is, 50 per cent below the median.

7. Again, with the first survey, the significance of partnerships without cohabitation needs stressing. This type of partnership applied to 25 per cent of parents with custody at the time of the first survey, half that number at the second, and concerned mainly working mothers who were highly qualified. Here one either has a lifestyle that has been deliberately chosen to safeguard the children and/or an autonomy that is considered precious, or else a stage in the process of reconstitution, but a precarious one which may lead to a new split (Martin, 1997).

8. More than half of parents with custody who have low educational attainment live within six miles of their own parents, a quarter of them within little over a mile, whereas the figures drop to 30 per cent and 14 per cent where baccalauréat level or above has been attained. Conversely – and evidently – these well-qualified parents having custody reside at a greater distance from their parents: 40 per cent of them more than 60 miles distant, as against only 13 per cent of those unqualified. A probable factor here is that of employment and career, either because, for the first ones, promotion requires evidence of mobility or because, for the others, proximity to the family and its supply of information is an aid in job-searching (Desveaux, 1991).

9. Thirty-six per cent of parents having custody but with no educational qualifications see their parents everyday, but with those who have attained at least baccalauréat level the figure drops to 15 per cent.

10. Nearly 60 per cent of parents having custody but no educational attainment see surviving grandparents at least once a fortnight, whereas only 14 per cent of those who have reached or gone beyond baccalauréat level do so.

11. A policy of 'non-involvement' and acceptance of the situation is mentioned in one case out of five. Disapproval or refusal to accept a break-up is minimal (5 per cent of cases).

12. Similarly, frequency of help on the part of siblings is in direct proportion to educational advantage. Thus, 52 per cent of parents with custody admit to having had no help from siblings following break-up: 65 per cent of these having no qualifications, 38 per cent having attained at least baccalauréat level.

11

FROM 'BEING OF USE' TO 'FINDING ONESELF': DILEMMAS OF VALUE TRANSMISSION BETWEEN THE GENERATIONS IN NORWAY

Marianne Gullestad

In Norwegian fiction, family life has long been a central focus. Henrik Ibsen's plays, in particular, highlight the problems of modern individuals as they struggle to find their place within families and other social collectivities. Ibsen also focused, with considerable foresight, on women's problematic roles within modern bourgeois family life. In his plays, families transmit values, as well as vices, bad habits, and disease. Ibsen's plays demonstrate that families are not centrally important only because they are positively viewed; for many people, families are sites of intense positive *and* negative feelings and experiences.

Since Ibsen wrote his plays at the end of the nineteenth century, many changes have occurred within family life in Norway.[1] In this chapter, I draw on the rapidly proliferating literature theorizing changing economic, social and cultural structures to explore an emerging common sense in the upbringing of children in Norwegian families. In these theories changing social and cultural structures are related to the accelerated transnational flows of capital, information, ideas, and lifestyles, as well as to changes in production processes.

I see the present changes as transformations within modern capitalist society, and I therefore use the terms 'advanced capitalism' and 'transformed modernity', taking into account that cultural changes occur gradually and do not necessarily reach all groups or all areas of life. The present is characterized by the presence of ideas and practices from many periods of time, which sometimes coexist, sometimes complement each other, and are sometimes in sharp conflict.

Children and young people are increasingly exposed to multiple forces of cultural production and transmission in kindergartens, schools, and organized leisure activities, as well as through TV and other mass media, and through the consumption of commercially marketed products. Being variously of a local, national and global provenance, such influences are often contradictory. What children learn from life in one context provides a reference point for interpreting experiences in others. When they experience disjunctures, children attempt reflexively to comprehend these differences, and the peer group takes on additional meanings as a forum for certain kinds of reflexivity. Nevertheless, I want to play with the counter-factual idea that the role of parents and other family members has *not* diminished in this process. Children's dependence on their families when it comes to developing moral values only seems smaller, because it has become more indirect and more complex. This is the first idea that I want to discuss.

The second idea is related to the double and ambiguous nature of modern family life. On the one hand, family life can be considered as a site for the transmission of certain kinds of morality, alternative social visions, new ideas, and resistance to the values of capitalist production, market liberalism, and state bureaucracy. On the other hand, family life is also instrumental in adapting individuals to productive roles. The second idea that I discuss is that there are some intriguing parallels between present changes in theories of management and work-life, on the one hand, and changes from a rhetoric emphasis on 'being of use' to an emphasis on 'being oneself' in the upbringing of children, on the other. In short, young people who are brought up to 'be themselves' seem in some ways to be in tune with the kinds of flexibility and creativity cherished by emerging production systems. In order to spell out these two ideas, I will first provide a brief overview over recent changes in Norway, and then move on to a detailed examination of two autobiographies.

Social transformations in Norway

Like other countries, but in slightly different ways, Norway displays a range of apparent contradictions and ambiguities: advanced capitalism and a social democratic welfare state; a welfare state based on rationality and social planning, and monarchy; close relations between state and nation, and a forceful popular resistance to government efforts for joining the European Union; a Lutheran state church, and low church attendance; high amounts of money used on developmental aid given to the Third World, and restrictive immigration policies; a romantic revital-ization of nationalism, and a considerable stress on rationality, foresight and planning; much popular support for the welfare state, and a perceived crisis of the welfare state. There are tensions between the fixity imposed by state regulations and the rapid and fluid motion of capital, humans, commodities, ideas, technologies and images. These tensions can work both ways: the state is both conceived as a protec-tion against unwelcome transgressions and a barrier to a flexible social organization of production and reproduction.

If we look at everyday life, there are important changes in family life as well as in the organization of production. Beginning in the 1960s and 1970s, considerable numbers of married women with small children started taking up regular paid work outside their homes. Women's employment was accompanied by new feminist movements and demands for restructurings of family life, work-life, and the welfare state. Women struggling to manage both a job and family argued for more flexibility, networks and egalitarian power structures at work, and for more egalitarian relations at home. This meant that egalitarian individualism was brought into the home with particular force when spouses began negotiating the division of household tasks using the discourse of equality conceived as sameness (Gullestad, 1984; 1992). By the 1980s, egalitarian individualism also started to reach children. As mothers go to work, children are increasingly expected to be independ-ent and equal in new ways, within families as well as in other social institutions (Gullestad, 1997). Children and adolescents move between worlds their parents barely know. These social changes challenge in fundamental ways hegemonic ideologies involving a separation of the domestic sphere from the market and the location of women, children and certain kinds of virtue in the home. Women are no longer equally suitable symbols of care and compassion. Children are no longer equally suitable symbols of certain kinds of innocence.

In my previous works, based on participant observation, I have explored changes in family life and neighbourhood. Concerning Nor-wegian work-life, I have never done any fieldwork myself. My observations are based on research reports as well as debates in the Norwegian mass media. The following remarks should therefore be regarded as tentative and provisional.

Many argue that changes are occurring in the relationship between employers and employees. The rhetorically pre-eminent models of work organization in Norway, as in the USA, are no longer mass production and mass marketing, but rather fleeting and fluid networks of alliances, a highly decoupled and dynamic form with great organizational flexibility (see Emily Martin, 1994, p.209 about the USA). Some aspects of changes within work-life are connected to flexibility and egalitarian power structures, and can be regarded as a convergence of organizational ideas long popular among feminists and new social movements. Other aspects, connected to new technologies and greater competition leading to delayering and unemployment, bring fear and suffering, even if the worst consequences in Norway are softened by welfare state policies. Efficiency, innovation, creativity, flexibility, and reducing the workforce are now rhetorically central keywords of the day. Neo-liberalist economic models for the management of private firms are also applied increasingly to state agencies and public sector organizations such as schools, universities, and hospitals. The rhetorical stress is put on increased effectiveness, competitiveness, quality control, and technological innovation.

These ideologies and practices seem partly to be imported from abroad and refashioned in Norway. Partly, the new ideologies are highly contested, and partly, they are just emerging as a new common sense. Issues such as management theories, the future of the welfare state, school policy, and the role of fathers and husbands are discussed in Norwegian mass media, as well as around the lunch-table at work. The times are such that it is not enough to live according to received moral values, accepted beliefs, and habitual practices.

'Being of use': Kari's story

I now turn to the first of two autobiographies that I focus on in this chapter. The empirical material is taken from a larger project in which I analyse constructions of self and society and the moral reasoning embedded in 630 Norwegian autobiographies written by 'ordinary' people in 1988/89.[2] The author, Kari, is an ageing woman looking back on her childhood and on her own childrearing. Her stage of life is one of resignation and tempered optimism. She was born in 1924 and is, in traditional economic terms, a working-class woman. Nevertheless, her story demonstrates how people adapt in creative ways to structural labels such as gender, class and age. Her childhood and youth took place before and during the Second World War. Her mother died early, and she was raised by her grandmother. The years of her life as a mother with children at home took place in the 1950s and 1960s, the culmination of 'classic modernity' in Norwegian cities. The welfare state was being built and labour organizations were strong. Like her grand-mother, Kari embodied the ideology of the housewife as the centre of her home, which meant that her various stints of paid work were always subordinated to her role as a housewife.

Kari's autobiographical reconstruction of family life in her childhood presents a world in which the teaching of practical household skills was intertwined with the teaching of moral values: responsibility and a Protestant work ethic, tied to the idea of 'being of use'. Kari strongly emphasizes the values of hard work and moderation with respect to consumption. Utterances like the following are typical: 'We made use of everything and wasted nothing'; 'We earned everything we got'; 'We were not so demanding'; 'At that time people trusted each other'. Her narrative contains numerous contrasts between the moral values of her childhood and the moral values of the present. Kari is often nostalgic, and, like many ageing autobiographical authors, she mourns values that seem lost today: trust, honesty, modesty, and hard work.

Grandmother taught her to 'do unto others as you want others to do unto you'. She was not religious, nor is Kari herself, but their values clearly derive from a secularized religious culture. It is a morality in which sharing and giving are emphasized, involving not only ritualized gifts at particular occasions, but also everyday gifts of services and commodities, as the need arose. These values are particularly well exemplified in the following account of events that occurred in the 1930s:

> One of my uncles had a family with three children. He was a bricklayer by trade. He was unemployed. That was bad, I felt, even if we did not miss anything at home. One late evening in the fall it rained outside, and I had gone to bed. My bed was, by the way, two chairs against each other, and that was OK. It was placed in the room in such a way that, when the door was partly open, I could see the big mirror in the hall. Then somebody rang the bell, and I became wide awake and peeked towards the mirror to see the person Grandmother met at the door. It was Uncle Gustav. He had a black raincoat which was dripping wet, and his black hair hung in strips over his forehead. I listened intently and heard very well that he said, with his head on his mother's shoulder: 'I have no food to give the kids tomorrow, Mother'. I see and hear it whenever I want to. They went into the kitchen and closed the door, but he did not return home empty-handed.
>
> . . . . She always had something to give away, and cared for everybody, and saved many meals. My uncle later got relief work and managed better, and the times improved little by little, but I have never forgotten that period.

Because of the mirror and because the door is only partly closed, the child is able to observe an adult man, her uncle, in a moment of despair. She was not meant to see this, and the kitchen door was later closed. Not to be able to provide food for his children is a striking image of male helplessness. Kari reconstructs his sad message in the local working-class dialect, thus providing it with even greater authenticity. At this point in the narrative she suddenly shifts to the present tense: 'I see and hear it whenever I want to'. For her the story did not happen only in the past; it retains a quality outside time and place.

Kari's recollection is emblematic of the morality of sharing. Over and over again, Grandmother is praised because she was helpful. 'She was not at home many hours each day, but what she gave us was whole and complete'. Grandmother had to go away to work, but her gift to her family was 'whole and complete', apparently because she did everything for her family, not for herself. Kari's understanding of Grandmother's paid work is shaped by an ideological separation between the home and the market as separate spheres divided by gender.

The notion of giving (*gi*) involves some interesting tensions between equality and hierarchy. Giving can be interpreted with an emphasis on sharing, involving equality and mutality, but also as 'giving away' (*gi bort*), involving a possible hierarchy and unidirectionality.

Kind and skilful (*snill og flink*) are the adjectives most often used to characterize the people to whom Kari feels close. *Snill* means kind, good, nice, gentle, while *flink* means skilful, able, clever, competent, and quick to learn. At home and at school Kari learned to value the ability to work, as well as goodness of character and an orientation to sharing. These are also the virtues by which she wants to be judged herself.

However, these values are not undisputed virtues in Norway, and such differences are present in Kari's narrative. In the 1970s, when she was in her fifties, she had a nervous breakdown and a short stay in a mental hospital. The hospital caused her to reflect on values she had previously taken for granted, by introducing her to new ways of thinking about herself and her actions in the world. The therapists told her that she was 'too obedient', 'too self-sacrificing' and 'not independent enough' and that she needed to 'let her anger out' and 'be herself'. However, Kari is not quite able to abandon her former values. In her narrative, she expresses tensions between being 'independent' and 'getting her anger out', on the one hand, and 'doing right' (*gjøre riktig*) and being 'kind' (*snill*) and considerate of other peoples feelings', on the other.

Kari suffers from many ailments and diseases, some of them of a serious nature. It is tempting to ask if her pains are related to the conflicts and contradictions of her life through complex psychosomatic processes. She seems to suffer from social and moral conflicts that manifest themselves through ailments.

Conflicting values

The conflicting values in Kari's life story are demonstrated particularly well in the following passage in which she discusses the upbringing of her daughter, Beate, in the 1950s.

> But she could also be very obstinate, and I, being the one who noticed, took her to task, because it could be an inheritance from my father and very negative. Today I think I was wrong, she should have been more herself. I continued to make her obedient, the way I was raised myself. This is the way it is, but today one knows better. Nevertheless, I think that she got a good upbringing, with lots of love and tenderness.

This short but extremely rich passage sums up well how Kari struggles to make sense of her life in terms of available cultural concepts. On the one hand she explicitly discusses alternative ideals of bringing up children. On the other hand the passage also illustrates very vividly how a new kind of taken-for-grantedness is in the process of emerging ('she should have been more herself', 'today one knows better'). Kari conducts a reflexive dialogue, discussing ideas and values that were current in her own childhood (in the 1930s) and ideas and values that are current at the moment of writing (1989). There is, in her account, a continuity between her own childhood (the 1930s) and Beate's childhood (in the 1950s), as well as a break between those childhoods and the values that are current today.

As a true descendant of Henrik Ibsen, Kari also juxtaposes a model of negative inheritance through blood with a model of negative inheritance through the social relations of family upbringing. While she does not question the model of blood relations, she does question her own attempts at making Beate obedient. In the passage there is an opposition between past and present childrearing ideologies and practices, with present ideologies and practices explicitly presented as better. This is one of the few passages where she is not nostalgic.

Within the new childrearing ideology, there is an opposition between being 'oneself' and being 'obedient'. Being oneself is valued, while being obedient, which was positive then, has become negative now. One should not be 'too obedient'. Within the former childrearing ideology, the opposition is one between being obedient and being obstinate (*egen*). Being *egen* literally means being 'one's own' in Norwegian, and can be translated as obstinate, inflexible, not social. Its meanings are negative, both in the past and now. On close inspection, however, the notion of being 'one's own' (*egen*) has the same meaning as the notion of 'being oneself'. The difference is only that one notion is negatively valued and the other is positively valued.

Kari's reflections point to an ideological change in which obedience, once a central notion, is no longer equally rhetorically central. When being obedient is valued, the individual is more clearly and explicitly a *social* being. Social contexts and relationships are paramount, and being egen (one's own) is to be inflexible, marginal and decentred. When 'being oneself' is valued, the centre is within each individual. The social anchoring of the individual becomes conceptually and ideologically less visible. But, of course, 'being oneself' is also indirectly anchored in social relations.

To some extent the conflicts of value in Kari's story represent cultural class conflicts, to some extent they represent inherent tensions in modern individualism, and to some extent they represent historical changes from 'classic modernity' to a 'transformed modernity'. These many strands of meaning make the analysis of changing moralities provocative and exasperatingly complex.

The clash of values can partly be understood as the confrontation between a working-class woman with cultural interests and much admiration for education, on the one hand, and the educated therapists in a state hospital, on the other. Since her childhood schooling, hegemonic ideas and practices have changed. The therapists embody new aspects of state hegemony, and their world views are reinforced by the mass media and other central institutions. Within their world view, many value conflicts are translated into psychological problems.

Conflicting values can also be understood as a central part of the experience of modernity. Kari has experienced a rupture between the values of her childhood and young adulthood and the values that are common now. The tension between solidarity with other people and individual self-realization is also a modern phenomenon. Kari is thus in several ways a typically modern woman.

She grew up and raised children in an era in which obedience and sharing were ideals, especially for women. In school and at home she learned to be 'kind and skilful'. There was (and to some extent still is) a stronger emphasis on raising girls to be capable of sharing and self-sacrifice. This is connected to the ideological separation between women's world and men's world. The home supplied the moral counter-weight to the insensibility and brutality of the market, and women were the guardian angels of morality. As a young woman Kari guarded the boundaries of her home by subordinating all her activities to the needs of her family, just like Grandmother. Now, the ideal is rather to be oneself. Women are no longer the guardian angels of morality to the same extent as before, and the ideological separation between home and market has been challenged. Kari must acknowledge this shift as well as face fundamental restructurings of home and neighbourhood because women and children are not present in the same ways or to the same extent as before. These changes can, in my view, be characterized as experiences of 'transformed modernity'.

Historical changes in Norway in the 1970s and 1980s have challenged Kari's sense of self and her moral concepts in fundamental ways. Today, she must not simply act in right ways, or interpret abstract norms situationally, but in fact, she must decide what is right in the first place. This is not only a question of situationally interpreting deeply felt moral values, but also, more fundamentally, of identifying moral values themselves.

'Finding oneself': Cecilia's life story

I now want to contrast Kari's narrative with the narrative of Cecilia, born in 1973. Cecilia grew up in the 1970s – the period when the present social and cultural transformations started to become pronounced in Norwegian social life. She is in a very different stage of life than Kari, and she has also grown up in a very different historical period. She was 15 years old when she wrote her autobiography in 1989, and her stage of life was characterized by the 'egocentrism' and 'identity crisis' of adolescence (Erikson, 1980). While Kari is a working-class woman who never got the education she wanted, Cecilia is a middle-class girl with many educational options. The two narratives of Kari and Cecilia are not comparable in any simple sense, but they give me the opportunity to explore certain ideas about cultural variation and change.

While Kari's story has a more or less linear and chronological form, Cecilia has given her story a fragmented, associative and non-chronological structure, framed by two parallel introductions and conclusions. The story reveals an underlying social model in which competition is central, not only competition for success, but, above all, competition for recognition. There is little sense of group solidarity, only of dyadic relations. Over and over again, Cecilia constructs a split between herself and 'the others', and between herself and her body. The life story is a narrative about how to create a self and establish social relations outside the family. This is, among other things, evident in the fact that she begins her childhood memories at the point in time when she leaves home to begin kindergarten. In contrast, Kari begins her story at the moment of her birth.

Most of the action in Cecilia's story takes place in institutions or in public places: kindergarten, school, and organized leisure activities. She recreates a rich social world where peer relations are central. No less than 57 different children and young persons are mentioned by name in her story. There is, however, a remarkable contrast between the sheer number of people who have some part to play and the precarious nature of a few really important dyadic relationships. The people in these important relationships are characterized as both 'unique' and as 'like me'. There is a particular Scandinavian flavour to this way of conceiving and resolving oppositions between difference and sameness (see Gullestad, 1984; 1992).

While Kari's story gives a rich picture of the larger society through the lenses of family, neighbourhood and kinship, Cecilia's story portrays relatively little of family life, or social life more generally. The members of her family are often just mentioned in passing, though in several passages their roles in her life are explicitly discussed. In the following passage her mother is in focus.

> She is silly, I would say. But I of course comply with her. If I protest, she becomes cross and makes trouble. She plays on my bad conscience towards her. Whatever it is, she manages to make me feel very guilty, even for minor issues. If I want something she doesn't want, she makes me feel guilty, and if I forget something, she makes me feel I have disobeyed her and done it on purpose. In this way she saddles me with bad conscience.
>
> She tells me what to think ... not deliberately, but by giving me a bad conscience if I wish something else than she does. I do not know if she understands this. She probably wants the best for me. But this is my life . . . . Maybe mamma wants me to be 'little' as long as possible. I am their youngest child, and they constantly express that they do not know what they would have done without me. It feels as if they want to 'keep' me. But I have to find myself, be an independent person, something others at my age have started doing long ago. I can still be 'little', maybe, but one day I have to be allowed to find out who I am. I cannot manage to do that while living as close to them as I do. I want more freedom, but I know that I cannot manage totally without them, especially emotionally ... of course.

I know that my view of my parents may be a little unfair, especially of mother. But this is the way it feels, unfair or not. On this point I am not less normal than other young people, I hope. I love my parents and my family, but I feel that I do not know who I am myself. I can be ever so self-centered and egotistical, but I am all the same still very unsure about who I really am.

This passage is a generalized reconstruction of events in a relationship, seen from the one-sided point of view of one of the participants. Still, it indicates many complexities in the transmission of values between parents and children.

Cecilia's parents apparently do not explicitly order her to stick to their values. In other words, they do not directly ask for obedience. But they seem to make use of various indirect means to influence her. For example, they set some of the conditions for what kinds of experiences she can have. They decide, for instance, that she is too young to go to school and live alone in another town.

It also seems as if her mother attempts, by more or less subtle means ('becomes cross', 'makes trouble') to influence Cecilia's values more directly. Cecilia frames her own loyalty, love and affection as 'bad conscience' to be 'played on' by her mother. The notion of obedience re-emerges in this passage, as Cecilia writes about her mother that 'she makes me feel I have disobeyed her'. Apparently Cecilia's mother does not say 'you have disobeyed me'. Nevertheless, Cecilia would not 'feel guilty' if her mother had not been successful in instilling values from her own generation in her. This suggests that in spite of considerable changes in organizing concepts, there is also a hidden continuity of reflexes and habits. Values do not only exist as explicit notions, but may also be reproduced in subtle ways through embodied practices in everyday life. Nevertheless, Cecilia's reflections demonstrate contested values and practices, just as Kari's reflections did, though from a very different point of view in terms of generation and stage in life.

Of particular interest is the centrality of the idea of independence and how it is linked to the idea of 'finding myself', of 'finding out who I really am'. While the ageing Kari seems to assume that the child should become what she already is, Cecilia focuses on her search to *find* what she already is.

The idea that a self can be 'found' seems to be ubiquitous in the Western world.[3] During one of my follow-up conversations with Cecilia in 1991, she expanded upon the notion of 'finding oneself':

'To find oneself is to feel whole. When I was 15, I had lost a part of myself in the sense that I was not able to get in touch with it. It was there inside me all the time, but it was difficult to find. I do not know what it was. The only thing I know is that now I am in touch with it, and therefore I understand more.'

The place where Cecilia 'found' herself is inside herself. In her way of formulating the process, there is no opposition between being oneself and finding oneself. The self holds an inner value which is, in a certain sense, both ascribed and achieved. The inside can be interpreted as a metaphor for aspects of life which are not usual parts of social interaction. These inner aspects are part of a reality which is difficult to acknowledge intersubjectively. Being 'in touch' may thus be understood as being potentially able to communicate these aspects of one's experiences, and 'finding oneself' is a question of opening up to the possibilities 'inside'. This model of self thus presupposes both an inner depth *and* a role for social relations in creating one's self. The passage thus underscores the relational nature of her sense of self.

The metaphor of being in touch with something inside herself that she had lost may also be interpreted as pointing back to family life – to childhood experiences and influences from her parents and other family members, such as grandparents. Cecilia has to leave her family in order to choose and refashion parts of what has been transmitted to her by her family.

An era of expressivity

However, there are still other meanings of 'finding oneself'. The following passage demonstrates both Cecilia's vulnerability in relation to 'the other', her sensitive bodily awareness, and the importance of music and dancing for a positive sense of her self.

Students' party at school. It is Wednesday, I have been to my jazz ballet class earlier this afternoon. I have never been to a students' party before, nor have I been to a school discoteque. I am completely alone. I know nobody enough to dare to go over and talk to them . . . . The others dance, but very carefully. Barely moving their legs. I, too, want to dance. I love it. But I feel so stupid in front of all these ... these people who are so *in*, who cannot stand that others are different. People come over to me and ask me if I am not going to dance instead of just looking. No, I do not want to. I do not dare, but that I do not say.

They drag me out on the floor, anyway. I do not think about being different from them. I just dance, the music is good and I feel that I and the music are one. I am *something*, I am something made of movements belonging to the music. I am not just me, I am dancing.

The value of dancing is connected to the forgetting of social boundaries ('I do not think about being different from them'), to the temporary healing of conflicts and tensions ('the music and I are one'), and to being able to create, express and thus objectify a positive identity ('I am something made of movements belonging to the music. I am not just me, I am dancing'). Through the use of her body, Cecilia is negotiating boundaries between the individual and group and between difference and sameness. Becoming one with the music means to become one with her body and also indirectly to become one with other people. The tensions between Cecilia and the others, between Cecilia and her body, and between difference and sameness, are temporarily resolved. Her experience is thus both individualistic and collectivistic. The music is common to all the dancers, and through this common experience a transcendent sensibility can be realized.

The music and the dancing constitute an intersubjective space within which Cecilia is able to be creative. While dancing she can experience wholeness instead of painful splits, and freedom from social and personal relations usually felt to be constraining. Through the creativity and expressivity of dancing she at once loses and finds her self.

Cecilia's story demonstrates how morality is being detached from the direct transmission of values, and illustrates some of the problems and challenges that this detachment raises. 'Being oneself' means that each person is, in an even more fundamental sense than before, responsible for his or her own morality. It can also mean that one renounces morality, but that does not apply in Cecilia's case. Nevertheless, because she wants to do things her own way, Cecilia is particularly vulnerable to the judgement of others, and also particularly dependent on finding 'special', and 'unique' friends who are 'like me' and therefore willing to support her.

Like Kari, Cecilia refers extensively to bodily practices and embodied experiences. Conflicts, contradictions and tensions, on the one hand, and blissful moments, on the other, are reconstructed in bodily terms. In both accounts there is somatization of moral tensions, but only Cecilia focuses explicitly on the body as a site for creativity. For her, being oneself is explicitly linked to creative self-fashioning.

Cecilia's story also exemplifies tensions between fragmentation and wholeness. On the one hand, there is a celebration of multiple identities. On the other hand, her story also exhibits a desire for coherence and integrity. Formally, Cecilia has created coherence in her narrative by framing her flickering fragments of memory with two parallel introductions and conclusions, and by a recurrent *leitmotiv* of tensions between herself and others and tensions within herself. Substantially she has found wholeness by exploring the rare and blissful moments when tensions are suspended.

Theorizing the relationship between parents and children

I have focused on moral diversity and change and their relation to family life within Norwegian society, particularly with respect to changing generational relationships. Nevertheless, there are important respects in which this analysis of Norway may also be seen as representing dilemmas of value transmission in contemporary Europe (and Western society more generally), brought on by a wide-ranging historical transition from 'classic modernity' to a 'transformed modernity', emerging roughly in the 1970s and early 1980s, in which the transmission of moral values has changed from requests for obedience to influence by means of persuasion and complex negotiations.

'Being obedient' and 'being of use' are challenged by 'being oneself' as moral values. In this process notions of duty and responsibility also acquire new meanings. There is a change of emphasis from discipline to expressivity – to 'finding oneself' and creating one's own identity through expressive activities.

The very idea of being oneself, and the associated notion that being oneself is being authentic, easily leads to the idea that in order to be oneself one needs to struggle against some externally imposed rules. Relations with parents are particularly important in this regard, since young people to a large extent develop their own values through resisting and reshaping the influences of their parents.

While the notion of obedience focuses on continuity and the open and legitimate transmission of values between parents and children, the notion of being oneself emphasizes separateness and discontinuity. This means, in other words, that there are not only changes in the values transmitted, but also in the ways of transmitting them. Finding and being oneself necessitates careful and subtle forms of interaction.

To attain the ideal of being oneself, children must justify their values in terms of their own individual convictions and preferences, not in terms of the convictions and preferences of their parents. Parents today should ideally transmit the ability to be oneself and to develop oneself, rather than specific ideas and specific values. These new tendencies resonate with the kinds of flexibility and creativity needed in the present stage of capitalism.

Raising children thus consists in getting them to freely choose to manage himself or herself in certain ways, though parents attempt to insure that children freely choose only within certain limits. Parents usually think it is wrong if children and young people stick to the parents' values just to please them. Then the children may be characterized as 'too obedient' and 'dependent'. But if they do something entirely different from what their parents want, this too is usually wrong. Then the children may be characterized as 'immature'. Children seem to have to learn indirect, flexible and finely attuned ways of paying attention to other people and to context, ways that are entirely different from the rigid power hierarchies of 'obedience'.

In the 'transformed modern' society, the individual life span is foregrounded, compared to the renewal of the family life cycle. Instead of individuals being resources for families, families are becoming resources out of which individuals construct their selves.

Friendship relations, expressive activities and love affairs help young people to become themselves by 'finding' themselves. Peer group relations mediate between family life and other institutional settings, and between inherited values and reflexively chosen values. Differences between generations are emphasized, both in the home and in the mass media. At the same time, former values and ideas survive submerged in the shadows of more rhetorically powerful notions. One example is the way Cecilia reconstructs certain aspects of her relationship to her mother as 'being made to feel disobedient'. Values also survive by being used in new contexts and may thus be reinforced as rhetorically powerful notions. This is in my view the case with the notions of independence and the home in Norway.

Raising children and transmitting values involve discourses of influence, seduction and guilt, teaching children to be attuned to indirect and subtle cues, to be a part of teamwork where the power-relations can be more or less hidden, to deal with and find one's own solutions in the midst of many conflicting messages, and to make use of a rich variety of cultural resources for creative purposes.

Closing note

Interesting similarities exist between the various skills related to 'being oneself' and the human qualities promoted by the discourses of recent management theories: flexibility, innovation, and flair. It should be stressed, however, that I am not arguing for a simple reflectionist theory about historical causality – that 'advanced capitalism' somehow calls for or demands corresponding changes in families and subjectivities. Rather, I am noting *constellations of changes* and I want in particular to call attention to what is happening between the generations concerning value transmission and the creation of the self. Further analyses of many kinds are necessary: analyses of changing discourses within family life, work-life and schools have to be grounded in practice; analyses of the complexities involved in the interrelations between production systems, the market, the welfare state, social movements, and family life are needed to describe the subtle processes of interaction within families, the complex interrelations between family life and other social fields, the global travelling of new ideas, the extent to which particular popular notions and practices are co-opted by management theory and capitalist enterprises, and the social and economic inequalities among families. I have not addressed questions of class difference, and this issue will also have to be discussed in the future.

Family studies easily become limited and parochial without a foundation in social theory. And family studies easily become normative and moralistic without fine-grained ethnographic analysis. In this chapter I have attempted to illuminate a few connections between an ethnographic approach to family relations and broader social theories. The analysis has led me to be more aware of the complex and often contradictory nature of value transmission in the present stage of modernity. It has also led me to be more aware of the embodied nature of value contradictions and ambiguities. The past lives on in the present, often in ways other than we think.

Notes

1. In spite of the centrality of family and kinship in Scandinavian fiction and daily life, these topics have not been equally central to anthropological studies in the Scandinavian countries. Family and kinship, together with religion, have been thought to be of minor importance by modern secularized academics. Some exceptions are Boholm (1983) on kinship, Borchgrevink and Melhuus (1985), Frykman and Löfgren (1987), Gullestad (1984, 1992), Holtedahl (1986), Solheim, Heen and Holter (1986) and Thorsen (1993) on family life. Kinship, in particular, has been little studied.
2. The data collection procedure is described in detail in Gullestad and Almås 1992 (English version) and 1991 (French version). The

project has so far resulted in an edited volume of six autobiographies (Almås and Gullestad, 1992, French version 1991), a monograph called *Everyday Life Philosophers* (Gullestad, 1996a), an edited book on autobiography and childhood (Gullestad, 1996b). An extended version of this chapter is to be found in (1996) *Journal of the Royal Anthropological Institute*, **2**, 1, pp.25–42.

3. The idea of finding oneself is not unique to Scandinavia. (For the USA see for example Bellah *et al.*, 1986, pp.55–85.) For young (and not so young) people in Norway the paradigmatic song text is Finn Kalvik's *Finne meg sjæl* ('*Find myself*') from 1969. The genre and the melody are inspired by Bob Dylan. This song has become so popular that it is now part of state hegemony by being part of the curriculum in Norwegian schools (in *Torbjørn Egners lesebok*).

SELECT BIBLIOGRAPHY

Åberg R. (ed.) (1990) *Industrisamhälle i omvandling*, Stockholm.

Allardt E. (1975) *Att ha, att ällska, att vara: omvälfärden i Norden*, Helsinki.

Allat P. and Yeandle S. (1986) 'It's not fair, is it?' Young Unemployment, Family Relations and the Social Contract', in Allen S., Watson A., Purcell K. and Wood S. (eds), *The Experience of Unemployment*, Macmillan, London.

Almås R. and Gullestad M. (1990) *Livshistorier*, Universitetsforlaget, Oslo.

Anderson M. (1980) *Approaches to the History of the Western Family 1500–1914*, London.

Andersson L. (1993) *Äldre i Sverige och Europa*, Ädelutvärderingen, 93:4, Socialstyrelsen.

Arrondel L. and Laferrère A. (1992) 'Les partages inégaux des successions entre frères et sœurs', *Économie et Statistique*, **250**, pp.29–42.

Attias-Donfut C. (1988) *Sociologie des générations, l'empreinte du temps*, PUF, Paris.

Attias-Donfut C. (1993) 'Coéducation des générations et effets en retour de la mobilité sociale', in Pronovost G., Attias-Donfut C. and Samuel N. (eds), *Temps libre et modernité. Mélanges en l'honneur de J. Dumazedier*, PUQ et L'Harmattan, Paris.

Attias-Donfut C. (1995a) 'Le double circuit des transmissions', in Attias-Donfut C. (ed.), *Les solidarités entre générations. Vieillesse, familles, État*, Nathan, Paris, pp.41–79.

Attias-Donfut C. (ed.) (1995b) *Les solidarités entre générations, Vieillesse, familles, État*, Nathan, Paris.

Aubert F. (1992) 'Compter ses amis. De quelques repères de l'amitié', in Aubert F. (ed.), *Variations sociologiques en hommage à Pierre Ansart*, L'Harmattan, Paris.

Audirac P. A. (1985) 'Les personnes âgées, de la vie de famille à l'isolement' *Économie et Statistique*, **175**.

Augustins G. (1990) *Comment se perpétuer? Devenir des lignées et destins des patrimoines dans les paysanneries européennes*. Société d'ethnologie, Paris.

Ball H. (1990, new edition) *Zur Kritik der deutschen Intelligenz*, Frankfurt.

Banfield E. C. (1958) *The Moral Bases of a Backward Society*, Free Press, Glencoe (Italian edition, 1976).

Baraille J.-P. (1993), 'L'âge de la retraite', *Données sociales*, pp.339–45.

Barbagli M. (1984) *Sotto lo stesso tetto. Mutamenti della famiglia in Italia dal xv al xx secolo*, Il Mulino, Bologna.

Barrera Gonzalez A. (1985) *La dialectica de la identitad en Catalunya* CIS, Madrid.

Bawin-Legros B. and Kellerhals J. (eds) (1994) *Relations intergénérationnelles. Parenté, transmission, mémoire*, actes du colloque de Liège, 17–18 May 1990, Association internationale des sociologues de langue française et Association des sociologues belges de langues française.

Beck U. and Beck-Gernsheim E. (1990) *Das ganz normale Chaos der Liebe*, Frankfurt.

Bellah R. N., Madsen R., Sullivan W. M., Swidler A. and Tipton S. M. (1986) *Habits of the Heart: Individualism and Commitment in American Life*, Harper & Row (Perennial Library), New York (first edition 1985).

Boholm Å. (1983) 'Swedish kinship. An exploration into cultural processes of belonging and continuity', *Gothenburg Studies in Social Anthropology*, **5**.

Borchgrevink T. and Melhuus M. (1985) 'Familie og arbeid. Fokus på sjøe-mannsfamilier', Report No.27, Work Research Institute, Oslo.

Bouquet M. (1993) *Reclaiming English Kinship*, Manchester University Press, Manchester.

Bourdieu P. (1984) *Questions de sociologie*, éd. de Minuit, Paris.

Bourdieu P. (1993) 'La famille comme catégorie réalisée', *Actes de la Recherche en Sciences Sociales*, **100**, pp.32–6.

Bourdieu P. (1994) 'Stratégies de reproduction et modes de domination', *Actes de la recherche en sciences sociales*, **105**, pp.3-12.

Bugarini F. and Vicarelli G. (1979), 'Interazione e sostegno parentale in ambiente urbano', *Rassegna italiana di sociologia*.

Burgoyne J. and Clark D. (1984) *Making A Go Of It*, Routledge, London.

Canceill G. (1982) 'Ressources et niveaux de vie des personnes âgées, de la vie de famille à l'isolement', *Économie et Statistique*, No.222.

Caplow T. *et al.* (1982) *Middletown Families. Fifty Years of Change and Continuity*, University of Minneapolis Press, Minneapolis.

Carlsson I. (1983) Förord in Barn(?) *Författare, forskare och skolungdomar diskuterar varför det föds så få barn*. Stockholm.

CBS (1986) *Personele vermogensoverdrachten 1981-1982*, Staatsuitgeverij, The Hague.

Cerc (1987) *Familles nombreuses, mères isolées, situation économique et vulnérabilité*, La Documentation française, Paris.

Cherlin A. (1978) 'Remarriage as an incomplete institution', *The American Journal of Sociology*, **84**, 3.

Cives G. (1990) *Il comune rustico. Storia sociale di un paese del Mezzogiorno nell'800*, Il Mulino, Bologna.

Coenen-Huther J. (1994) *La mémoire familiale: un travail de reconstruction du passé*, L'Harmattan, Paris.

Coenen-Huther J., Kellerhals J. and Von Allmen M. (1994) *Les réseaux de solidarité dans la famille. Réalités sociales*, Lausanne.

Collomp A. (1984) 'Tensions, Dissensions and Ruptures inside the Family in Seventeeth- and Eighteenth-Century Haute-Provence', in Medick H. and Sabean W. (eds), *Interests and Emotions*, Cambridge University Press, Cambridge, pp.145-70.

Cozijn C. (1978) *Meningen van de bevolking over de vederling van nalatenschappen onder het abinsstaat erfrecht*, WODC, The Hague.

Davidoff L. and Hall C. (1987) *Family Fortunes: Men and Women of the English Middle Class 1780-1850*, Hutchinson, London.

Déchaux J.-H. (1994) 'Les trois composantes de l'économie cachée de la parenté: l'exemple français', *Recherches sociologiques*, 3, pp.37-52.

Delaisi G. and Verdier P. (1994) *Enfant de personne*, Odile Jacob, Paris.

Desplanques G. (1993) 'Les familles en 1990', *Solidarité, Santé, Études Statistiques*, No. 4, pp.39-50.

Desveaux E. (1991) 'De l'embauche à l'usine comme de la dévolution d'un patrimoine', in Segalen M. (ed.), *Jeux de famille*, Éditions du CNRS, Paris.

Drulhe M. and Clément S. (1992) 'Transmission du patrimoine et prise en charge des parents âgés dans le Sud-Ouest rural', *Sociétés contemporaines*, No. 10: Solidarité entre générations au temps de la retraite, pp.93–109.

Dumont L. (1986) *Essays on Individualism: Modern Ideology in Anthropological Perspective*, University of Chicago Press, Chicago.

Edwards J., Franklin S., Hirsh E., Price F. and Strathern M. (1993) *Technologies of Procreation: Kinship in the Age of Assisted Conception*, Manchester University Press, Manchester.

Eekelaar J. and Maclean M. (1986) *Maintenance After Divorce*, Clarendon, Oxford.

Elder G., Robertson E., Skinner M. and Conger R. (1994) 'La transmission d'un mode de vie dans l'Amérique rurale', *Communications*, No. 59: Générations et filiation, pp.101–18.

Erikson E. (1980) *Identity and the Life Cycle*, W. W. Norton & Company, New York (first edition 1959).

Erni M. (1965) *Das Vaterbild der Tochter*, Cologne.

Eurostat (1989) CEE, Luxemburg.

Faus I. and Condomines J. (1907) 'Els capitols matrimonials a la Comarca de Guissona', *Revista Juridica de Catalunya*.

Festy P. (1991) 'Biographies après divorce', in Himbert T. and Roussel L. (eds), *La nuptialité. Évolution récente en France et dans les pays développés*, INED/PUF, coll. 'Congrès et colloques', No. 7, Paris.

Finch J. (1989) *Family Obligations and Social Change*, Polity Press, Cambridge.

Finch J. and Hayes L. (1995) 'Gender Inheritance and Women as Testators', in Lyon S. and Morris L. (eds), *Gender Relations in Public and Private: Changing Research Perspectives*, Macmillan, London.

Finch J. and Mason J. (1993) *Negotiating Family Responsibilities*, Routledge, London.

Finch J., Hayes L., Mason J., Masson J. and Wallis L. (1996) *Wills, Inheritance and Property*, Oxford, Oxford University Press.

Firth, R., Hubert, J. and Forge, A. (1970) *Family and their Relatives*, Routledge, London.

Flaquer L. *et al.* (1992) *Enquesta de la Regio Metropolitana de Barcelona 1990. Condicions de vida i habits de la poblacio*, Diputacio de Barcelona.

Fortes M. (1969) *Kinship and the Social Order: the Legacy of L. H. Morgan*, Aldine, Chicago.

Frykman, J. and Löfgren O. (1987) *Culture Builders: A Historical Anthropology of Middle Class Life*, New Brunswick, NJ., Rutgers University Press.

Gähler M. (1994) 'Svensk familjeupplösning och några av dess konsekvenser', in Fritzell J. and Lundberg O. (eds), *Vardagens villkor. Levnadsförhållanden i Sverige under tre decennier*, Stockholm, pp.59–86.

Galland O. (1991) *Sociologie de la jeunesse, l'entrée dans la vie*, Armand Colin, coll. 'U', Paris.

Gaunt D. (1983) *Familjeliv i Norden*, Stockholm.

Gaunt D. (1991) *Krigsåsens barn-minnen, möten, myter*, Gävle.

Geffray C. (1990) *Ni père ni mère. Critique de la parenté: le cas Makhuna*, Le Seuil, Paris.

Giddens, A. (1992) *The Transformation of Intimacy: Sexuality, Love and Eroticism in Modern Society*, Polity Press, Cambridge.

Girod de L'Ain B. (1983) 'Kein Aufstand gegen die Familie. Erfahrungen des "Mai 68" und danach', *Dokumente*, special issue, pp.61–70.

Godelier M. (1993) 'L'Occident, miroir brisé. Une évaluation partielle de l'anthropologie sociale assortie de quelques perspectives', *Annales ESC*, **5**, pp.1183–1207.

Gokalp C. (1978) 'Le réseau social', *Population*, pp.1077–1093.

Golini A. (ed.) *Tendenze demografiche e politiche per la popolazione*, Il Mulino, Bologna.

Goody J. (1976) *Family and Inheritance: Rural Society in Western Europe*, Cambridge University Press, Cambridge.

Goody J. (1985) *L'évolution de la famille et du mariage en Europe*, Armand Colin, Paris.

Goody J. (1994) Préface au 3ᶜ tome de *Histoire de la Famille*, Livre de poche, Paris.

Goody J., Thirsk J. and Thompson E. P. (eds) (1976), *Family and Inheritance: Rural Society in Western Europe 1200–1800*, Cambridge University Press, Cambridge.

Gribaudi G. (1993) 'Familismo e famiglia a Napoli e nel Mezzogiorno', *Meridiana*, **17**, pp.13–42.

Gribaudi G. (1994) 'Il paradigma del "familismo amorale" ', in Macry P. and Massafra A. (eds), *Fra storia e storiografia*, Il Mulino, Bologna.

Gubrium J. F. (1968) *Reclaiming English Kinship*, Manchester University Press, Manchester.

Gullestad M. (1984) *Kitchen-Table Society*, Scandinavian University Press, Oslo/Oxford University Press, Oxford.

Gullestad M. (1992) *The Art of Social Relations: Essays on Culture,*

Social Action and Everyday Life in Modern Norway, Scandinavian University Press, Oslo/Oxford University Press, Oxford.

Gullestad M. (1996a) *Everyday Life Philosophers: Modernity, Morality and Autobiography in Norway*, Scandinavian University Press, Oslo.

Gullestad M. (1996b) 'Modernity, Self and Childhood in the Analysis of Life Stories', in Gullestad M. (ed.), *Imagined Childhoods: Self and Society in Autobiographical Accounts*, Scandinavian University Press, Oslo.

Gullestad M. (1997) 'A Passion for Boundaries: Reflections on Connections between the Everyday Lives of Children and Discourses on the Nation in Contemporary Norway', *Childhood*, 4, 1, pp.19-41.

Gullestad M. and Almås R. (1992) 'Write your Life, A Norwegian Life Story Contest', *Oral History*, 20, 2, pp.61-5. French version, 'Écrivez votre vie', *Cahiers de sémiotique textuelle*, 20, pp.43-64.

Hagestad G. (1988) 'Demographic Change and the Life Course: Some Emerging Trends in the Family Realm', *Family Relations*, 37, pp.405-10.

Hagestad G. (1995) 'La négociation de l'aide: jeux croisés entre familles, sexes et politiques sociales', in Attias-Donfut C. (ed.), *Les solidarités entre générations. Vieillesse, familles, État*, Nathan, Paris, pp.157-66.

Hajnal J. (1965) 'European Marriage Patterns in Perspective', in Glass D. and Eversley D. (eds), *Population and History*, E. Arnold, London.

Hammarström G. (1989) *Möten mellan generationer*, Uppsala.

Hanssen B. (1978) *Familj, hushåll, släkt*, Stockholm.

Hantrais L. and Letablier M.-T. (1994) 'Construction et déconstruction de la famille en Europe: une analyse comparative', *Recherches et prévisions*, 37, pp.1-10.

Hareven T. and Adams K. (1994) 'Génération intermédiaire et aide aux parents âgés dans une communauté américaine', *Gérontologie et Société*, 68, pp.83-97.

Holcombe L. (1983) *Wives and Property*, Martin Robertson, Oxford.

Höllinger F. (1989) Familie und soziale Netzwerke in fortgeschrittenen Industriegesellschaften', *Soziale Welt*, 40, 4, pp.513-37.

Höllinger F. and Haller M. (1990), 'Kinship and Social Network in Modern Societies: a Cross-Cultural Comparison among Seven Nations', *European Sociological Review*, pp.103-24.

Holtedahl L. (1986) *Hva mutter gjør er alltid viktig*, Universitetsforlaget, Oslo.

Iglesias de Ussel J. (1993) Vivienda y familia', in Garrido L. and Gil E. (eds), *Estrategias Familiares*, Allianza, Madrid.

Infratest (1992) *Möglichkeiten and Grenxen selbstädiger Lebensführung*, Munich.

Istat (1985) *Indagine sulle strutture e sui comportamenti familiari*, Rome.

Istat (1993) *Indagine sulle strutture e sui comportementi familiari*, Rome.

Istat (1994) *Indagine multiscopo sulle famiglie. Volume 2: Famiglia, popolazione e abitazioni*, Rome.

Iszaevich A. (1981) 'Corporate Household and Ecocentric Kinship Group in Catalonia', *Ethnology*, **20**, pp.272–90.

Jahoda M. *et al.* (1977) *Die Arbeitslosen von Marienthal*, Frankfurt.

Kommission Der E. G. (1979) *Die Europäer und ihre Kinder*, Brussels.

König R. (1957), 'Family and Authority: The German Father in 1955', *The Sociological Review*, **5**, pp.107–25.

Laferrère A. (1991) Les donations: surtout de l'immobilier', *Insee Première*, No. 169.

Lallemand S. (1993) *La circulation des enfants en société traditionnelle. Prêt, don, échange*, L'Harmattan, Paris.

Lamaison P. (1988) 'La diversité des modes de transmission: une géographie tenace', *Études rurales*, Nos 110, 111, 112.

La Mendola, S. (1991a) 'I rapporti di parentela in Veneto', *Polis*, pp.49–70.

La Mendola (1991b) *Gente commune. La famiglia coniugale in Veneto*, Fondazione Corazzin, Venice.

Lave J. and Wenger E. (1991) 'The Family as Project', *Sociological Review*, pp.273–96.

Leach E. (1980) 'Les vierges-mères', in Leach E. (ed.), *L'unité de l'homme et autres essais*, Gallimard, Paris, pp.77–107.

Lefaucheur N. (1993) 'Sur la scène de l'anormalité familiale', in Meulders-Klein M.-T. and Théry I. (eds), *Les recompositions familiales aujourd'hui*, Nathan, Paris.

Lefaucheur N. and Martin C. (1993) 'Lone Parent Families in France. Situation and Research', in Hudson J. and Galoway B (eds), *Lone Parent Families. Perspectives on Research and Policy*, Thomson Educational Publishing, Toronto.

Le Bras H. and Todd E. (1981) *L'invention de la France*, Hachette, Paris.

Le Gall D. (1992) 'Secondes amours. Aimer la raison?', *Revue inter-nationale d'action communautaire*, Montreal, 27/67.

Le Gall D. (1993) *Formes de régulation conjugale et familiale à la suite d'unions fécondes*, habilitation à diriger des recherches en sociologie (edited by F. de Singly), université René Descartes, Paris.

Le Gall D. (1996), 'Beaux-parents au quotidien et par intermittence', in Le Gall D. and Martin C. (eds), *Familles, droits et politiques sociales*, L'Harmattan, coll. 'Logiques sociales', Paris.

Le Gall D. and Martin C. (1989) *Familles monoparentales, Évolution et traitement social*, ESF, Paris.

Le Gall D. and Martin C. (1991), 'Recomposition familiale et production normative', in Bawin-Legros B. and Kellerhals J. (eds), *Relations inter-générationnelles*, AISLF, Universities of Geneva and Liège.

Le Gall D. and Martin C. (1993), 'Transitions familiales, logiques de recomposition et modes de régulation conjugale', in Meulders-Klein M.-T. and Théry I. (eds), *Les recompositions familiales aujourd'hui*, Nathan, Paris.

Le Gloannec A.-M. (1989) *La nation orpheline: les deux Allemagne en Europe*, Calmann-Lévy, Paris.

Le Play F. (1855) *Les ouvriers européens*, Imprimerie impériale, Paris.

Le Play F. *et al.* (1994) *Les Mélouga. La famille-souche, questions de méthode*, Nathan, Paris (first edition 1855).

Macfarlane A. (1978) *The Origins of English Individualism*, Blackwell, Oxford.

Marshall V., Mathews S. and Rosenthal C. (1993) 'Elusiveness of Family Life: A Challenge for Sociology of Aging', *Annual Review of Gerontology and Geriatrics*, **13**, pp.39–72.

Martin C. (1993) 'Risque solitude. Divorces et vulnérabilité relation-nelle', *Revue internationale d'action communautaire*, Montreal, Nos 29/69.

Martin C. (1994) 'Diversité des trajectoires post-désunion. Entre le risque de solitude, la défense de son autonomie et la recomposition familiale', *Population*, **6**, pp.1557–84.

Martin C. (1997) *L'après-divorce*, Presses de l'université de Rennes, Rennes.

Martin E. (1992) 'The End of the Body?', *American Ethnologist*, **19**, 1, pp.121–41.

Martin E. (1994) *Flexible Bodies: Tracking Immunity in American Culture – From the Days of Polio to the Age of AIDS*, Beacon Press, Boston.

Maspons i Anglasell F. (1935) *La llei de la familia catalana*, Barcino, Barcelone.

McLanahan S. and Sandefur G. (1994) *Growing Up with a Single Parent*, Harvard University Press, Cambridge (Mass.).

Medick H. and Sabean D. (eds) (1984) *Interest and Emotions*, Cambridge University Press, Cambridge.

Mellows A. R. (1983) *The Law of Succession*, Butterworth, London.

Mendras H. (1995) *Comment devenir sociologue. Mémoires d'un vieux mandarin*, Actes Sud, Arles.

Meulders-Klein M.-T. and Théry I. (eds) (1993) *Les recompositions familiales aujourd'hui*, Nathan, Paris.

Millar J. (1992) 'Lone Mothers and Poverty', in Glendinning C. and Millar J. (eds), *Women and Poverty in Britain. The 1990s*, Harvester Wheatsheaf, London.

Minicuci M. (1989) *Qui e altrove. Famiglie di Calabria e di Argentina*, Angeli, Milan.

Mitscherlich A. (1973) *Auf dem Wege zur vaterlosen Gesellschaft*, Munich.

Moqvist I. (1990) 'Familjen-beständig och föränderlig', in Åberg R. (ed), *Industrisamhälle i omvandling*, Stockholm, pp.115-62.

Moss M. S. and Moss S. Z. (1988) 'Reunion between Elderly Parents and their Distant Children', *American Behavioral Scientist*, **31**, pp.654-66.

Murru Corriga G. (1993) 'Di madre in figlia, di padre in figlio. Un caso di "discendeza parallela" in Sardegna', *La ricerca folklorica*, **27**, pp.53-74.

Noëlle-Neumann E. (1983) *Eine desmoskopische Deutschstunde*, Zurich.

Noëlle-Neumann E. and Köcher R. (1989) *Die verletzte Nation*, Stuttgart.

Odén B., Alvar S. and Tornstam L. (1993) *Att åldras i Sverige*, Stockholm.

Oppo A. (1990a) ' "Where there's no woman there's no home": Profile of the Agropastoral Family in Nineteenth-Century Sardinia', *Journal of Family History*, pp.483-502.

Oppo A. (ed.) (1990b), *Famiglia e matrimonio nella società sarda tradizionale*, La Tarantola, Cagliari.

Oppo A. (1991) 'Madri, figlie e sorelle: solidarietà parentali in Sardegna', *Polis*, pp.21-48.

Paci M. (1980) 'Introduzione: struttura e fonzioni della famiglia nello sviluppo industriale "periferico" ', *Famiglie e mercato del lavoro in un 'economia periferica*, Angeli, Milan, pp.9–69.

Palumbo B. (1992) 'Casa di mugliera, casa di galera', *La ricerca folklorica*, pp.7–25.

Petitat A. (1991) 'Les circuits du don: Kula, charité et assurances', *Cahiers internationaux de sociologie*, **90**.

Pina-Cabral J. de (1989) 'L'Héritage de Maine: L'érosion des categories d'analyse dans l'étude des phénomènes familiaux en Europe', *Ethnologie Française*, **19**, pp.329–40.

Pina-Cabral J. de (1991) *Os contextos da Antropologia*, Difel, Lisbon.

Pina-Cabral J. de (1992) 'The primary social unit in Mediterranean and Atlantic Europe', *Journal of Mediterranean Studies*, **2**, 1, pp.25–41.

Pina-Cabral J. de (1994) 'Personal Identity and Ethnic Ambiguity: Naming Practices among the Eurasians of Macau', *Social Anthropologist*, **2**, 2.

Pitrou A. (1977) 'Le soutien familial dans la société urbaine', *Revue française de sociologie*, pp.47–84.

Pitrou A. (1992) *Vivre sans famille? Les solidarités familiales dans le monde d'aujourd'hui*. Privat, Toulouse (first edition 1978).

Poster M. (1978) *Critical Theory of the Family*, Pluto Press, London.

Rein M. (1994) 'Solidarity between Generations: A Five-Country Study of the Social Process of Aging', manuscript, Berlin.

Riehl W. (1855) *Die bürgerliche Gesellschaft*, Stuttgart.

Rosenmaryr L. and Kockeis E. (1963) 'Essai d'une théorie sociologique de la vieillesse et de la famille', *Revue internationale des sciences sociales*, **15**, 2, pp.432–48.

Rosser C. and Harris C. (1965) *The Family and Social Change. A Study of Family and Kinship in a South Wales Town*, Routledge and Kegan Paul, London.

Rossi A. S. and Rossi P. H. (1990) *Of Human Bonding: Parent–Child Relations Across The Life Course*, Aldine de Gruyter, New York.

Roussel L. and Bourguignon O. (1976) *La famille après le mariage des enfants*, INED, Travaux et documents, Cahier No. 78, PUF, Paris.

Sandre P. de (1986) 'Quando i giovani lasciano la famiglia', *Studi interdisciplinari sulla famiglia*, pp.63–84.

Santamaria i Tous V. (1901) *Derecho Consuetudinario y economia popular de las Provincias de Tarragona y Barcelona con indicacion de las de Gerona y Lerida*, Memoria de la Real Academia de Ciencias Morales y Politicas, Madrid.

Schaffner B. (1948) *Father Land. A study of Authoritarianism in German Family*, New York.

Schneider D. M. (1968) *American Kinship: A Cultural Account*, Prentice Hall, Englewood Cliffs, NJ.

Schneider D. M. (1984) *A Critique of the Study of Kinship*, University of Michigan Press, Ann Arbor.

Schultheis F. (1990) 'Body and Soul', *The Times Literary Supplement*, 2, pp.13-14.

Segalen M. (1984) ' "Avoir sa part": Sibling Relations in Partible Inheritance, Brittany', in Medick H. and Sabean D. (eds), *Interest and Emotions*, Cambridge University Press, Cambridge, pp.129-44.

Segalen M. (1986) *Historical Anthropology of the Family*, Cambridge University Press, Cambridge.

Segalen M. (ed.) (1991) *Jeux de Familles*, Éditions du CNRS, Paris.

Segalen M. (1996) *Sociologie de la famille*, Armand Colin, coll. 'U', Paris (fourth edition).

Serra i Pagès R. (1992) 'Consideracions generals sobre "I Folklore" ', in Rius M. (ed.), *Alguns escrits del Professor Serra i Pagès*, M. Rius, Barcelona.

Siebert S. and Sutter J. (1963) 'Attitudes devant la maternité: une enquête', *Population*, 4, pp.665-82.

Singly F. de and Schultheis F. (eds) (1991) *Affaires de famille, affaires d'État*, IRAS-Goethe Institut.

Smith R. M. (1984) 'Some Issues Concerning Families and their Property in Rural England 1250-1800', in Smith R. M. (ed.), *Land, Kinship and Life Cycle*, Cambridge University Press, Cambridge.

Solheim J., Heen H. and Holter Ø. G. (1980) 'Nordsjøliv og hjemmeliv', report No. 35, Work Research Institute, Oslo.

Solinas P. (1987) 'La dot et la part. Transmission des biens, fils et filles dans les familles polynucléaires des métayers siennois', in Ravis-Giordani G. (ed.), *Femmes et patrimoine*, Éditions du CNRS, Paris, pp.169-88.

Stacey, J. (1990) *Brave New Families: Stories of Domestic Upheaval in Late Twentieth-century America*, Basic Books, New York.

Strathern M. (1992) *After Nature, English Kinship in the Late Twentieth Century*, Cambridge University Press, Cambridge.

Sweetser D. A. (1966) 'The Effect of Industrialization on Intergeneration Solidarity', *Rural Sociology*, pp.156-70.

Théry I. (1991) 'Trouver le mot juste. Langage et parenté dans les recompositions familiales après divorce', in Segalen M. (ed.), *Jeux de famille*, Presses du CNRS, Paris.

Théry I. (1993) *Le démariage*, Odile Jacob, Paris.

Thorsen L. E. (1993) *Det fleksible kjønn. Mentalitets- endringer i tre generasjoner bondekvinner*, Universitetsforlaget, Oslo.

Tornstam L. (1989) 'Gerotranscendence: a reformulation of the disengagement theory', *Aging*, 1, pp.55–63.

Törnqvist E. (1993) *Filmdiktarenn Ingemar Bergman*, Stockholm.

Tosi A. (1991) 'Condizioni e processi educativi', in Irer, *Social Survey in Lombardia*, Angeli, Milan, pp.239–79.

Townsend P. (1957) *The Family Life of Old People*, London, Penguin.

Trost J. (1993) *Familjen i Sverige*, Stockholm.

Viegas, Susana D. de Matos (1994) *Enigmas. A Experiência Social do Envelhecimento*, Dissertation (Provas de Aptidão Científica e Capacidade Pedagógica), Faculty of Sciences and Technology, University of Coimbra.

Vinke P. and Berghuis-Van Der Wijk I. J. (1975) *Rechtsgevoel in de ervaring van verschillende bevolkingsgroepen*, Kluwer, Deventer.

Vives V. J. (1954) *Noticia de Catalunya*, Destino, Barcelona.

Willmot P. and Young M. (1960) *Family and Class in a London Suburb*, Routledge and Kegan Paul, London.

Wilterdink N. (1984) *Vermogensverhoudingen in Nederland*, Arbeiderspers, Amsterdam.

Wrigley, E. A. and Schofield, R. S. (1981) *The Population History of England 1541-1871. A Reconstruction*, Harvard University Press, Cambridge, Mass.

Yanagisako S. and Collier J. (eds) (1987) *Gender and Kinship*, Stanford University Press, Stanford.

Young M. and Willmott P. (1957) *Family and Kinship in East London*, Routledge and Kegan Paul, London. (French translation) *Le village dans la ville*, CCI, Paris, 1985.

INDEX